D0084271

Case Studies in Health Information Management

Case Studies in Health Information Management

Charlotte McCuen, MS, RHIA

Nanette B. Sayles, EdD, RHIA, CCS, CHP, FAHIMA

Patricia Schnering, RHIA, CCS

THOMSON

DELMAR LEARNING™

Australia   Canada   Mexico   Singapore   Spain   United Kingdom   United States

THOMSON
™
DELMAR LEARNING

Case Studies in Health Information Management
by Charlotte McCuen, Nanette B. Sayles and Patricia Schnering

Vice President,
Health Care Business Unit:
William Brottmiller

Director of Learning Solutions:
Matthew Kane

Managing Editor:
Marah Bellegarde

Senior Acquisitions Editor:
Rhonda Dearborn

Marketing Director:
Jennifer McAvey

Marketing Channel Manager:
Michele McTighe

Production Director:
Carolyn Miller

Content Project Manager:
Thomas Heffernan

Marketing Coordinator:
Andrea Eobstel

COPYRIGHT © 2008 Thomson Delmar Learning, a part of the Thomson Corporation. Thomson, the Star logo, and Delmar Learning are trademarks used herein under license.

Printed in Canada

1 2 3 4 5 6 7 8 XXX 11 10 09 08 07

For more information, contact Thomson Delmar Learning, 5 Maxwell Drive, Clifton Park, NY 12065 Or find us on the World Wide Web at http://www.delmarlearning.com

ALL RIGHTS RESERVED. No part of this work covered by the copyright hereon may be reproduced or used in any form or by any means—graphic, electronic, or mechanical, including photocopying, recording, taping, Web distribution or information storage and retrieval systems—without the written permission of the publisher.

For permission to use material from this text or product, contact us by
Tel (800) 730-2214
Fax (800) 730-2215
www.thomsonrights.com

Library of Congress Cataloging-in-Publication Data

McCuen, Charlotte.
 Case studies in health information management / Charlotte McCuen, Nanette B. Sayles, Patricia Schnering.
  p. ; cm.
 ISBN-13: 978-1-4180-5546-2
 ISBN-10: 1-4180-5546-8
 1. Medical records–Management–Case studies.
 2. Medical informatics–Case studies.
 3. Information resources management–Case studies. 4. Health facilities–Information services–Management–Case studies. I. Sayles, Nanette B. II. Schnering, Patricia. III. Title.
 [DNLM: 1. Information Management–organization & administration. 2. Medical Informatics–organization & administration.
 3. Practice Management.
W 26.5 M4782c 2008]
 RA976.M33 2008
 651.5'04261–dc22

                                    2007028548

Notice to the Reader

Publisher does not warrant or guarantee any of the products described herein or perform any independent analysis in connection with any of the product information contained herein. Publisher does not assume, and expressly disclaims, any obligation to obtain and include information other than that provided to it by the manufacturer.

The reader is expressly warned to consider and adopt all safety precautions that might be indicated by the activities described herein and to avoid all potential hazards. By following the instructions contained herein, the reader willingly assumes all risks in connection with such instructions.

The publisher makes no representations or warranties of any kind, including but not limited to, the warranties of fitness for particular purpose or merchantability, nor are any such representations implied with respect to the material set forth herein, and the publisher takes no responsibility with respect to such material. The publisher shall not be liable for any special, consequential, or exemplary damages resulting, in whole or part, from the reader's use of, or reliance upon, this material.

Contents

Section 3 | Statistics and Quality Improvement 127

Section 4 Healthcare Privacy, Confidentiality, Legal, and Ethical Issues 160

Section 5 Information Technology and Systems 231

Section 6   Management and Health Information Services 291

Section 7   Project and Operations Management **345**

Preface

Case Studies in Health Information Management answers the educational need for a comprehensive case study workbook for Health Information Management (HIM) educators and students. The case format will help the student move from theory to application and analysis. The more than 240 comprehensive case studies are designed to provide both the AS or BS student with an opportunity to experience a wide range of HIM situations.

Case Study Framework

The cases are based on real-life HIM scenarios and demand thought and action from the HIM student. Critical thinking is a cornerstone to HIM practice. These case studies were designed to assist students of all levels develop and strengthen their critical-thinking skills. Each case brings the user into the HIM setting and invites him or her to consider all of the variables that influence the information management situation. The students are then expected to utilize HIM principles in making decisions based on these multiple variables.

Case Studies in Health Information Management provides instructors with a transitional tool to help guide students in "bridging the gap" between content knowledge and on-the-job performance in actual HIM practice. The cases represent a unique set of variables to offer a breadth of learning experiences and to capture the reality of HIM practice. So the students should not expect to be able to just look up the answers in the textbooks. They will have to draw on everything that they have learned to answer many of the questions in the case study.

Organization

The cases are grouped into parts based on seven major HIM topics:

- Health Data Management
- Clinical Classification Systems and Reimbursement Methodology
- Statistics and Quality Improvement
- Healthcare Privacy, Confidentiality, Legal, and Ethical Issues
- Information Technology and Systems
- Management and Health Information Services
- Project and Operations Management

Within each section, we attempted to organize cases by subject area and then from less to more difficult. The classification of the cases is subjective and, as we all know, many of the HIM principles pertain to more than one HIM topic. For example, some cases in different sections may be quite similar but were included in the section for a different focus on the subject (e.g., personal health record [PHR] is addressed in Privacy and Security as well as in information systems [IS]). Although reimbursement issues and coding go hand in hand, we have not included a variety of coding questions because there are a myriad of excellent coding texts and workbooks. Our focus is on principles and compliance rather than specific codes.

Features

- *A Case Study Correlation Grid,* found before the first section, illustrates at a glance which case studies contain principles related to the various American Health Information Management Association (AHIMA) Registered Health Information Administrator (RHIA) and Registered Health Information Technician (RHIT) competency statement domains.

- *Case study questions* are written in such a way that the answers cannot be looked up in a textbook but instead must be found by drawing on the knowledge acquired during the course of study, promoting critical thinking.

- *True-to-life scenarios* are used throughout, including actual forms, codes, and the like that the HIM professional will utilize on the job.

Online Instructor's Manual

The *Online Instructor's Manual* is a password-protected instructor website containing answers or suggested answers to every question found in the workbook. The *Online Instructor's Manual* contains Word files that can be easily manipulated by instructors so they can alter the information to meet their individual needs.

Also Available

Case Studies for Health Information Management on DVD, ISBN: 1-4180-5235-3:

This five-program series focuses on applying critical-thinking skills to real events and situations that occur in the workplace. Each case study dramatizes a real situation, provides a discussion checkpoint, and follows with an outcome that reflects how the scenario would be resolved in the real world. The programs align to the five health information management curriculum domains and include 20 case studies for review and discussion.

Features

- 20 case studies mapping to curriculum domains, subdomains, and knowledge clusters
- Promotes application of concepts to real-world problems and situations
- Realistic presentation and dialogue to prepare students for situations they may encounter on the job
- Aligns to Commission on Accreditation of Health Informatics and Information Management Education (CAHIIM) standards for accreditation
- Designed to capture student interest with stimulating and fresh graphics
- Instructor's manual provides outlines, question prompts, and quizzes

Program 1: Health Data Management
Program 2: Health Statistics, Biomedical Research, and Quality Management
Program 3: Health Services Organization and Delivery
Program 4: Information Technology and Systems
Program 5: Organization and Management

About the Authors

Charlotte McCuen, MS, RHIA

Charlotte McCuen, MS, RHIA, is an Associate Professor at Macon State College. She has a master's degree from Mercer University in Health Care Policy and Administration and a bachelor's degree from the Medical College of Georgia in Health Information Management. She is the Clinical Coordinator at Macon State College and teaches in the associate and bachelor programs in Health Information. She has 15 years' experience as a health information manager in acute care hospitals. Charlotte has also worked as an independent consultant in the management of patient care data for long-term care facilities, behavioral health facilities, physician offices, and renal dialysis centers.

Nanette B. Sayles, EdD, RHIA, CCS, CHP, FAHIMA

Nanette Sayles is a 1985 graduate of the University of Alabama at Birmingham Medical Record Administration (now Health Information Management) program. She earned her Master's of Science in Health Information Management (1995) and her Master's in Public Administration (1990) from the University of Alabama at Birmingham. She earned her doctorate in Adult Education from the University of Georgia (2003). She is currently the Program Director/Associate Professor for the Health Information Management and Technology programs at Macon State College in Macon, Georgia. She has a wide range of health information management experience in hospitals, consulting, system development/implementation, and education. She won the 2005 American Health Information Management Association Triumph Educator Award.

Patricia J. Schnering, RHIA, CCS

Patricia Schnering was the founder of PRG Publishing, Inc., and Professional Review Guides, Inc. She has worked as owner, author, and publisher for Professional Review Guides, Inc., and PRG Publishing, Inc. Mrs. Schnering is a 1995 graduate of the Health Information Management Program at St. Petersburg College in St. Petersburg, Florida. In 1998 she was certified as a CCS and in 1999 she received her RHIA certification. Her education includes a bachelor's degree from the University of South Florida in Tampa, Florida, with a major in business administration. Since 1993, she has worked in health information services supervisory positions, as an HIM consultant and as an adjunct HIM instructor at St. Petersburg College. She has been involved in her local, state, and national HIM associations since 1992 and has served on various committees and as a director for the Florida Health Information Management Association (FHIMA). She was the recipient of the FHIMA Literary Award in 2000 and 2006.

Acknowledgments

I would like to extend my sincere thanks to my cohorts, Dr. Nanette Sayles and Mrs. Patricia Schnering, for their professional experience, dedication, and contribution to the development of this book. Their input of real-world experiences and knowledge of working in the health information field helped in the development of the case studies presented. I also would like to thank the peer reviewers for their comments and suggestions for making improvements in the development of the cases and format of the book.

I would like to give thanks to special people in my life. First, I thank my husband and children for their understanding throughout the development of the book. I also extend gratitude to my parents who have always encouraged me to strive for my dreams. Their example of work ethic, diligence and determination have shown me that your goals can be achieved. Without their support, the text would not have been possible.

Charlotte McCuen, MS, RHIA

This case study book is one that I have wanted to do for a long time. It is a product that I believe will be useful to both health information management educators and students. For this goal to be realized, it took a lot of support from a number of people:

- My husband, Mark, is supportive of the various projects that I am working on, including this project.
- My parents, George and Jeanette Burchfield, who taught me to work hard and the importance of education.
- My coauthors, Pat Schnering and Charlotte McCuen, for their hard work on this book.

Without their hard work, this case study book would not exist. I'm not sure any of us knew what we were getting ourselves into when we decided to commit to this project.

To the students, it is my hope that you find this book a useful part of your preparation to enter the exciting and challenging world of health information management.

To the educators, I hope that you will find this case study book valuable as you develop and continue to refine your courses.

Nanette B. Sayles, EdD, RHIA, CCS, CHP, FAHIMA

XVI ACKNOWLEDGMENTS

I especially wish to express my gratitude to Nanette Sayles and Charlotte McCuen who were instrumental in creating this book. At the AOE meetings, instructors have been asking for a case study book for HIM. Nanette and Charlotte said they would love to do the book. I was very excited! Nanette and Charlotte are seasoned professionals and instructors at the HIA and HIT programs at Macon State College. Their level of energy and dedication to the profession is amazing.

There are some very special people in my life who make the work possible.

- My husband, Bob, as always, continues to keep me grounded, as I tend to spin off in space while I work on the books.
- My mother, Emma Miller, is my role model for perseverance leading to success. She embodies grace, courage, strength, and endurance.

My thanks would not be complete without acknowledging all the HIM/HIT professionals, educators, and students who support our efforts by letting us know what would be useful to them and how we can improve the products we produce. Thank you for the letters and words of encouragement.

My reward is knowing that the materials you use here may assist you in preparing for the challenge of the workplace. I wish you the very best now and throughout your career.

Until we meet...

Patricia J. Schnering, RHIA, CCS

SECTION ONE

Health Data Management

Subjective, Objective, Assessment, and Plan (SOAP) Statements and the Problem-Oriented Medical Record (POMR)

Review each of the following unrelated statements abstracted from problem-oriented medical record (POMR) documentation. Determine whether each statement is a subjective (S), objective (O), assessment (A), or plan (P) entry from the patient records.

_____Patient complains of pain in the left ear and upon neck movement.

_____Compare baseline mammogram 2006 to current mammogram.

_____Uncontrolled hypertension.

_____Pedal edema was 2+.

_____Rule out cancerous tumor following biopsy of thyroid lesion.

_____Patient complained of headache, fatigue, and photosensitivity.

_____Patient states, "I am thirsty all the time."

_____BUN 21.0 mg/dL, ALB 6.0 gm/dL, bilirubin total 6.3 mg/dL.

_____Percussion was normal.

_____Complaining of pain in the low back.

_____Laceration measured 2 cm above right brow.

_____Determine treatment following results of radiology studies.

CASE 1-2

Problem-Oriented Medical Record (POMR) Record Format

Read the patient visit report shown in Figure 1-1 and answer the following questions.

1. What is the patient's chief complaint?

2. What information in the scenario is "subjective"?

3. What information in the scenario is "objective"?

4. Does Dr. Jenkins have a definitive assessment of Ms. Gerry's problem?

5. What is the plan for this patient?

Patient Visit Report

HISTORY OF PRESENT ILLNESS: Ms. Gerry is an 85 year old female who fell out of a wheelchair today. She comes in complaining of severe pain in her left hip. X-ray reveals an intertrochanteric fracture of the left hip.

PAST MEDICAL HISTORY: Alzheimer's disease, GERD, COPD, coronary artery disease.

MEDICATIONS: Zantac 75 mg in the AM; Synthroid 88 mcg in the AM; Norvasc 2.5 mg in the AM; Nebulizer QID; Coumadin 2.5 mg Monday, Wednesday, Friday and Saturday.

PHYSICAL EXAM: Shortening of the left leg; good bilateral pedal pulses.

PLAN: Medical clearance. Vitamin K to decrease protime. Bucks traction. Open reduction and internal fixation of left hip if cleared for surgery.

X-ray after surgery: Diffuse osteopenia present. Patient is post placement of a dynamic hip screw within the proximal left femur. There is near anatomical alignment of the intertrochanteric femoral neck fracture.

Figure 1-1 *Patient Visit Report*

CASE 1-3

Master Patient Index (MPI) and Duplicate Medical Record Number Assignment

The ad hoc report shown in Table 1-1 (Master Patient Index [MPI] Discrepancy Report) is a function of the MPI system. This system function applies weights for the probability, on a scale from 1 to 15, of whether the two patient encounters in each case are likely to pertain to the same patient or not. The policy of the hospital is to retain the survivorship record number when correcting duplicate number assignments on the same patient.

Review the ad hoc report provided in Table 1-1 for analysis of duplicate medical record number assignments.

Which enumerated pair listed can be determined as being for the same patient, and which medical record number should be retained based on the hospital policy?

Which numbers listed do you think will require further documentation review to determine if the patients are the same or not?

Table 1-1 *MPI Discrepancy Report*

			MPI Discrepancy Report			
Case	Patient Name	MR#	SSN	DOB	Residence	Wt
1	John Carmichael	016792	256-14-9876	1-5-1982	111 Holly Dr.	14.1
	J.D. Carmichael	019156	256-14-9876	1-5-1982	295 Stream Dr.	
2	Susan A. Pherris	042121	031-55-8642	5-4-2002	Hwy. 24, Box 11	5.0
	Susan Ferris	050377	386-12-7854	5-4-1962	456 First St.	
3	Amanda Johns	114682	487-09-4210	8-2-1984	219 Bates St.	10.4
	Amanda Willis	143022	487-09-4211	8-2-1984	532 Jesse Dr.	
4	Jonathan Allen, III	015467	276-22-9768	1-9-1955	131 Oaks Rd.	2.5
	Jonathan Allen	139878	297-46-2089	9-8-2006	197 Trey Cir.	
5	William Jones	122199	698-28-7667	2-6-2004	100 Windy Rd.	13.0
	Bill Jones	140981	698-28-7661	2-6-2004	100 Windy Rd.	
6	Tracy Lemon	130961	209-88-0120	1-9-2001	28 Hillman Ave.	1.5
	Treina Lemon	098972	462-90-0156	8-5-2006	101 Troy Ct.	

CASE 1-4

Enterprise MPI

As the assistant health information management (HIM) director of a growing health system network, you are a member on the Information Systems Committee. You have been asked to oversee the development of a standardized, systemwide-enterprise master patient index (MPI).

Research the recommended core elements of a MPI through professional journals (e.g., *Journal of AHIMA*).

1. Develop a data dictionary, defining each of the data elements needed.

2. Design a data display screen.

Chart Check-Out Screen Design and Data Quality

You have been recently hired by a vendor who is developing electronic health record (EHR) software. In your role as the subject matter expert, it is your responsibility to ensure that the system will meet the needs of the users in the HIM department. One of your first duties is to evaluate the screens that have been designed over the past few months when they did not have an HIM professional on staff. The first one that you review is the chart check-out screen for the chart locator.

Evaluate the screen design in Figure 1-2 to identify ways to improve data quality. This should include the comprehensiveness and appropriateness of the fields on the screen. Make recommendations for improvement.

To help you in your project, you may reference the general design principles described in the textbook *Health Information Management Technology: An Applied Approach* (2007), edited by Merida Johns.

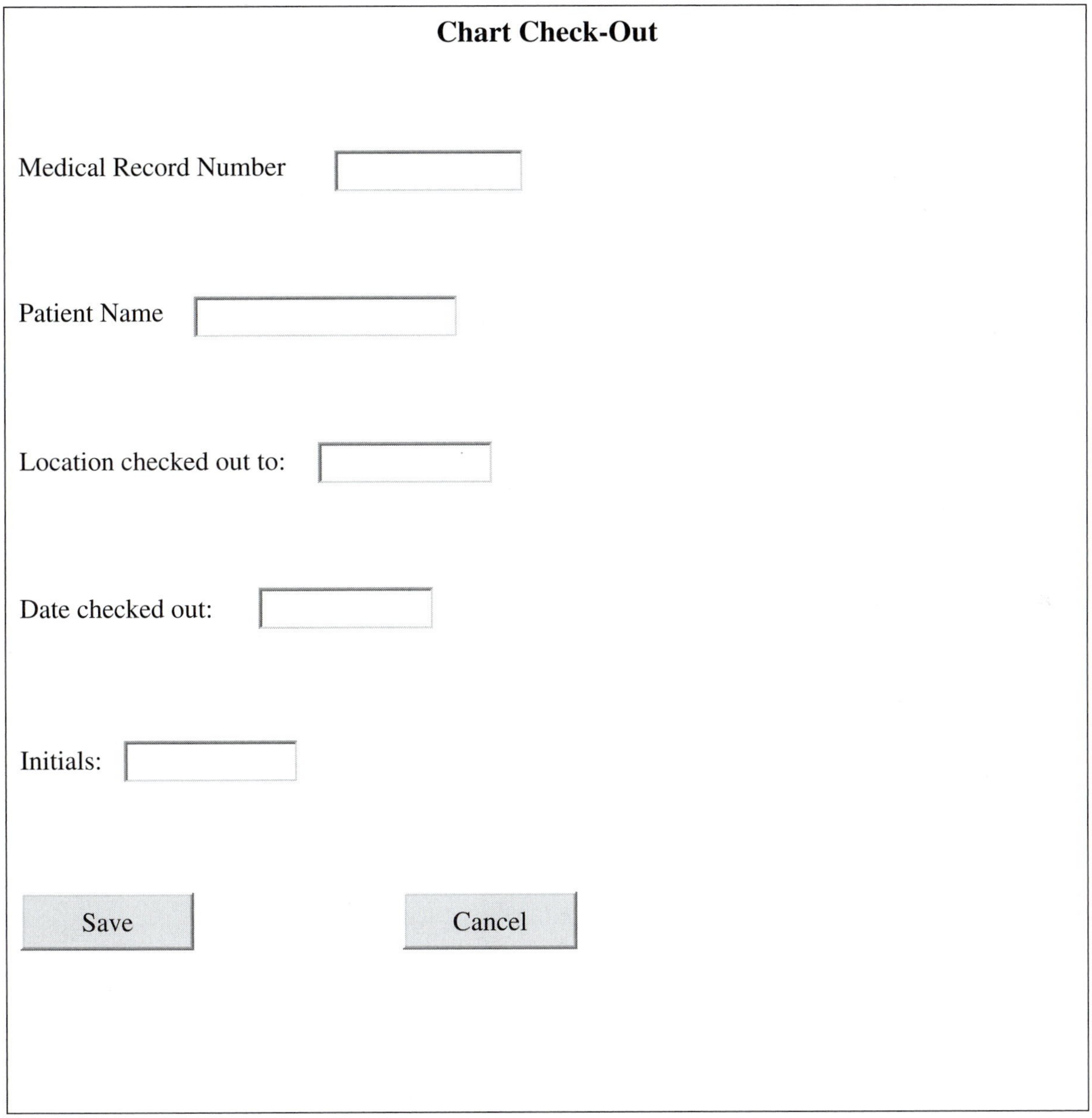

Chart Check-Out

Medical Record Number

Patient Name

Location checked out to:

Date checked out:

Initials:

[Save]   [Cancel]

Figure 1-2 *Chart Check-Out Screen*

CASE 1-6

Patient Demographic Data Entry Screen Design and Data Quality

You are the assistant HIM director and you are on the Health Information Systems (HIS) Committee for overseeing screen design for data entry. A screen request for a patient demographic data entry screen has been submitted by the supervisor of the chart locator system.

Employ good design principles for data entry and data quality to critique the screen design in Figure 1-3.

Evaluate the screen design and content in Figure 1-3 to identify ways to improve data quality, including the comprehensiveness and appropriateness of the data fields as well as field names.

To help you in your project, you may reference the general design principles described in the textbook *Health Information Management Technology: An Applied Approach* (2007), edited by Merida Johns.

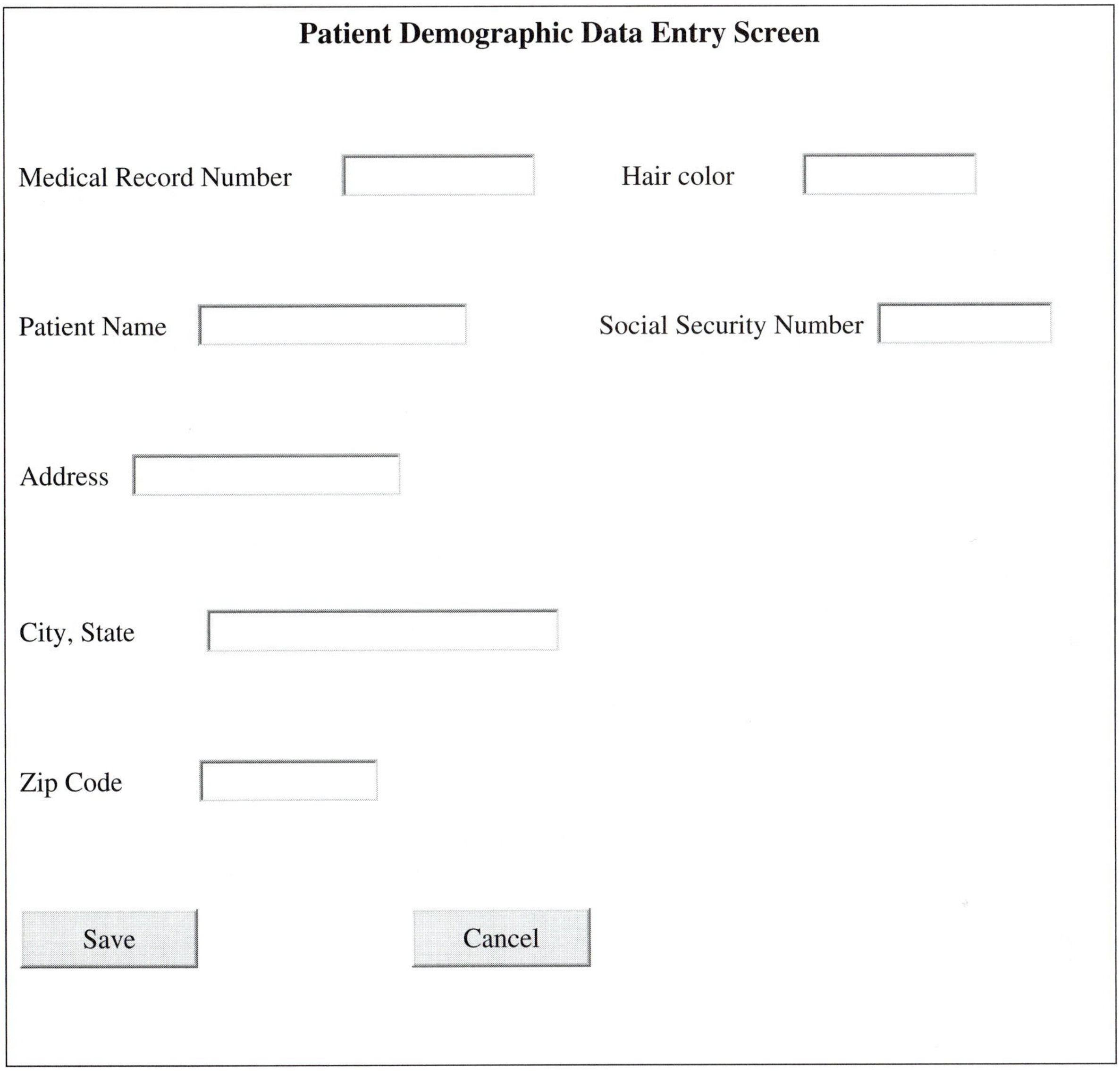

Patient Demographic Data Entry Screen

Medical Record Number [   ]   Hair color [   ]

Patient Name [   ]   Social Security Number [   ]

Address [   ]

City, State [   ]

Zip Code [   ]

[Save]   [Cancel]

Figure 1-3 *Patient Demographic Data Entry Screen*

Encounter Abstract Screen Design and Data Quality

You are the assistant HIM director and you are on the HIS Committee for overseeing screen design for data entry. A screen request for an encounter data entry screen has been submitted by the supervisor of the chart locator system.

Employ good design principles for data entry and data quality to critique the screen design in Figure 1-4.

Evaluate the screen design and content in Figure 1-4 to identify ways to improve data quality, including the comprehensiveness and appropriateness of the data fields as well as field names.

To help you in your project, you may reference the general design principles described in the textbook *Health Information Management Technology: An Applied Approach* (2007), edited by Merida Johns.

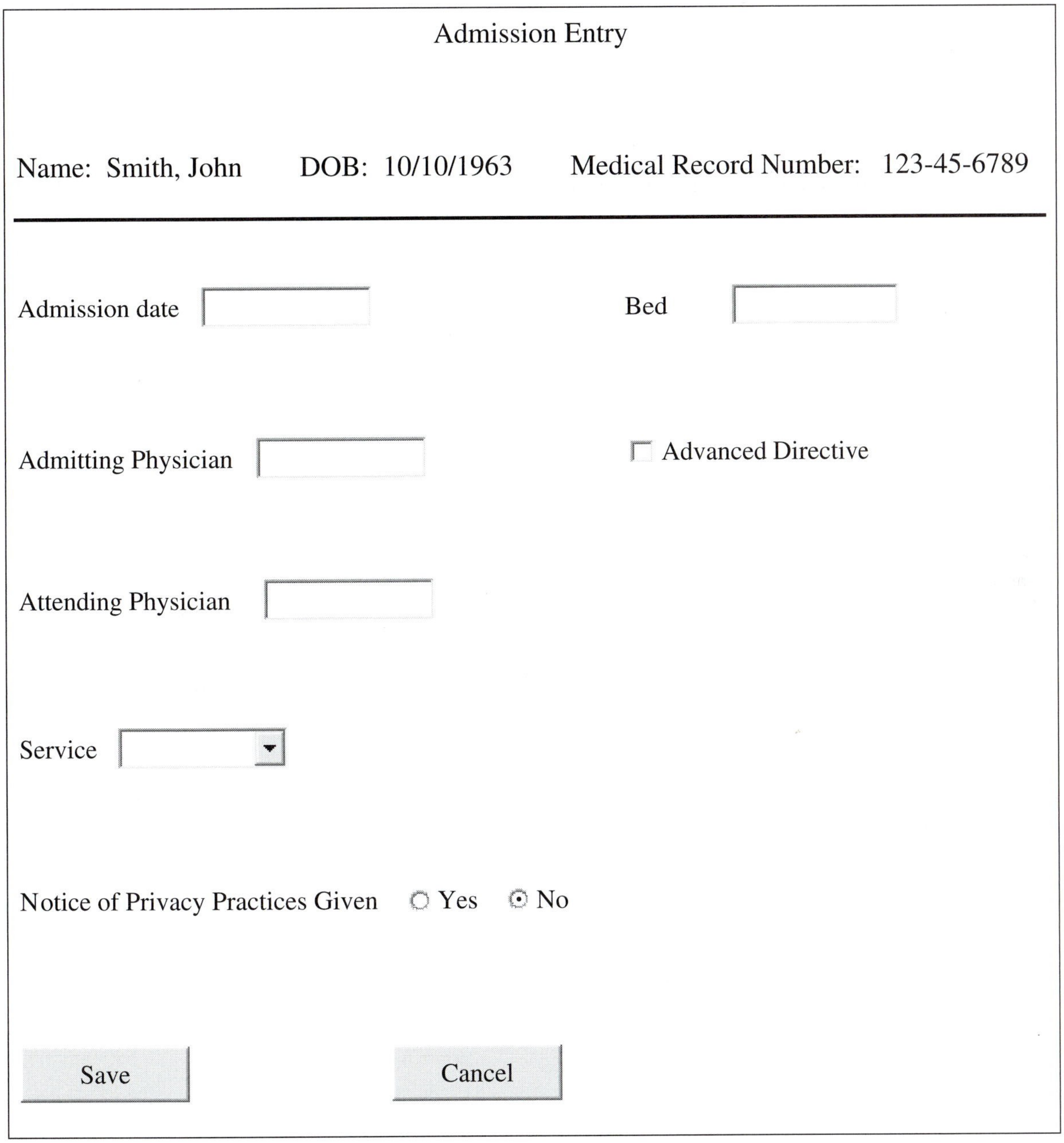

Admission Entry

Name: Smith, John   DOB: 10/10/1963   Medical Record Number: 123-45-6789

Admission date [   ]   Bed   [   ]

Admitting Physician [   ]   ☐ Advanced Directive

Attending Physician [   ]

Service [▼]

Notice of Privacy Practices Given   ○ Yes   ⊙ No

[Save]   [Cancel]

Figure 1-4 *Encounter Abstract Screen*

Coding Abstract Data Entry Screen Design and Data Quality

You are the assistant HIM director and you are on the HIS Committee for overseeing screen design for data entry. A screen request for a coding abstract screen has been submitted by the supervisor of the chart locator system.

Employ good design principles for data entry and data quality to critique the screen design in Figure 1-5.

Evaluate the screen design and content in Figure 1-5 to identify ways to improve data quality, including the comprehensiveness and appropriateness of the data fields as well as field names.

To help you in your project, you may reference the general design principles described in the textbook *Health Information Management Technology: An Applied Approach* (2007), edited by Merida Johns.

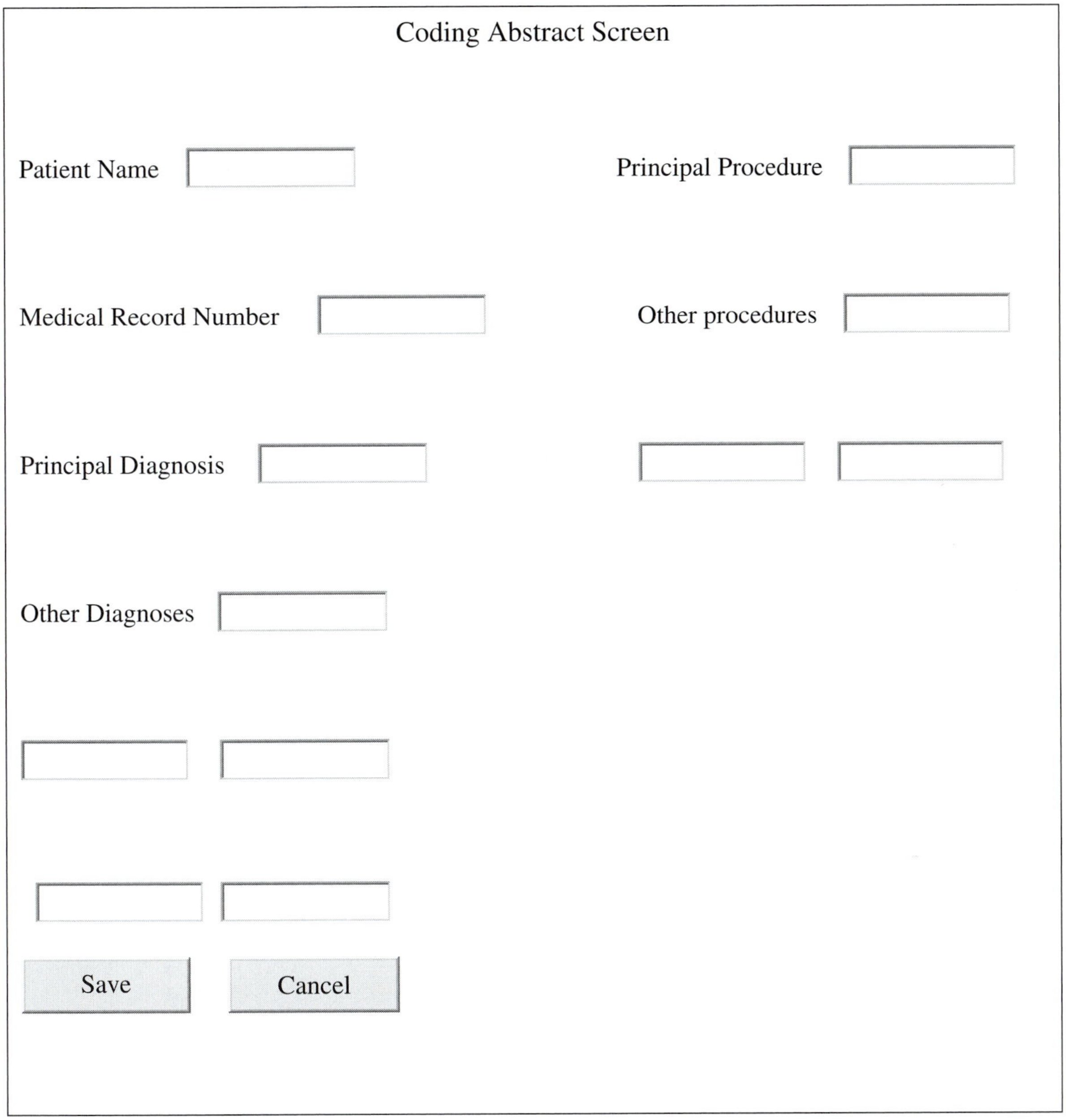

Coding Abstract Screen

Patient Name [   ]   Principal Procedure [   ]

Medical Record Number [   ]   Other procedures [   ]

Principal Diagnosis [   ]   [   ] [   ]

Other Diagnoses [   ]

[   ] [   ]

[   ] [   ]

[Save]   [Cancel]

Figure 1-5 *Coding Abstract Data Entry Screen*

Designing a Report for Radiology and Imaging Service Examinations

You are a member of the Forms Committee of an ambulatory diagnostic center. You have been assigned the task of developing a requisition and imaging report to be used for radiology and imaging service exams. The new report form needs to combine both the requisition and radiology interpretative report on the same form. Utilize Microsoft Access, Microsoft Excel, or Microsoft Word to develop this form, and include all data elements specified in the following list.

- Patient Name
- Date of Birth
- Medical Record Number
- Encounter Number
- Attending Physician
- Referring Physician
- Encounter Date
- Diagnosis/Condition
- Interpretation

CASE 1-10

Documentation Requirements for the History and Physical Report

As the chart completion supervisor, you are to meet with the HIM director to discuss documentation requirements among various agencies, such as the timeliness of the History and Physical Report, by which the hospital abides.

Research the history and physical report documentation requirements for the Joint Commission on Accreditation of Healthcare Organizations (Joint Commission) and the American Osteopathic Association (AOA).

Create a table to report the differences in requirements.

Documentation Requirements for the Autopsy Report

You are the chart completion supervisor. You are preparing for a meeting with the HIM director to discuss the documentation requirements for timeliness of the Provisional and Final Autopsy Report. There are various agencies with requirements that the hospital must meet.

Research the Provisional and Final Autopsy Report documentation requirements for the Joint Commission on Accreditation of Healthcare Organizations (Joint Commission) and the American Osteopathic Association (AOA).

Create a table to report the differences in requirements.

CASE 1-12

Data Collection in Long-Term Care: Minimum Data Set Version 2.0 (MDS 2.0)

The company that you work for owns 25 long-term nursing and rehabilitation homes throughout the state. The CEO has asked you to develop a corporate compliance program to adhere to the Minimum Data Set Version 2.0 (MDS 2.0) requirements for completing the (comprehensive) Full Assessment Form. The final written plan will standardize data collection among the corporation's homes for more efficient collection and reporting of the MDS data to CMS for reimbursement of care.

For information on the MDS and to download a PDF copy of the MDS 2.0, visit the CMS website at http://www.cms.hhs.gov.

Review the comprehensive MDS form and identify required data sections collected on the form. Develop a check sheet (listing the required data sections) to be used as an audit tool in your survey of MDS forms' completeness.

Visit three nursing homes and audit a representative sample (one record from each nursing home) containing completed comprehensive MDS Full Assessment Forms. In the audit, use your check sheet to determine which document form was used for collecting data to complete the comprehensive MDS.

Data Collection for the Health Plan Employer Data and Information Set (HEDIS) in Managed Care

The managed care delivery system you have been employed with over the past few months is struggling in some areas of patient care and information systems for capture and reporting patient care. You sit on a committee to develop an organizational quality improvement program for the organization. In preparation for the next administrative staff meeting, you are to report on the most prevalent health plan employer data and information set (HEDIS) elements found to be deficient among the U.S. population–enrolled managed care organizations (MCOs).

As the HIM manager, you initially plan to visit www.ncqa.org and review professional literature to research HEDIS data element requirements.

Develop a list of the top 5 most deficient care measures (i.e., relative resource use measures) in the U.S. population from "The State of Health Care Quality 2006: Executive Summary," National Committee for Quality Assurance, Washington, DC. Visit http://www.ncqa.org to view the summary.

Explain why these deficient care measures are important in terms of number of deaths and cost of care.

CASE 1-14

Birth Certificate Reporting Project

Cabbage County is a rural community in Georgia that still completes and mails birth certificates to the county health department and state vital records office once a week. The hospital had one live birth yesterday. You are the birth certificate coordinator at Cabbage Patch Hospital and are responsible for completing birth certificates on the newborn babies in the hospital. Pertinent identity information was obtained from an interview with the mother and from her obstetric record.

Valid information from the interview is given in Figure 1-6. The remainder of the prenatal, perinatal, and postnatal information can be found in the mother's medical record (obstetric record) provided in Figure 1-7. Use the information in the interview and abstract information from the obstetric record provided to complete the birth certificate shown in Figure 1-8.

The obstetrician who delivered the baby was James Mercy, MD, license number 52443. His office is at 210 Cabbage Patch Circle, Cleveland, Georgia 31402. The certifier field on the birth certificate will be left blank; notify the doctor to sign before mailing the certificate.

The registrar with the state vital records office will sign the registrar field of the completed birth certificate, when it is received, and maintain it on file at the vital records office in Cabbage County, where the baby was born.

Interview with Mother

The mother's name is Diana Lynn Prince, maiden name Quinn, DOB 9-1-71, Social Security number 251-XX-XXXX. Ms. Prince is a homemaker who was born in Arizona, where she completed her high school education. She later relocated to her new hometown, the city of Cleveland, Georgia. She lives with her husband, Charles Anthony Prince, at 100 Windy Lane, Cleveland, GA 31402. The record indicates Ms. Prince was admitted 10-13-93 in labor. Charles Anthony Prince was born in Maryland on 10-5-67 and has the Social Security number 231-XX-XXXX. Mr. Prince is a black male of American descent who completed 4 years of college with a bachelor's degree in business. Ms. Prince and her husband chose to name their baby boy Lawrence Anthony Prince. The mother did give consent to release information to the Social Security Administration for issuance of a Social Security number for the baby.

Figure 1-6 *Interview with Mother*

Figure 1-7 *Mother's Obstetric Record*

Cabbage Patch Hospital

Admission Information INPATIENT

Admit Date	Admit Time	Location	Room/Bed	Accom.	Bill. Type	Rel. Info.	Med. Rec. Number	Fin. Cl.
10-13-93	0530	322	224/03	P	00	Y	09 09 99	8

Patient Name	Nick Name	Maiden Name	Account Number	Donor
Diana Lynn Prince			1003215	N

Street Address	County	City	State	Zip Code	Facility ID
100 Windy Lane	Cabbage	Cleveland	GA	31402	88888

Sex	Race	Marital	Date of Birth	Age	SSN
F	B	M	9-1-1971	22	251-00-8888

Religion	Place of Worship	City	State
Non			

Patient Employer	Occupation	Work Phone
N/A	homemaker	

Address	City	State	Zip Code

Emergency Contact	Relationship	Home Phone	Work Phone
Charles Anthony Prince			

Address	County	City	State	Zip Code
100 Windy Lane	Cabbage	Cleveland	GA	31402

Insurance Co. 1	Authorization Number	Phone
Blue Cross/Blue Shield	0123456 78 PZ	(912) 999-0000

Insurance Co. 2	Authorization Number	Phone
N/A		

Insurance Co. 3	Authorization Number	Phone

Admission Physician	Service	Doctor Code	Answering Serv. Phone	Beeper	
James Mercy	OBS	018	799-8888	032	UPIN 52443

Referring Physician	City	State	Phone Number

Admit Diagnosis	Admit Type	Admit Source	Accident Date	Accident Time
OB for delivery at term	1	1	N/A	

Pre-Admit Clerk	Admit Clerk	Memos
	APT	

Normal Vaginal Delivery, spontaneous
Tubal Ligation

Consulting Physicians:		
		Assembly
		Code/Abstract
		Entered
Discharge Date 10-14-93 Discharge Time Days Stay		Deficiency
Results: ☐ Alive ☐ Post Op Death +48 Hrs. ☐ Death +48 Hrs. ☐ Death with Autopsy		Final Analysis
☐ AMA ☐ Post Op Death −48 Hrs. ☐ Death −48 Hrs.		

Figure 1-7 *Mother's Obstetric Record (continued)*

Prince, Diana Lynn
DOB 9/1/71
MR 09 09 99, 10032145

Cabbage Patch Hospital

Obstetric Admitting Record

ASSESSMENT

Admission Date: 10 / 13 / 1993 Time 0535 Age 22

G	T	P	A	L

EDC 10-16-93 EGA 39+
LMP 1-8-93

Perinatal Transfer (From-Place) N/A

Arrival on Unit: ☐ Ambulatory ☐ Wheelchair ☐ Stretcher

Reason for Admission _rule out labor_

Allergies _No known drug allergies_

Labor Began: Date 10-13-93 Time 0500

Membranes on Admission:
☑ Intact ☐ Ruptured: Date _____ Time _____
Fluid: ☐ Clear ☐ Meconium ☐ Foul Smelling
Vaginal Bleeding: ☑ None ☐ Normal Show
☐ Bleeding (Describe): _____

Patient: ☑ Recent URI ☐ Dentures
☐ Been vomiting ☐ Glasses
☐ Exposed to infection ☐ Contact lenses

Prenatal: Care: ☐ No ☑ Yes
Prev. Adm. L&D: ☐ No ☑ Yes Record: ☐ No ☑ Yes
Education: ☑ No ☐ Yes

RISK ASSESSMENT

Risk Factors: ☑ None

_____
_____
_____

Antepartum Tests: ☐ None
Sonogram X2

Hx Herpes Virus: ☑ No ☐ Yes
+Culture and/or Herpes Lesion:
☐ No ☐ Yes Date _____
Hx Blood Transfusions: ☑ No ☐ Yes
Previous Alcohol and/or Drug Use: ☑ No ☐ Yes
Other _____
Smoker: ☑ No ☐ Yes
Hx Hepatitis: ☑ No ☐ Yes
Blood Type: _A+_
Last Oral Intake:
Fluids - Date 10-12-93 Time 2100
Solids - Date 10-12-93 Time 2100
Current Medications: ☐ None

Name/Type of Medication	Last Taken	Brought In

PHYSICAL ASSESSMENT

HT. 5'2"	WT. 149	BP 156/70	FHR 150
T 37	P 115	R 24	

DTR'S + 2°

Mental Status _alert & appropriate_

Dilation 4 cm.
Effacement 80 %
Station _____
Presentation vertex

Urine dipstick: Protein _____

Glucose _____ Ketone _____

Other: _none obtained at admission._

PLAN

Plans for Anesthesia:

Specify Type _____ ☐ None planned

Pt. has: Living Will: ☐ No ☐ Yes Durable Power of Attorney: ☐ No ☐ Yes
☐ Information regarding Advance Directives given to patient.
☐ Advised of video broadcast
☐ Referred to resource group
☐ Referred to physician

Patient Orientation: ☐ Fetal Monitor
☐ Nurses Call Light
☐ Visiting Policy
Consent Forms: ☐ NA
☐ Preanesthesia Evaluation ☐ Support Person
☐ Metabolic Screening ☐ Sibling Visitation

Pediatrician _Jim Jelanski, MD._
Support Person _father of baby_
Tubal Ligation: ☐ No ☑ Yes
Desires Circumcision: ☐ No ☑ Yes
Pt. plans: ☐ Private ☐ Breast feeding
☑ Mother/Baby ☑ Bottle feeding

INTERVENTION

Procedures _EFM/VE_

Disposition: _Admit_

Physician's Name _James Mercy, M.D._

Notified by _____
Date 10-13-93 Time 0610

RN SIGNATURE _Lucy Aiken, RN_

Figure 1-7 *Mother's Obstetric Record (continued)*

Prince, Diana Lynn
DOB 9/1/71
MR 09 09 99, 10032145

Cabbage Patch Hospital

Obstetric Admitting Record

ASSESSMENT

Admission Date: _10_ / _10_ / _1993_ Time _0130_ Age _22_

G	T	P	A	L	EDC _10-16_ EGA _39_
3	2	0	0	2	LMP _1-8-93_

Perinatal Transfer (From-Place) _____

Arrival on Unit: ☐ Ambulatory ☑ Wheelchair ☐ Stretcher

Reason for Admission _rule out labor_

Allergies _no known drug allergies_

Labor Began: Date _10-9-93_ Time _2300_

Membranes on Admission:

☑ Intact ☐ Ruptured: Date _____ Time _____

Fluid: ☐ Clear ☐ Meconium ☐ Foul Smelling

Vaginal Bleeding: ☑ None ☐ Normal Show

☐ Bleeding (Describe): _____

Patient: ☑ Recent URI ☐ Dentures
☐ Been vomiting ☐ Glasses
☐ Exposed to infection ☐ Contact lenses

Prenatal: Care: ☐ No ☑ Yes
Prev. Adm. L&D: ☑ No ☐ Yes Record: ☐ No ☐ Yes
Education: ☑ No ☐ Yes

RISK ASSESSMENT

Risk Factors: ☑ None _____

_____

_____

Antepartum Tests: ☐ None

OB sonogram X 2

_____

Hx Herpes Virus: ☑ No ☐ Yes
+Culture and/or Herpes Lesion:
☐ No ☐ Yes Date _____

Hx Blood Transfusions: ☑ No ☐ Yes
Previous Alcohol and/or Drug Use: ☑ No ☐ Yes
Other _____

Smoker: ☑ No ☐ Yes

Hx Hepatitis: ☑ No ☐ Yes

Blood Type: _A +_

Last Oral Intake:
Fluids - Date _10-9-93_ Time _2200_
Solids - Date _10-9-93_ Time _2000_

Current Medications: ☐ None

Name/Type of Medication	Last Taken	Brought In
PNV's + FESO4	_10-9-93_	

PHYSICAL ASSESSMENT

HT. _5'2"_	WT. _149½_	BP _153/75_	FHR _____
T _37.3 c_	P _82_	R _20_	Dilation _____

DTR'S _____
Mental Status _alert + oriented_

Effacement _____
Station _____
Presentation _____

Urine dipstick: Protein _N_

Glucose _N_ Ketone _N_

Other: _____

PLAN

Plans for Anesthesia:

Specify Type _epidural_ ☐ None planned

Pt. has: Living Will: ☐ No ☐ Yes Durable Power of Attorney: ☑ No ☐ Yes
☐ Information regarding Advance Directives given to patient.
☐ Advised of video broadcast
☐ Referred to resource group
☐ Referred to physician

Patient Orientation: ☑ Fetal Monitor
☑ Nurses Call Light
☑ Visiting Policy

Consent Forms: ☐ NA
☑ Preanesthesia Evaluation ☑ Support Person
☑ Metabolic Screening ☑ Sibling Visitation

Pediatrician _Jim Jelanski, M.D._
Support Person _father of baby_
Tubal Ligation: ☐ No ☐ Yes
Desires Circumcision: ☐ No ☐ Yes
Pt. plans: ☐ Private ☐ Breast feeding
☑ Mother/Baby ☑ Bottle feeding

INTERVENTION
Procedures _____

Disposition: _____

Physician's Name _____

Notified by _J. Jones, RN_
Date _10-10-93_ Time _0200_

RN SIGNATURE _J. Jones, RN._

Figure 1-7 *Mother's Obstetric Record (continued)*

Prince, Diana Lynn DOB 9/1/71 MR 09 09 99, 10032145	Cabbage Patch Hospital
	OBSTETRIC HISTORY & PHYSICAL

Date _10-13-93_ Time _0200_ (24 Hr.)

Age _22_ Race _B_ FPAL _2002_
LMP _1-8-93_ EDC _10-16-93_ EGA _39_
Prev C/S ☐ No ☐ Yes: LTCS ☐ No ☐ Yes ☐ Unknown
Ultrasound ☐ No ☑ Yes
   Date _3-12_ EDC _10-16_ EGA _8.2 mo._
   Date _____ EDC _____ EGA _____
Drug Allergies ☑ No ☐ Yes _____
ACOG Criteria for Elective Delivery Met?
☐ Yes ☐ No ☐ N/A _____ Initials

OBSTETRIC LAB PROFILE
ABO _A_ Rh _⊕_ MSAFP _____ Cytol _____
Last Hgb/Hct _____ Date _____ Hgb Screen _____
Antibody Screen _____
Rubella _immune_ HBSAg _____
Urine Culture _____
1° Glucose Screen _94_
RPR _WNL_ Date _____ Chlamydia _⊖_
Other Lab(s) _____
   HIV ⊖

HISTORY

Past Medical History _∅_

Family History _∅_   Social History _⊖ cigarette, ⊖ ETOH, ⊖ drugs_

ROS _∅_

Admission History _22 y/o, P2002, admitted with occasional contractions. Had uneventful antepartum course._

PHYSICAL EXAMINATION

General _WDWN_   Vital Signs T _37.3 c_ P _82_ R _20_ BP _153/75_
Mental Status ☐ Normal ☐ Abnormal _____ Skin _____
HEENT _pupils equal, round, reactive to light_ Neck _____
Heart _regular rate and rhythm_
Lungs _____ Breasts _soft/non-tender_
Abdomen Fundal Ht _____ FHR _130_ EFW _____ Presentation/Lie _vertex_ Other _____
Cervix Dil _3 cm_ Eff _70%c_ Stn _-2_ Consist _____ Cx Position _____ Other _____
Pelvic Assessment ☐ Adequate ☐ Borderline ☐ Contracted _____
Membranes ☐ Intact ☐ Ruptured _____ Date _____ Time _____ (24 Hr.)
Rectal _____ Extremities _____ Neuro _____
Other _____

Fetal Monitor Assessment _reactive_

Impressions _39 wks._   Plans _anticipate NSVD_

PHYSICIAN SIGNATURE _James Mercy, M.D._

Figure 1-7 *Mother's Obstetric Record (continued)*

Prince, Diana Lynn DOB 9/1/71 MR 09 09 99, 10032145	Cabbage Patch Hospital Labor and Delivery Summary

Labor Summary

G	T	Pt	A	L	Type & Rh
3	2	0	0	2	A+

Maternal transport ☐ Yes ☐ No

Presentation ☐ Position

☑ Vertex
☐ Face or brow
☐ Breech: ___
☐ Transverse lie ☐ Compound
☐ Unknown

Complications ☑ None
☐ No prenatal care
☐ Preterm labor (<37 weeks)
☐ Postterm (>42 weeks)
☐ Febrile (> 100.4°) when adm.
☐ PROM (> 12 hrs. preadmit)
☐ Meconium
☐ Foul smelling fluid
☐ Hydramnios
☐ Abruption
☐ Placenta previa
☐ Bleeding-site undetermined
☐ Toxemia (mild) (severe)
☐ Seizure activity
☐ Precipitous labor (< 3 hrs.)
☐ Prolonged labor (> 20 hrs.)
☐ Prolonged latent phase
☐ Prolonged active phase
☐ Prolonged 2nd stage (> 2.5 hrs.)
☐ Secondary arrest of dilation
☐ Cephalopelvic disproportion
☐ Cord prolapse
☐ Decreased FHT variability
☐ Extended fetal bradycardia
☐ Extended fetal tachycardia
☐ Multiple late decelerations
☐ Acidosis (pH 7.2)
☐ Anesthetic complications
☐ Multiple variable decelerations
☐ HSV

☐ _____
☐ _____

Scalp pH: ☐ Yes ☐ No
Induction ☑ None
☐ ARM ☐ Oxytoc. ☐ Prostin
☐ Serial X: _____ days
Augmentation ☑ None
☐ ARM ☐ Oxytoc.
☐ _____

Monitor ☑ LR ☑ DR ☐ None
External: ☐ FHT ☐ UC
Internal: ☐ FHT ☐ UC

Medications	Total dose
fentanyl	0.1mg

Time of last narcotic: 0615

Delivery Data

Method of Delivery
☐ VBAC
Cephalic
☑ Spontaneous
☐ Low forceps ⎫
☐ Mid forceps ⎬ Type: _____
☐ Rotation: ___ to ___
☐ Vacuum Extractor

Breech
☐ Spontaneous
☐ Partial extraction (assisted)
☐ Total extraction
☐ Forceps to A.C. head

Cesarean (details in operative notes)
☐ Primary ☐ Repeat
☐ Low cervical: transverse
☐ Low cervical: vertical
☐ Classical
☐ Cesarean hysterectomy

Placenta	Blood Loss
☑ Spontaneous	☐ < 500 ml.
☐ Expressed	☐ > 500 ml.
☐ Manual	Specify amt.
☐ Adherent	(ml.)
☐ Ut. exploration	Detail in remarks
☐ Configuration	
☐ Normal	

☐ Abn.: _____
☐ To pathology ☐ Yes ☑ No

Cord
☐ Nuchal cord X: N/A
☐ True knot
2 ☑ Umbilical vessels
Cord blood: ☑ Lab ☐ Not obt.
Cord blood gas: No
pH ___ pCO2 ___ pO2 ___ B.E. ___

Episiotomy ☑ None
☐ Median suture: _____
☐ Mediolateral _____
☐ Degree: _____

Laceration ☐ None
☑ 2 3 4 Degree perineal
☐ Vaginal
☐ Cervical
☐ Uterine rupture
☐ Other: vaginal

Del. room no.: 03

father of baby
Support persn
Maternal BP: ___ P: ___
FHT: ___ Time: ___
James Mercy, MD
Attending physician

_____
Assisting physician

Delivery Data (Cont.)

Surgical Procedures ☐ None
☑ Tubal ligation ☐ Curettage
☐ Specimen to Pathology

Delivery Anesthesia ☐ None
1=Local 2=Pudendal
3=Paracervical ④=Epidural
5=Spinal 6=General
Administered by: _____

Delivery Room Meds ☐ None

Agent/Drug	Dose	Route

Time/Signature

Agent/Drug	Dose	Route

Time/Signature

IV Fluids: _____

Time/Signature _____

Maternal O2: ☐ Yes ☐ No
☐ LR ☐ DR

Chronology
EDC date: 10 / 16 / 93
Gestation: 39 weeks

	Date	Time
• Admit to hospital	10-13	0535
• Membranes ruptured	10-13	0652
• Onset of labor	10-13	0500
• Complete cervical dil.	10-13	0558
• Delivery of infant	10-13	0659
• Delivery of placenta	10-13	0703

Remarks: _____
_____
RN signature: *L. Mimbs, RN.*
Physician signature: *James Mercy, MD*

Infant Data

Assessment

- crying vigorously.
- movement good.

Plan & Intervention
☐ Term ☐ IMC ☐ NICU ☑ MB
_____
_____
_____

Apgar Scores

	Heart rate	Respiration	Muscle tone	Reflex irritation	Skin color	Totals
1 min	2	2	2	1	1	8
5 min	2	2	2	2	1	9

Basic Infant Data
Medical rec. no.: _____
ID bracelet no.: 9850
☑ Male ☐ Female
Birth order: 1 of ① 2 3 4
Weight: 6 lbs 11 ozs.
3050 Grams
Length: 19½ in
☑ Erythromycin oint.
RN: P. Smith, RN
Deceased N/A
Date: __/__/__ Time: _____
☐ Antepartum ☐ Intrapartum
☐ Neonatal (in delivery room)

White - Mother's Chart   Yellow - Baby's Chart   Pink - physician

Figure 1-7 *Mother's Obstetric Record (continued)*

Prince, Diana Lynn
DOB 9/1/71
MR 09 09 99, 10032145

Cabbage Patch Hospital

Labor & Delivery Admission Orders

Admission Date: _10-13-93_   Time: _0630_

RN Init.	Time	
		Admit to Labor & Delivery
		Allergies: _NKDA_
		Patient may ambulate if desired and labor uncomplicated.
		NPO except for ice chips and medications.
		Measure intake q 8h and output q void.
		Obtain external fetal monitor strip for 30 minutes on admission.
la	0630	Activity: ☑ Bedrest
		☐ Bathroom privileges
		☐ May ambulate ☐ with fetal monitor ☐ without fetal monitor
		Fetal Monitor: ☐ No ☑ External ☐ Internal
la	0634	Labs: ☑ Hemoglobin & Hematocrit: ☐ STAT ☐ Routine
		☑ Urinalysis: ☐ None ☑ Routine ☐ Microscopic ☐ Culture & Sensitivity
		☑ Dipstick urine for protein, glucose, ketone, and nitrite.
		☐ Biochemical Profile I for patient desiring PPS.
		☐ RPR
		☑ Type and Screen
la	0638	☐ Other Labs
		IV Fluids: _D5LR_ @ _125_ cc/hr through 18 gauge intravenous
		catheter. May adjust IV rate as indicated for hydration.
		IV Fluids for epidural bolus: RL only (at least 1500cc intake before epidural placement)
		Maternal and fetal vital signs per intrapartum standard of care.
		Catheterize PRN: if patient bladder distended and patient unable to void.
		Sedation: _Fentanyl 0.1mg IVF q 1-2hr prn pain_

Physician Signature: _James Merry, MD._

RN Init./Signature: _Lucy Aiken, RN._

Figure 1-7 *Mother's Obstetric Record (continued)*

Prince, Diana Lynn DOB 9/1/71 MR 09 09 99, 10032145	Cabbage Patch Hospital
Date: mo/day/yr	Health History Summary

Age 22 Date of birth 9-1-71 Race or ethnicity Black Religion (non) Years married 7 yrs

Social Security Number 251-00-1333 Work Tel. no. ___ Home Tel. no. ___ Work Tel. no. ___ Home Tel. no. ___

Referring physician ___ Attending physician James Mercy, MD. OPTIONAL FOR INSURANCE, ETC.,

Medical History

Check and detail positive findings including date and place of treatment. Precede findings by reference number.

	Patient	Family	
1. Congenital anomalies	☐	☐	
2. Genetic diseases	☐	☐	
3. Multiple births	☑	☐	Patient is a twin.
4. Diabetes mellitus	☐	☑	Mother, Maternal G'mother.
5. Malignancies	☐	☐	
6. Hypertension	☐	☑	Maternal G'mother.
7. Heart disease	☐	☑	Maternal G'mother.
8. Rheumatic fever	☐	☐	
9. Pulmonary disease	☐	☑	Sister.
10. GL problems	☐		
11. Renal disease	☐	☐	
12. Genitourinary tract problems	☐		
13. Abnormal uterine bleeding	☐		
14. Infertility	☐		
15. Venereal disease	☐	☐	
16. Phlebitis, varicosities	☐		
17. Neurologic disorders	☐	☐	
18. Metabol./endocrine disorders	☐	☐	
19. Anemia/hemoglobinopathy	☐	☐	
20. Blood disorders	☐	☐	
21. Drug abuse	☐		
22. Smoking/alcohol use	☐		
23. Infectious diseases	☐		
24. Operations/accidents	☐		
25. Allergies/meds sensitivity	☐		NKDA
26. Blood transfusions	☐		
27. Other hospitalizations	☐		
28. ___	☐	☐	
29. ___	☐	☐	
30. No known disease/problems	☐	☐	

Preexisting Risk Guide

Indicates pregnancy/outcome at risk

31. ☐ Age< 15 or > 35	
32. ☐ < 8th grade education	
33. ☐ Cardiac disease (class I or II)	
34. ☐ Tuberculosis, active	
35. ☐ Chronic pulmonary disease	
36. ☐ Thrombophlebitis	
37. ☐ Endocrinopathy	
38. ☐ Epilepsy (on medication)	
39. ☐ Infertility (treated)	
40. ☐ 2 abortions (spontaneous/induced)	
41. ☐ ≥ 7 deliveries	
42. ☐ Previous preterm or SGA infants	
43. ☐ Infants ≥ 4,000 gms	
44. ☐ Isoimmunization (ABO, etc.)	
45. ☐ Hemorrhage during previous preg.	
46. ☐ Previous preeclampsia	
47. ☐ Surgically scarred uterus	
48. ☐ Preg. without familial support	
49. ☐ Second pregnancy in 12 months	
50. ☐ Smoking (≥ 1 pack per day)	
51. ☐ ___	
52. ☐ ___	
53. ☐ ___	

Indicates pregnancy/outcome at high risk

54. ☐ Age ≥ 40
55. ☐ Diabetes mellitus
56. ☐ Hypertension
57. ☐ Cardiac disease (class III or IV)
58. ☐ Chronic renal disease
59. ☐ Congenital/chromosomal anomalies
60. ☐ Hemoglobinopathies
61. ☐ Isoimmunization (Rh.)
62. ☐ Alcohol or drug abuse
63. ☐ Habitual abortions
64. ☐ Incompetent cervix
65. ☐ Prior fetal or neonatal death
66. ☐ Prior neurologically damaged infant
67. ☐ Significant social problems
68. ☐ ___
69. ☐ ___
70. ☐ ___

Menstrual History	Onset 13 age	Cycle q. 28 days	Length 3 days	Amount	L M P 1-8-93 mo/day/yr quality

Pregnancy History	Grav 3	Term 2	Pret 0	Abort 0	Live 2	E D C 10-16-93 mo/day/yr

No.	Month/year	Sex	Weight at birth	Wks gest	Hrs. in labor	Type of delivery	Details of delivery: Include anesthesia and maternal or newborn complications. Use Risk Guide numbers where applicable.
1.	9-87	F	5lb 6oz	38		NSVD	without complication
2.	8-89	M	7lb 1oz	39		NSVD	without complication
3.							
4.							
5.							
6.							
7.							
8.							

Historical Risk Status

71. ☑ No risk factors noted
72. ☐ At risk
73. ☐ At high risk

Signature *Lucy Aiken, RN*

Figure 1-7 *Mother's Obstetric Record (continued)*

Prince, Diana Lynn DOB 9/1/71 MR 09 09 99, 10032145 Date: *3-10-93* mo/day/yr	Cabbage Patch Hospital Initial Pregnancy Profile

History Since LMP (/) Check and detail all positive findings below: Use reference numbers

1. Headaches ☐
2. Nausea/vomiting ☑ *occasional*
3. Abdominal pain ☐
4. Urinary complaints ☐
5. Vaginal discharge ☐
6. Vaginal bleeding ☐
7. Edema (specify area) ☐
8. Febrile episode ☐
9. Rubella exposure ☐
10. Other viral exposure ☐
11. Radiation exposure ☐
12. _____ ☐
13. _____ ☐
14. Contraception prior to conception ____ None ☐

Type *D. Novum 1/35*
Last used ____ mo/day/yr

15. Nutritional Assessment

☑ Adequate   ☐ Inadequate
☐ Nutritional counseling

Remarks: _____
_____
_____

16. Medications Since LMP

☑ None   ☐ Exposure to drugs

Describe: _____
_____
_____

Initial Physical Examination   Height *5'2"*   Weight *140*   Pregravid weight *137*   B.P. *120/72*   Pulse *82*

OPTIONAL

SYSTEM	Normal	Abn	Check and detail all abnormal findings below: Use reference numbers.
17. Skin	☑	☐	
18. EENT	☑	☐	
19. Mouth	☑	☐	
20. Neck	☑	☐	
21. Chest	☑	☐	
22. Breast	☑	☐	
23. Heart	☑	☐	
24. Lungs	☑	☐	
25. Abdomen	☑	☐	
26. Musculoskeletal	☑	☐	
27. Extremities	☑	☐	
28. Neurologic	☑	☐	

Pelvic Examination

	Normal	Abn
29. Ext. genitalia	☑	☐
30. Vagina	☑	☐
31. Cervix	☑	☐
32. Uterus (describe)	☑	☐
33. Adnexa	☑	☐
34. Rectum	☑	☐
35. Other	☐	☐

Bony   36. Diag. conj. _____   37. Shape sacrum _____   38. S.S. notch _____   39. Ischial spines _____
40. Pubic arch _____   41. Trans. outlet _____   42. Post sag.diam. _____   43. Coccyx _____

Pelvis   44. Classification ☐ Gynecoid ☐ Android ☐ Anthropoid ☐ Platypelloid
45. Estimation ☐ Adequate ☐ Borderline ☐ Contracted

Exam done on mo/day/yr *3-10-93* by: *James Mercy MD*

Figure 1-7 *Mother's Obstetric Record (continued)*

Prince, Diana Lynn
DOB 9/1/71
MR 09 09 99, 10032145

Cabbage Patch Hospital

Prenatal Flow Record

Historical Risk Factors and Assessment

Chlamydia ⊕, history

[0] Has no known risk
[1] Is "at risk"
[2] Is at high risk

Continuing Risk Assessment Guide Irevise RISK STATUS)

Date	At risk factors	Date	High risk factors
/	Uterine/cervical malformation	/	Diabetes mellitus
/	Suspect pelvis	/	Hypertension
/	Rh negative (nonsensitized)	/	Thrombophlebitis
/	Anemia (Hct <30%: Hgb <10%)	/	Herpes (type 2)
/	Venereal disease	/	Rh sensitization
/	Acute pyelonephritis	/	Uterine bleeding
/	Failure to gain weight	/	Hydramnios
/	Abnormal oresentation	/	Severe preeclampsia
/	Postterm pregnancy	/	Fetal growth retardation
/	Alcohol use	/	Premature rupt. membranes
/	_____	/	Multiple pregnancy (preterm)
/	_____	/	Alcohol and drug abuse
/		/	
/		/	

Initial Prenatal Screen / **Additional Lab Findings**

Date: mo/day/yr	Test	Date	Result	Date	Result
Hct/Hgb	12/39	Hct/Hgb			
Patient's Blood type and Rh	A+	Blood sugar			
Antibody	NR	Antibody			
Serology	NR				
Rubella titer	Imm				
Urinalysis micro		AFP	WNL		
Pap test		HIV	3/10 neg		
Cervical culture		HEP B	3/10 neg		
		chlamydia status neg.			

L M P: 1-8-93   Quickening date _____ mo/dy/yr

Medication Sensitivity   ☐ None known or. _____

☐ Initial prenatal instructions
☐ Attends prenatal classes
☐ Do herpes culture
☐ Do antenatal RhoGam
☐ For sterilization
☐ Circumcision
☐ Needs rubella vaccine
☐ Breast ☐ Bottle feeding

Amniocentesis
Explained on ____ mo/day
☐ Accepted ☐ Rejected by patient
VBAC or C-Section
☐ OR records reviewed
Explained on ____ mo/day
☐ Candidate for VBAC
☐ For Cesarean section

G	T	Pt	A	L
3	2	0	0	2

Age _____

Visit date 19 **93**

Columns: Weight this visit / Pre-gravid / Blood pressure / Base line / Urine protein / Urine Sugar / Est weeks gestation / Fundal height (dates/size) / Fetal heart rate/quadrant / Edema / RISK STATUS (0,1,2)

Baby's physician _____   Return visit / Sig.

Visit date	Weight	Blood pressure		Est weeks		Risk Status
						+
3/10	144	120/72		8		+
/		/		/		+
/		/		/		+
/		/		/		+
/		/		/		+
/		/		/		+
/		/		/		+
/		/		/		+
/		/		/		+
/		/		/		+
/		/		/		+

Patient desires prenatal care. Will obtain prenatal labs, HIV consent and OB ultrasound for estimated gestational age.

① Return to lab 4 wks for exam
② PN Vitamins, FESO4 given
      ℞ 3-10-93 Vitamins   D. Berry, RN
* Need urine C+S next visit.
Urine 3-10-93 ⊕ WBC and 2+ bacteria

Physician's signature James Mercy MD

Figure 1-8 *Manual Birth Certificate*

U.S. STANDARD CERTIFICATE OF LIVE BIRTH

LOCAL FILE NO.

BIRTH NUMBER:

C H I L D	1. CHILD'S NAME (First, Middle, Last, Suffix)		2. TIME OF BIRTH (24 hr)	3. SEX	4. DATE OF BIRTH (Mo/Day/Yr)

	5. FACILITY NAME (If not institution, give street and number)	6. CITY, TOWN, OR LOCATION OF BIRTH	7. COUNTY OF BIRTH

M O T H E R	8a. MOTHER'S CURRENT LEGAL NAME (First, Middle, Last, Suffix)	8b. DATE OF BIRTH (Mo/Day/Yr)

8c. MOTHER'S NAME PRIOR TO FIRST MARRIAGE (First, Middle, Last, Suffix)   8d. BIRTHPLACE (State, Territory, or Foreign Country)

9a. RESIDENCE OF MOTHER-STATE   9b. COUNTY   9c. CITY, TOWN, OR LOCATION

9d. STREET AND NUMBER   9e. APT. NO.   9f. ZIP CODE   9g. INSIDE CITY LIMITS? ☐ Yes ☐ No

F A T H E R	10a. FATHER'S CURRENT LEGAL NAME (First, Middle, Last, Suffix)	10b. DATE OF BIRTH (Mo/Day/Yr)	10c. BIRTHPLACE (State, Territory, or Foreign Country)

CERTIFIER   11. CERTIFIER'S NAME: _____

TITLE: ☐ MD ☐ DO ☐ HOSPITAL ADMIN. ☐ CNM/CM ☐ OTHER MIDWIFE

☐ OTHER (Specify)_____

12. DATE CERTIFIED _____ / _____ / _____   MM   DD   YYYY

13. DATE FILED BY REGISTRAR _____ / _____ / _____   MM   DD   YYYY

INFORMATION FOR ADMINISTRATIVE USE

M O T H E R   14. MOTHER'S MAILING ADDRESS: ☐ Same as residence, or: State: City, Town, or Location:

Street & Number: Apartment No.:   Zip Code:

15. MOTHER MARRIED? (At birth, conception, or any time between) ☐ Yes ☐ No
IF NO, HAS PATERNITY ACKNOWLEDGEMENT BEEN SIGNED IN THE HOSPITAL? ☐ Yes ☐ No

16. SOCIAL SECURITY NUMBER REQUESTED FOR CHILD? ☐ Yes ☐ No

17. FACILITY ID. (NPI)

18. MOTHER'S SOCIAL SECURITY NUMBER: 19. FATHER'S SOCIAL SECURITY NUMBER:

INFORMATION FOR MEDICAL AND HEALTH PURPOSES ONLY

M O T H E R

20. MOTHER'S EDUCATION (Check the box that best describes the highest degree or level of school completed at the time of delivery)

☐ 8th grade or less

☐ 9th - 12th grade, no diploma

☐ High school graduate or GED completed

☐ Some college credit but no degree

☐ Associate degree (e.g., AA, AS)

☐ Bachelor's degree (e.g., BA, AB, BS)

☐ Master's degree (e.g., MA, MS, MEng, MEd, MSW, MBA)

☐ Doctorate (e.g., PhD, EdD) or Professional degree (e.g., MD, DDS, DVM, LLB, JD)

21. MOTHER OF HISPANIC ORIGIN? (Check the box that best describes whether the mother is Spanish/Hispanic/Latina. Check the "No" box if mother is not Spanish/Hispanic/Latina)

☐ No, not Spanish/Hispanic/Latina

☐ Yes, Mexican, Mexican American, Chicana

☐ Yes, Puerto Rican

☐ Yes, Cuban

☐ Yes, other Spanish/Hispanic/Latina

(Specify)_____

22. MOTHER'S RACE (Check one or more races to indicate what the mother considers herself to be)

☐ White
☐ Black or African American
☐ American Indian or Alaska Native (Name of the enrolled or principal tribe)_____
☐ Asian Indian
☐ Chinese
☐ Filipino
☐ Japanese
☐ Korean
☐ Vietnamese
☐ Other Asian (Specify)_____
☐ Native Hawaiian
☐ Guamanian or Chamorro
☐ Samoan
☐ Other Pacific Islander (Specify)_____
☐ Other (Specify)_____

F A T H E R

23. FATHER'S EDUCATION (Check the box that best describes the highest degree or level of school completed at the time of delivery)

☐ 8th grade or less

☐ 9th - 12th grade, no diploma

☐ High school graduate or GED completed

☐ Some college credit but no degree

☐ Associate degree (e.g., AA, AS)

☐ Bachelor's degree (e.g., BA, AB, BS)

☐ Master's degree (e.g., MA, MS, MEng, MEd, MSW, MBA)

☐ Doctorate (e.g., PhD, EdD) or Professional degree (e.g., MD, DDS, DVM, LLB, JD)

24. FATHER OF HISPANIC ORIGIN? (Check the box that best describes whether the father is Spanish/Hispanic/Latino. Check the "No" box if father is not Spanish/Hispanic/Latino)

☐ No, not Spanish/Hispanic/Latino

☐ Yes, Mexican, Mexican American, Chicano

☐ Yes, Puerto Rican

☐ Yes, Cuban

☐ Yes, other Spanish/Hispanic/Latino

(Specify)_____

25. FATHER'S RACE (Check one or more races to indicate what the father considers himself to be)

☐ White
☐ Black or African American
☐ American Indian or Alaska Native (Name of the enrolled or principal tribe)_____
☐ Asian Indian
☐ Chinese
☐ Filipino
☐ Japanese
☐ Korean
☐ Vietnamese
☐ Other Asian (Specify)_____
☐ Native Hawaiian
☐ Guamanian or Chamorro
☐ Samoan
☐ Other Pacific Islander (Specify)_____
☐ Other (Specify)_____

Mother's Name

Mother's Medical Record No.

26. PLACE WHERE BIRTH OCCURRED (Check one)
☐ Hospital
☐ Freestanding birthing center
☐ Home Birth: Planned to deliver at home? ☐ Yes ☐ No
☐ Clinic/Doctor's office
☐ Other (Specify)_____

27. ATTENDANT'S NAME, TITLE, AND NPI

NAME: _____ NPI:_____

TITLE: ☐ MD ☐ DO ☐ CNM/CM ☐ OTHER MIDWIFE
☐ OTHER (Specify)_____

28. MOTHER TRANSFERRED FOR MATERNAL MEDICAL OR FETAL INDICATIONS FOR DELIVERY? ☐ Yes ☐ No
IF YES, ENTER NAME OF FACILITY MOTHER TRANSFERRED FROM:

_____

REV. 11/2003

Figure 1-8 *Manual Birth Certificate (continued)*

MOTHER	29a. DATE OF FIRST PRENATAL CARE VISIT _____ / _____ / _____ □ No Prenatal Care M M D D YYYY	29b. DATE OF LAST PRENATAL CARE VISIT _____ / _____ / _____ M M D D YYYY	30. TOTAL NUMBER OF PRENATAL VISITS FOR THIS PREGNANCY _____ (If none, enter A0".)

31. MOTHER'S HEIGHT _____ (feet/inches)	32. MOTHER'S PREPREGNANCY WEIGHT _____ (pounds)	33. MOTHER'S WEIGHT AT DELIVERY _____ (pounds)	34. DID MOTHER GET WIC FOOD FOR HERSELF DURING THIS PREGNANCY? □ Yes □ No

35. NUMBER OF PREVIOUS LIVE BIRTHS (Do not include this child)		36. NUMBER OF OTHER PREGNANCY OUTCOMES (spontaneous or induced losses or ectopic pregnancies)	37. CIGARETTE SMOKING BEFORE AND DURING PREGNANCY For each time period, enter either the number of cigarettes or the number of packs of cigarettes smoked. IF NONE, ENTER A0".	38. PRINCIPAL SOURCE OF PAYMENT FOR THIS DELIVERY
35a. Now Living Number _____ □ None	35b. Now Dead Number _____ □ None	36a. Other Outcomes Number _____ □ None	Average number of cigarettes or packs of cigarettes smoked per day. # of cigarettes # of packs Three Months Before Pregnancy _____ OR _____ First Three Months of Pregnancy _____ OR _____ Second Three Months of Pregnancy _____ OR _____ Third Trimester of Pregnancy _____ OR _____	□ Private Insurance □ Medicaid □ Self-pay □ Other (Specify) _____

35c. DATE OF LAST LIVE BIRTH _____ / _____ MM Y Y Y Y	36b. DATE OF LAST OTHER PREGNANCY OUTCOME _____ / _____ MM Y Y Y Y	39. DATE LAST NORMAL MENSES BEGAN _____ / _____ / _____ M M D D YYYY	40. MOTHER'S MEDICAL RECORD NUMBER

MEDICAL AND HEALTH INFORMATION	41. RISK FACTORS IN THIS PREGNANCY (Check all that apply) Diabetes □ Prepregnancy (Diagnosis prior to this pregnancy) □ Gestational (Diagnosis in this pregnancy) Hypertension □ Prepregnancy (Chronic) □ Gestational (PIH, preeclampsia) □ Eclampsia □ Previous preterm birth □ Other previous poor pregnancy outcome (Includes perinatal death, small-for-gestational age/intrauterine growth restricted birth) □ Pregnancy resulted from infertility treatment-If yes, check all that apply: □ Fertility-enhancing drugs, Artificial insemination or Intrauterine insemination □ Assisted reproductive technology (e.g., in vitro fertilization (IVF), gamete intrafallopian transfer (GIFT)) □ Mother had a previous cesarean delivery If yes, how many _____ □ None of the above 42. INFECTIONS PRESENT AND/OR TREATED DURING THIS PREGNANCY (Check all that apply) □ Gonorrhea □ Syphilis □ Chlamydia □ Hepatitis B □ Hepatitis C □ None of the above	43. OBSTETRIC PROCEDURES (Check all that apply) □ Cervical cerclage □ Tocolysis External cephalic version: □ Successful □ Failed □ None of the above 44. ONSET OF LABOR (Check all that apply) □ Premature Rupture of the Membranes (prolonged, ≥12 hrs.) □ Precipitous Labor (<3 hrs.) □ Prolonged Labor (≥ 20 hrs.) □ None of the above 45. CHARACTERISTICS OF LABOR AND DELIVERY (Check all that apply) □ Induction of labor □ Augmentation of labor □ Non-vertex presentation □ Steroids (glucocorticoids) for fetal lung maturation received by the mother prior to delivery □ Antibiotics received by the mother during labor □ Clinical chorioamnionitis diagnosed during labor or maternal temperature ≥38°C (100.4°F) □ Moderate/heavy meconium staining of the amniotic fluid □ Fetal intolerance of labor such that one or more of the following actions was taken: in-utero resuscitative measures, further fetal assessment, or operative delivery □ Epidural or spinal anesthesia during labor □ None of the above	46. METHOD OF DELIVERY A. Was delivery with forceps attempted but unsuccessful? □ Yes □ No B. Was delivery with vacuum extraction attempted but unsuccessful? □ Yes □ No C. Fetal presentation at birth □ Cephalic □ Breech □ Other D. Final route and method of delivery (Check one) □ Vaginal/Spontaneous □ Vaginal/Forceps □ Vaginal/Vacuum □ Cesarean If cesarean, was a trial of labor attempted? □ Yes □ No 47. MATERNAL MORBIDITY (Check all that apply) (Complications associated with labor and delivery) □ Maternal transfusion □ Third or fourth degree perineal laceration □ Ruptured uterus □ Unplanned hysterectomy □ Admission to intensive care unit □ Unplanned operating room procedure following delivery □ None of the above

NEWBORN INFORMATION

NEWBORN	48. NEWBORN MEDICAL RECORD NUMBER 49. BIRTHWEIGHT (grams preferred, specify unit) _____ 9 grams 9 lb/oz 50. OBSTETRIC ESTIMATE OF GESTATION: _____ (completed weeks) 51. APGAR SCORE: Score at 5 minutes: _____ **If 5 minute score is less than 6,** Score at 10 minutes: _____ 52. PLURALITY - Single, Twin, Triplet, etc. (Specify) _____ 53. IF NOT SINGLE BIRTH - Born First, Second, Third, etc. (Specify) _____	54. ABNORMAL CONDITIONS OF THE NEWBORN (Check all that apply) □ Assisted ventilation required immediately following delivery □ Assisted ventilation required for more than six hours □ NICU admission □ Newborn given surfactant replacement therapy □ Antibiotics received by the newborn for suspected neonatal sepsis □ Seizure or serious neurologic dysfunction □ Significant birth injury (skeletal fracture(s), peripheral nerve injury, and/or soft tissue/solid organ hemorrhage which requires intervention) 9 None of the above	55. CONGENITAL ANOMALIES OF THE NEWBORN (Check all that apply) □ Anencephaly □ Meningomyelocele/Spina bifida □ Cyanotic congenital heart disease □ Congenital diaphragmatic hernia □ Omphalocele □ Gastroschisis □ Limb reduction defect (excluding congenital amputation and dwarfing syndromes) □ Cleft Lip with or without Cleft Palate □ Cleft Palate alone □ Down Syndrome □ Karyotype confirmed □ Karyotype pending □ Suspected chromosomal disorder □ Karyotype confirmed □ Karyotype pending □ Hypospadias □ None of the anomalies listed above

(left margin: Mother's Name   Mother's Medical Record No.)

56. WAS INFANT TRANSFERRED WITHIN 24 HOURS OF DELIVERY? 9 Yes 9 No IF YES, NAME OF FACILITY INFANT TRANSFERRED TO: _____	57. IS INFANT LIVING AT TIME OF REPORT? □ Yes □ No □ Infant transferred, status unknown	58. IS THE INFANT BEING BREASTFED AT DISCHARGE? □ Yes □ No

CASE 1-15

Clinical Coding Systems and Technology

Research literature to collect information to use in distinguishing similarities and differences among the encoder's technology of a logic-based automated codebook, to the automated code assignment technology in natural language processing (NLP).

Reference resources would likely include the American Health Information Management Association (AHIMA) website (www.ahima.org), the *Journal of AHIMA*, or the FORE Library: Body of Knowledge.

Compare and contrast how each might be used differently.

Summarize your analysis to state which technology you feel is most advantageous and why. Include reference sources you utilized in your analysis.

External Administrative Requirements: ORYX^{TM} *Performance Measures for the Joint Commission*

You will be having a meeting with the community's medical society to present information on external administrative requirements of hospitals and ORYX^{TM} Performance Measures for the Joint Commission.

What have been the ORYX^{TM} performance measure requirements in the past for hospitals?

Explain how ORYX^{TM} and performance measure data is used in the accreditation process.

One resource to use is the Joint Commission website: www.jcaho.org or http://www.jointcommission.org.

CASE 1-17

Joint Commission Mock Survey

You are on a Mock Joint Commission Survey Team for the hospital. The hospital will conduct an unannounced mock survey in the next 3 months. The team leader has asked you to bring suggestions of activities to include in the upcoming internal (mock) survey to share at the next meeting. You want to include activities that simulate a real Joint Commission on-site survey. You have several ideas from networking with your peers on the regional and state levels of your professional associations and by participating in AHIMA's COP for Joint Commission Accreditation. Your next step is to visit the Joint Commission website at www.jointcommission.org and review the current survey process to gain a better understanding of what is being done during the on-site survey.

What suggestions would you include in the next mock survey conducted?

Clinical Classification Systems and Reimbursement Methods

CASE 2-1

Official Coding Resource

You are training a new coder, Elizabeth. She is a new graduate and just passed her registered health information technician (RHIT) exam last month. Elizabeth is a delight to work with and is anxious to learn everything that she can. One of the things you noticed in working with her is that she is having trouble using the coding references. Specifically, she does not understand how to use *Coding Clinic, CPT Assistant,* and the official coding guidelines. The encoder has these resources built into the system, so it is not a problem with knowing where to find them. She does know how to access and use the encoder but just does not understand how Coding Clinic, *CPT Assistant,* and other resources tie into the coding software. Help her identify which official coding reference can help her assign the proper codes to the diagnoses and procedures listed in Table 2-1.

What other training issues should you address with Elizabeth?

Table 2-1 *Coding Resources for Diagnosis and/or Procedure*

Coding Resources for Diagnosis and/or Procedure	
Diagnosis and/or Procedure	Proper Code According to Official Coding Resources
Uvulopalatoplasty—laser assisted	
Tangent bone grafts	
Needle aspiration of the intervertebral disk using CT guidance	
Vertebral stapling	

CASE 2-2

ICD-9-CM Text

Your physicians hate the verbiage on the ICD-9-CM code 496, "Chronic Airway Obstruction, not elsewhere classified." They prefer the phrase "Chronic Obstructive Pulmonary Disease," so you changed the verbiage in the encoder.

Later that day, another physician came up and asked you to change the verbiage on code 584.9, "Acute Renal Failure, unspecified," to "End Stage Renal Disease." When you refused to change the text, the physician became irate. You were accused of favoring the pulmonologists but not helping the nephrologists.

After you were able to calm him down, you explained why you were able to change the text in one code but not the other.

What did you tell him to justify why you made the first change but not the second?

CASE 2-3

Coding Quality

You have been the coding supervisor for about 6 months. You are settling in and getting a strong grasp of what has been happening in the areas of quality, quantity, work ethic, policies, etc.

You have been there long enough to know that there is a problem with the quality of the coding. You know that you need to strengthen the quality audits that you are performing, so that you have an even better understanding of the coding quality problems. There is a lot of work ahead to get the process where it needs to be—at a 98% accuracy rate. The last audit showed only an 87% accuracy rate.

You decide to begin by conducting face validity audit of the codes. You start reviewing the latest diagnosis index to see if you can identify any glaring problems.

Perform a face validity review of the cases shown in Table 2-2 to determine if any coding quality issues can be identified.

Table 2-2 *Worksheet for Identifying Coding Quality Problems*

Worksheet for Identifying Coding Quality Problems
Case 1   Principal Diagnosis: 041.4 E. Coli infection   Secondary Diagnosis: 599.0 Urinary tract infection (UTI)
Problem(s) Identified:
Case 2   Principal Diagnosis: 038.10 Staphylococcal septicemia   Secondary Diagnosis: 041.10 Staphylococcal infection
Problem(s) Identified:
Case 3   Principal Diagnosis: 414.01 Coronary artery disease (CAD)   Principal Procedure: 36.12 Coronary artery bypass graft (CABG) 2 vessel
Problem(s) Identified:
Case 4   Principal Diagnosis: 550.92 Bilateral inguinal hernia   Principal Procedure: 53.14 Repair, bilateral inguinal hernia
Problem(s) Identified:
Case 5   Principal Diagnosis: 402.90 Hypertensive heart disease   Secondary Diagnosis: 401.9 Hypertension
Problem(s) Identified:

Case 6   Principal Diagnosis: 780.01 Coma
               Secondary Diagnosis: 191.9 Adenocarcinoma brain
               Secondary Diagnosis: M8104/3

Problem(s) Identified:
Case 7   Principal Diagnosis: 850.0 Concussion   Secondary Diagnosis: 784.0 Headache
Problem(s) Identified:

Case 8   Principal Diagnosis: V58.11 Admission for chemotherapy
               Secondary Diagnosis: 174.9 Adenocarcinoma breast
               Secondary Diagnosis: M8140/3 Adenocarcinoma
               Principal Procedure: 99.25 Chemotherapy

Problem(s) Identified:
Case 9   Principal Diagnosis: 426.0 Atrioventricular block, complete   Principal Procedure: 37.81 Initial insertion of permanent pacemaker
Problem(s) Identified:

CASE 2-4

Documentation Support for Principal Diagnosis

You are the coding supervisor at Vale Community General Hospital. A HIM student, Javier, is working with you today. He is looking at some charts and has asked you how you determine if the documentation supports the codes. You decide to walk through the charts with him and explain each one. The principal diagnoses are shown in Table 2-3.

What would you tell Javier about each one?

Table 2-3 *Principal Diagnosis and Explanation*

Principal Diagnosis and Explanation
Principal Diagnosis: Pneumonia Explanation:
Principal Diagnosis: Septicemia Explanation:
Principal Diagnosis: Respiratory failure Explanation:
Principal Diagnosis: Congestive heart failure Explanation:
Principal Diagnosis: Cholecystectomy with cholelithiasis Explanation:
Principal Diagnosis: Preeclampsia Explanation:
Principal Diagnosis: Thrombophlebitis Explanation:
Principal Diagnosis: Cerebrovascular accident (CVA) Explanation:

Improving Coding Quality

Coding quality is your responsibility as coding supervisor. Lately you have been doing a lot of coding audits and have recognized some patterns in the coding errors that you have identified. You have found three problem areas where coders are consistently miscoding: skin coronary artery bypass grafts (CABGs), respiratory failure, and heart catheterizations.

What can you do to improve coding quality?

What role can the encoder play in coding quality?

CASE 2-6

Chargemaster Audit

You are part of the chargemaster maintenance team, but the day-to-day operations tend to fall to you. As the chargemaster coordinator, you spend a lot of your time each day auditing the chargemaster. You printed out a portion of the chargemaster to review. These entries from the Chargemaster Report shown in Table 2-4 are to be audited; the audit will look for comprehensiveness of information and data quality.

What problem(s) can you identify?

Table 2-4 *Chargemaster Report to Audit*

Chargemaster Report to Audit			
CM#	Description	Current Procedure Terminology (CPT) Code	Charge
12355	EKG—12 lead	93000	$78.00
12356	Echocardiology—transesophageal (TEE)	93318	$379.00
12357	R heart catheterization	93501	$1,234.00
12358	L heart catheterization retrograde-percutaneous	93546	$1,234.00
12359	Bundle of HIS	93600	$257.00

Chargemaster Maintenance

You are the assistant director of the HIM department. You have just been given the responsibility of maintaining the chargemaster. The person who was maintaining the chargemaster just quit, and to save money, administration has decided to add this to your current duties instead of filling the position. You only spent 1 day with the person who resigned to learn about what you need to do. This is what you learned:

- The chargemaster coordinator did 100% of the maintenance on the chargemaster.
- If she had a question, she would call and ask the appropriate department.
- She was about 3 months behind in her maintenance.
- When departments started new services, she usually learned about them a week after they started, when billing problems arose.
- The reason that she quit was because she was so frustrated with her job.

You are concerned about what you have gotten yourself into. You know that you cannot do this alone, especially on top of your other duties, which were not decreased when this responsibility was added. You drag out your old textbooks, surf the Internet, and order a new book out on the chargemaster. After studying up on the subject, you decided to draft a proposal on a better way to manage the chargemaster. You want to do a good job because the director has agreed to send the final report to administration.

What plan would you come up with?

CASE 2-8

Selecting Coding Classification Systems

You are the director of HIM. The administrator, Stan, comes to you to discuss a change that he wants to make. Stan wants you either to stop using ICD-9-CM and CPT codes and start coding all of your records in Systematized Nomenclature of Medicine (SNOMED) or to add SNOMED to your coding responsibilities, without additional staff of course. He has heard that SNOMED is much more detailed. He wants to use it so that he can have as much information as possible to make decisions affecting the hospital.

How would you respond?

Presentation on ICD-10-CM and ICD-10-PCS

You have been assigned the responsibility of giving a presentation on ICD-10-CM and ICD-10-PCS to people within your hospital who are involved with reimbursement. This includes the business office staff, coders, chargemaster committee, and others. The goal of the presentation is not to teach them how to code, but to get them to understand the importance of ICD-10-CM, the information provided by the code and ICD-10-PCS, and the impact that it will have on your organization.

Develop PowerPoint slides to be used for your lecture.

CASE 2-10

Encoder Functional Requirements

You are part of a team charged with the selection of the new encoder. You are in the process of developing the request for proposal—specifically, the functional requirements. Last week you sent out a questionnaire asking coders and coding managers about their needs in an encoder. The questionnaires have been returned and combined, and the responses to what functional requirements the coders and coding managers want in an encoder are shown in Table 2-5.

Your job is to identify which of these functions are mandatory and which are optional requirements for the system that you choose. Justify your classification for each functional requirement.

Table 2-5 *Encoder Functional Requirements*

Response to Questionnaire
• Connect to MPI for demographic information download
• Ability to update codes each year when new codes come out
• Coding resources online
• Shows estimated reimbursement for our facility
• Shows list of charts not coded
• Ability to enter code(s) directly
• Ability to write notes
• Ability to transfer codes and other information back into hospital financial system
• Ability to sort codes
• Ability to create and print out physician queries
• Save codes when you are unable to complete the coding
• Multiple groupers

CASE 2-11

Encoder Selection

Administration wanted a choice for encoders made quickly, so the decision was to have the process be as informal as possible. There are two encoder systems to choose from: PerfectCode and JustCoding.

PerfectCode is an automated codebook with numerous reference materials, and it has an interface with the hospital information system and the ability to enter facility policies.

JustCoding is a logic-based system and also has reference materials, an interface with the hospital information system, and the ability to enter hospital policies into the system.

The coders are adamant about their choice. Half of your coders want PerfectCode and half want JustCoding. It was decided that the coders would vote for their choice, and that you, as the coding supervisor, would cast the deciding vote in the event of a tie.

How would you handle this?

What questions would you ask as part of the investigation?

If price, quality of system, references, and other evaluations are relatively equal, which would you choose and why? Be sure to include management, computer, and reimbursement issues.

CASE 2-12

Request for Information (RFI) for Encoder Systems

As part of the encoder selection team, you have been asked to identify four encoders on the market that your facility can investigate further. A request for information (RFI) will be sent to these vendors. You have been asked to gather some basic information on the vendors and their products. The specific information to be collected for each encoder is listed in Table 2-6.

Table 2-6 *Information for Request for Information (RFI) on Encoders*

Information for RFI on Encoders				
Information	Vendor 1	Vendor 2	Vendor 3	Vendor 4
Name of company				
Name of product				
Logic or automated				
Phone number of vendor				
Address				
Summary of additional coding/compliance resources beyond encoder				
Number of years on market				

CASE 2-13

Physician Query Policy

You have suspected there are problems in the physician query process for a while now, and you have planned to review the policy and query form to look for any compliance issues. You would rather find the problems yourself before the Office of the Inspector General (OIG) finds them. Your task today is to evaluate the physician query process at your facility.

Review Figures 2-1 and 2-2 for appropriateness.

Evaluate the policy and procedure on all aspects including:

- standards for completion of a proper physician query
- appropriate format of the policy
- grammar
- form design
- process described
- need to meet discharged not final billed (DNFB) standards

Honolulu General Hospital

Policy Title: Physician Queries

Policy: Physician Queries are used as the sole method of communication between coders and physicians. It should be used when there are problems with incomplete documentation, conflicting diagnoses, recommendations for improvement in medical practices, incomplete histories and physicals, incomplete discharge summaries, and other documentation issues.

Procedure:

Task	Person Responsible
1. Review medical record to determine principal diagnoses, secondary diagnoses, principal procedure, and other procedures	Coder
2. Complete physician query form (see attached)	Coder
3. Complete envelope with physician's mailing address	Coder
4. Mail physician query with a self-addressed, stamped envelope enclosed	Coder
5. When query is returned, review physician documentation and make the necessary adjustments to the code assignment	Coder
6. File the physician query in the medical record	Coder
7. Give copy of the completed query to the coding supervisor	Coder

Effective date: May 1, 2007

Figure 2-1   *Policy and Procedure for Physician Queries*

Honolulu General Hospital
Physician Query Form

Patient Name: _____

Dr. _____

Upon review of the above-mentioned chart for the purpose of coding, the following issue(s) were identified:

Please answer the above question(s) and return to Macon General Hospital in the enclosed stamped, self-addressed envelope. If you have any questions, please contact:

Coder: _____ Phone: (___)___-_____ Date:___/___/_____

Response:

Physician Signature: _____ Date: ___/___/_____

Figure 2-2 *Physician Query Form*

CASE 2-14

Physician Query Evaluation

As coding supervisor, you are responsible for monitoring the queries generated by the coders. You want to make sure that the queries are written appropriately with regard to content, appropriately worded questions, and documentation.

Review the sample queries in Figures 2-3 through Figure 2-10 and critique the content of each of these queries.

Is the query well written?

What recommendations do you have for improvement?

Do you see any trends?

Which coders are better at writing physician queries?

Physician Query

Patient name:	Timothy Brown
MRN:	1125851
Dates of service:	8/12–8/14/05
Attending physician:	Johnson
Query:	Please add Pneumonia, as it is indicated by the CXR.
Financial impact:	$357.25
Coder:	Sabrina

Figure 2-3 *Physician Query 1*

Physician Query

Patient name:	Tyler Smith
MRN:	1257863
Dates of service:	8/14–8/17/05
Attending physician:	Grant, James, MD

Query:

Dr. Grant, the progress note dated 8/15 states that the patient has new onset of asthma. The progress note on 8/16 states that the patient has chronic asthma with status asthmaticus. Please advise me on the proper diagnosis.

Financial impact:	$542.24
Coder:	Toni

Figure 2-4 *Physician Query 2*

Physician Query

Patient name: Tiffany Bradford

MRN: 0985688

Dates of service: 8/23–8/26/05

Attending physician: Rogers, Anthony, MD

Query:

Dr. Rogers, the pathology report states that the patient had cervical dysplasia. Dr. Brown wrote that the patient had carcinoma in situ. Please advise regarding the proper diagnosis.

Financial impact: $1.256.10

Coder: Clarice

Figure 2-5 *Physician Query 3*

Physician Query

Patient name: Grover Lake

MRN: 1015483

Dates of service: 8/01–8/03/05

Attending physician: Finebaum, Frederick, MD

Query:

Does the electrolyte imbalance indicate dehydration? Please circle: Yes or No.

Financial impact: $854.22

Coder: Lonna

Figure 2-6 *Physician Query 4*

Physician Query

Patient name:	Simone Hardcastle
MRN:	1122557

Dates of service: 08/10–8/21/05

Attending physician: Colgate, James, MD

Query:

Dr. Colgate if you will document the BBB in the progress notes, we can increase reimbursement.

Financial impact: $2,345.98

Coder: Claire

Figure 2-7 *Physician Query 5*

Physician Query

Patient name:	Harold Sykes
MRN:	0865521

Dates of service: 8/1–8/5/05

Attending physician: Dodd, Geraldine, MD

Query:

The low potassium is significant isn't it?

Financial impact: $567.98

Coder: Glenda

Figure 2-8 *Physician Query 6*

Physician Query

Patient name:	Susan Stokes
MRN:	1054437
Dates of service:	08/27–08/30/05
Attending physician:	Lawrence, Lynne, MD
Query:	Should hematuria be coded?
Financial impact:	$1,123.87
Coder:	Bob

Figure 2-9 *Physician Query 7*

Physician Query

Patient name:	Frank Byron
MRN:	1597799
Dates of service:	8/13–8/16/05
Attending physician:	Zeigler, Clark, MD

Query:

The operative report indicates that 1130 ccs of blood was lost. A CBC on the first POD shows a low RBC. Does this indicate a postoperative complication?

Financial impact:	$2,321.65
Coder:	Jennie

Figure 2-10 *Physician Query 8*

CASE 2-15

Physician Education

Two of your physicians are constantly writing urosepsis as the principal diagnosis. You send a physician query every time, but they still keep doing it. Both you and the two physicians have become very frustrated. Obviously, the informal education through the physician query process is not working, so you need to try another approach.

What would you recommend?

Why did you choose this method?

CASE 2-16

Using Workflow Technology in Physician Query Management

Janice, the coding supervisor, is excited about the implementation of the new EHR. Currently, to get responses to their queries, the coders have to wait for physicians to come in and complete their charts. This can sometimes take several weeks. With administration asking why the DNFB is not lower, Janice plans to use workflow technology to assist in the query process.

How can this help?

Physician Orders for Outpatient Testing

You are an admissions clerk in an acute care hospital. A patient comes to your facility and says that Dr. Jackson has sent him over to have a chest x-ray. You ask the patient for the order for the test, and the patient tells you that Dr. Jackson did not give him a written order for the test.

How should the admissions clerk handle this situation?

Why is having the order so important?

CASE 2-18

Report Generation

Dr. Smith came to the HIM department research coordinator and asked for a list of all of his patients with a diagnosis code of 486. The coordinator promptly printed out a list and presented it to him. Dr. Smith exploded, "I have lots more pneumonia patients than this!"

How should the research coordinator respond?

What could the research coordinator have done to get Dr. Smith the information that he wanted in his request without upsetting the physician?

CASE 2-19

Potential Compliance Issue

As compliance coordinator, you spend a lot of time looking for compliance issues that need correcting. Today, you are looking at various reports and charts. You cannot tell from the information provided to you if there is a compliance problem, but you can identify areas that need further investigation.

Review the information in Table 2-7 for potential compliance issues. Write a Y if the situation indicates a potential compliance problem; write an N if the situation describes a simple error or insignificant finding. Justify your responses.

Table 2-7 *Potential Compliance Problems*

Potential Compliance Problems	
Situation	Potential Compliance Problem Yes/No? Why?
Principal Diagnosis (Dx): fractured humerus Secondary Dx: crushed larynx Procedure: repair larynx and temporary tracheostomy	
Principal Dx: septicemia Secondary Dx: urinary tract infection Procedure: none	
National percent of simple pneumonia: 76% Your hospital's is 77%	
Your case mix index (CMI) is 1.5678 The average CMI for a comparable facility is 1.2094.	
98% of physician queries ask questions that would increase reimbursement.	
The number of advance beneficiary notices (ABNs) for the past year: 1	
Medicare reviewed 100 heart cath charts. The DRG was changed on two of the cases.	
A review of the remittance advice shows 50 denials over the past month, with 42 of these denials for medical necessity.	
An audit was performed on rebills; 62% were for higher-weighted DRGS, 38% were for lower.	
The annual report of compliance activities shows the following: • number of discharges: 22,000 • 50% of the medical services were audited • only inpatient services were audited • 50 charts were audited	
A new compliance software package was installed in January. In March, HR evaluated salary ranges for all of the jobs in the hospital. The admissions coordinator position's salary was dropped by 25%. The new hires have a high school education and strong typing skills.	
The coding supervisor reviews a random sample of inpatient, outpatient, and ER records for correct coding.	
The sample is taken from all services, all physicians, and all coders.	

CASE 2-20

Discharge Planning

The utilization review (UR) coordinator has been following a patient who has been in your facility for about a month now. The patient was critical at one time, but has now progressed to a point where the hospital can do little more to help the patient. The patient is going to need 24-hour nursing care, but not at a level that requires acute care hospitalization. Since the patient does not meet criteria to remain in the facility, the UR coordinator refers the patient to the physician advisor for review. The physician advisor agrees that the patient does not need acute care hospitalization.

What do you recommend?

What actions do you hope have been taking place over the past month for the patient's expected discharge?

CASE 2-21

Documentation Improvement

Laura just finished a documentation audit. She was not surprised to learn that there were significant documentation problems. The top three problems identified were:

- History and physicals (H&Ps) do not meet Joint Commission and medical staff regulations for time of completion and content.
- Discharge summaries do not meet Joint Commission and medical staff regulations for completion and content.
- Progress notes are very brief and do not adequately describe the patient's improvement or lack thereof.

What should Laura recommend to the HIM director to improve documentation?

Who should be involved in this documentation improvement program?

What else would you want to know?

What type of follow-up should be performed? When?

Coder Education

As the coding supervisor, you have the responsibility of training your staff on the new ICD-9-CM and diagnosis-related groups (DRGs) changes. A date and time for training has been scheduled for the following week. The next step is to develop PowerPoint slides, a script, and handouts to use in the training session.

Identify the changes and develop the materials described.

CASE 2-23

Developing a Coding Quality Plan

You have just been promoted to coding supervisor. The previous supervisor was terminated for incompetence. The coding section is a disaster: there is no coding quality program in place, and there are no coding standards for either quality or productivity. Your job is to clean up the coding section. Since you have been promoted from within the facility, you are already aware of many of the problems. Your facility is in serious trouble with the Quality Improvement Organization (QIO), and you fear that the OIG will show up on your doorstep soon. Although not all of the financial difficulties the hospital is having can be related to coding, many can.

What should you do?

High-Risk Diagnosis-Related Groups (DRGs)

You are the coding supervisor at a 250-bed acute care hospital. The facility averages about 1,050 discharges per month. About 41% of these discharges are Medicare. You have been given the responsibility of ensuring there are no problems with the OIG's high-risk DRGs.

The high-risk DRGs for this year are:

DRG 127
DRG 143
DRG 182
DRG 183
DRG 296
DRG 014
DRG 079
DRG 243
DRG 416
DRG 089

Create a plan for your monitoring of these DRGs. Include at least the types of monitoring, sample size, frequency, case selection, documentation, reporting, and corrective action plans.

CASE 2-25

Diagnosis-Related Group (DRG) Comparisons

Your chief financial officer (CFO) has asked you to gather some information for him. He wants to know the average length of stay (ALOS), average charges, and average reimbursement for specific DRGs. He wants you to compare this data to the national data and determine if there are any statistically significant differences at the 0.5 level. Calculate the ALOS information using Table 2-8. Calculate the average charges information using Table 2-9. Calculate the average reimbursement information using Table 2-10. Use the national data on these DRGs that is presented in Table 2-11. The number of patients at our facility for each DRG is:

DRG	Number of Patients
DRG 88	324
DRG 89	212
DRG 213	132
DRG 276	78
DRG 302	69
DRG 478	99

What does this data tell you?

Table 2-8 *Average Length of Stay (ALOS)*

Diagnosis-Related Group	Average LOS		
	Hospital	National	Statistically Significant
088	4.6		
089	5.6		
213	10.0		
276	3.6		
302	7.9		
478	7.4		

Table 2-9 *Average Charges*

Average Charges			
Diagnosis-Related Group	Hospital	National	Statistically Significant
088	$13,952		
089	$16,205		
213	$35,452		
276	$11,842		
302	$68,235		
478	$25,789		

Table 2-10 *Average Reimbursements*

Average Reimbursements			
Diagnosis-Related Group	Hospital	National	Statistically Significant
088	$3,960		
089	$4,900		
213	$10,425		
276	$33,521		
302	$24,753		
478	$14,573		

Table 2-11 *Medicare Provider Analysis and Review (MEDPAR) 2003 Diagnosis-Related Groups*

Centers for Medicare and Medicaid Services
100% MEDPAR Inpatient Hospital National Data for Fiscal Year 2003, 6/04 Update

Short Stay Inpatient Diagnosis-Related Groups

DRG	Total Charges	Covered Charges	Medicare Reimbursement	Total Days	Number of Discharges	Average Total Days
088	5,669,182,255	5,630,698,366	1,625,123,716	1,983,852	399,007	5.0
089	8,561,664,390	8,513,117,352	2,527,415,468	2,986,606	522,560	5.7
213	329,020,889	324,224,434	108,767,633	93,703	10,333	9.1
276	16,992,378	16,719,658	4,418,783	6,578	1,390	4.7
302	973,840,943	959,396,922	200,261,791	76,418	9,325	8.2
478	4,432,319,240	4,403,795,427	1,446,790,803	806,494	110,942	7.3

Extracted from http://www.cms.hhs.gov/MedicareFeeforSvcPartsAB/Downloads/DRG03.pdf, 100% MEDPAR Inpatient Hospital National Data for Fiscal Year 2003, 6/04 Update.

CASE 2-26

Diagnosis-Related Group (DRG) Changes

You just received a DRG change letter from the QIO. The medical record shows that the patient was admitted to the hospital with a high fever and difficulty breathing. A chest x-ray was taken and showed no signs of pneumonia. White blood count (WBC) was 17.4; blood cultures grew pseudomonas; arterial blood gases (ABGs) CO_2 rate was 49.6; and the O_2 rate was 53.2. The patient was diagnosed with septicemia and new onset asthma. The patient was treated with intravenous (IV) antibiotics, respiratory therapy, and bronchodilators. Since both of the diagnoses met the definition of principal diagnosis, the coder chose septicemia as the principal diagnosis since it paid more money. The DRG change notice said that the principal diagnosis should have been the asthma.

Write a letter to support your choice of principal diagnosis.

Complication/Comorbidity (CC) Diagnosis-Related Group (DRG) Analysis

As compliance coordinator, it is important that you compare your facility to other facilities and the national figures. One of your analyses is to compare the compliance/comorbidity (cc) rate of DRGs for your facility to the national average.

Use the information in Table 2-12 to determine if there is a statistically significant difference between the two figures at the 0.05 level.

Table 2-12 *Complication/Comorbidity Diagnosis-Related Group (DRG) Analysis*

Complication/Comorbidity DRG				
DRG	Number of Cases	National % with cc	% with cc	Possible Over/ Undercoding
DRG 10	157	87.0%	82.2%	
DRG 11	24			
DRG 16	123	78.4%	85.5%	
DRG 17	155			
DRG 24	21	69.3%	70.2%	
DRG 25	18			
DRG 31	2	71.5%	65.5%	
DRG 32	5			
DRG 79	55	65.4%	72.0%	
DRG 80	43			
DRG 99	123	84.1%	83.0%	
DRG 100	175			
DRG 182	54	71.2%	74.0%	
DRG 183	78			
DRG 253	175	37.2%	38.0%	
DRG 254	154			
DRG 304	63	83.5%	81.0%	
DRG 305	54			
DRG 493	32	62.4%	64.0%	
DRG 494	45			

CASE 2-28

Estimated Diagnosis-Related Group (DRG) Payments

Administration wants to know the estimated DRG payment for several DRGs. The grouper on your system is causing problems. Because administration needs this information immediately, you are given the go-ahead to calculate the DRG payments manually. Although manual calculation does not take add-ons into consideration, it will give administration an idea of how much money to expect. The hospital's base rate is $6,321.67. The DRGs that administration is concerned about are shown in Table 2-13. Use Table 2-13 to enter the relative weight from Table 2-14 and calculate the estimated payment.

Table 2-13 *Diagnosis-Related Groups (DRGs) with Relative Weight and Estimated Payment*

DRGs with Relative Weight and Estimated Payment			
DRG	DRG Title	Relative Weight	Estimated Payment
088	Chronic Obstructive Pulmonary Disease		
089	Simple Pneumonia & Pleurisy Age>17 w cc		
123	Circulatory Disorders w AMI, Expired		
143	Chest Pain		

Table 2-14 *Relative Weights*

Relative Weights						
DRG V22	MDC	Type	DRG Title	Relative Weights	Geometric Mean LOS	Arithmetic Mean LOS
88	04	MED	Chronic Obstructive Pulmonary Disease	0.9089	4.1	5.0
89	04	MED	Simple Pneumonia & Pleurisy Age>17 w cc	1.0479	4.8	5.8
123	05	MED	Circulatory Disorders w Ami, Expired	1.5421	2.9	4.7
143	05	MED	Chest Pain	0.5643	1.7	2.1

CASE 2-29

Case Mix Index (CMI) Trends

You have a committee meeting tomorrow where you have to report on any patterns that are appearing in the case mix index (CMI) for your facility. You have been asked to compare your CMI to the national CMI graphically. The national CMI for 2005 was 1.3638 and for 2006 it was 1.4279. Use the data in Table 2-15 to review the CMI for 2005 and 2006.

Table 2-15 *Quarterly Case Mix Index (CMI)*

Quarterly CMI	
Quarter	CMI
First quarter 2005	1.2354
Second quarter 2005	1.2456
Third quarter 2005	1.2156
Fourth quarter 2005	1.4354
First quarter 2006	1.3541
Second quarter 2006	1.3251
Third quarter 2006	1.3296
Fourth quarter 2006	1.3357

Create a line graph.

What trend(s) do you see?

What information would you want to know if you were analyzing the reasons behind the trends?

Give three possible reasons that would explain any trend(s).

CASE 2-30

Case Mix Index (CMI) Investigation

The CFO just called. He was supposed to have asked you to get him the CMI for 2004, 2005, and 2006 a month ago. He just remembered now that he is preparing for the board of directors meeting that takes place in 3 hours, but he needs the information in an hour so that it can be copied and placed in the packet for the board members. He needs you to create a bar graph to show the trending. He also needs you to provide an analysis of the trends so that he can report it to the board.

Use the information in Table 2-16 to make a line graph of the CMI for calendar years 2004, 2005, and 2006.

What trends can you identify?

Can you identify any cause for concern?

What investigation would you want to conduct?

Table 2-16 *Case Mix Index (CMI) for Years 2004, 2005, and 2006 by Month*

Month	CMI by Month Years 2004, 2005, and 2006		
	2004	2005	2006
January	1.4321	1.3276	1.3756
February	1.3215	1.2535	1.4544
March	1.2487	1.2478	1.2489
April	1.5789	2.2435	1.2570
May	1.5789	1.5248	1.5278
June	1.5321	1.4245	1.5741
July	1.2635	1.2857	1.2576
August	1.5227	1.4456	1.5700
September	1.4568	1.2357	1.2768
October	1.2748	1.2575	1.2578
November	1.3578	1.3574	1.4456
December	1.2357	1.6574	1.5788
Annual			

CASE 2-31

Top 10 Diagnosis-Related Groups (DRGs)

Your facility has been investigating your patient population's age, insurance type, and other demographic characteristics. The focus is now turning to services provided. The first round of reports is looking at the top 10 DRGs based on the number of discharges and the revenue brought in. You have been asked to report on this at the department director's meeting next week. You have run a report that shows the relative weight for each DRG and the number of discharges for each DRG. Even though you are using the Medicare grouper and DRGs for the report, all patients are included—not just Medicare patients. Other items of information that you have collected to use are:

- the hospital's base rate: $5,792.38
- the total add-on amount: $268.00
- the ALOS: 3.5
- 43% of your patients are Medicare
- you have 209 physicians as active members of your medical staff

Use Table 2-17 to identify the top 10 DRG for your facility based on:

- number of discharges
- revenue brought in

Table 2-17 *Diagnosis-Related Group (DRG) Relative Weights*

DRG	DRG TITLE	WEIGHTS	DISCHARGES
1	CRANIOTOMY AGE>17 W CC	3.4347	2
2	CRANIOTOMY AGE>17 W/O CC	1.9587	2
3	CRANIOTOMY AGE 0-17	1.9860	0
4	CARPAL TUNNEL RELEASE	0.7878	0
5	PERIPH & CRANIAL NERVE & OTHER NERV SYST PROC W CC	2.6978	17
6	PERIPH & CRANIAL NERVE & OTHER NERV SYST PROC W/O CC	1.5635	23
7	SPINAL DISORDERS & INJURIES	1.4045	1
8	NERVOUS SYSTEM NEOPLASMS W CC	1.2222	1
9	NERVOUS SYSTEM NEOPLASMS W/O CC	0.8736	1
10	DEGENERATIVE NERVOUS SYSTEM DISORDERS	0.8998	51
11	MULTIPLE SCLEROSIS & CEREBELLAR ATAXIA	0.8575	30
12	INTRACRANIAL HEMORRHAGE OR CEREBRAL INFARCTION	1.2456	79
13	NONSPECIFIC CVA & PRECEREBRAL OCCLUSION W/O INFARCT	0.9421	100
14	NONSPECIFIC CEREBROVASCULAR DISORDERS W CC	1.3351	128
15	NONSPECIFIC CEREBROVASCULAR DISORDERS W/O CC	0.7229	53

(Continued)

Table 2-17 *(Continued)*

DRG	DRG TITLE	WEIGHTS	DISCHARGES
16	CRANIAL & PERIPHERAL NERVE DISORDERS W CC	0.9903	86
17	CRANIAL & PERIPHERAL NERVE DISORDERS W/O CC	0.7077	21
18	NERVOUS SYSTEM INFECTION EXCEPT VIRAL MENINGITIS	2.7865	7
19	VIRAL MENINGITIS	1.4451	2
20	HYPERTENSIVE ENCEPHALOPATHY	1.1304	0
21	NONTRAUMATIC STUPOR & COMA	0.7712	0
22	SEIZURE & HEADACHE AGE>17 W CC	0.9970	7
23	SEIZURE & HEADACHE AGE>17 W/O CC	0.6180	17
24	SEIZURE & HEADACHE AGE 0-17	1.8191	1
25	TRAUMATIC STUPOR & COMA, COMA>1 HR	1.3531	23
26	TRAUMATIC STUPOR & COMA, COMA <1 HR AGE>17 W CC	1.3353	54
27	TRAUMATIC STUPOR & COMA, COMA <1 HR AGE>17 W/O CC	0.7212	123
28	TRAUMATIC STUPOR & COMA, COMA <1 HR AGE 0-17	0.3359	12
29	CONCUSSION AGE>17 W CC	0.9567	175
30	CONCUSSION AGE>17 W/O CC	0.6194	123
31	CONCUSSION AGE 0-17	0.2109	23
32	OTHER DISORDERS OF NERVOUS SYSTEM W CC	1.0062	7
33	OTHER DISORDERS OF NERVOUS SYSTEM W/O CC	0.6241	87
34	RETINAL PROCEDURES	0.7288	0
35	ORBITAL PROCEDURES	1.1858	0
36	PRIMARY IRIS PROCEDURES	0.6975	0
37	LENS PROCEDURES WITH OR WITHOUT VITRECTOMY	0.7108	0
38	EXTRAOCULAR PROCEDURES EXCEPT ORBIT AGE>17	0.9627	0
39	EXTRAOCULAR PROCEDURES EXCEPT ORBIT AGE 0-17	0.3419	0
40	INTRAOCULAR PROCEDURES EXCEPT RETINA, IRIS & LENS	0.7852	0
41	HYPHEMA	0.6141	0
42	ACUTE MAJOR EYE INFECTIONS	0.6874	0
43	NEUROLOGICAL EYE DISORDERS	0.7474	0
44	OTHER DISORDERS OF THE EYE AGE>17 W CC	0.7524	0
45	OTHER DISORDERS OF THE EYE AGE>17 W/O CC	0.5203	0
46	OTHER DISORDERS OF THE EYE AGE 0-17	0.3012	0
47	MAJOR HEAD & NECK PROCEDURES	1.6361	75
48	SIALOADENECTOMY	0.8690	1
49	SALIVARY GLAND PROCEDURES EXCEPT SIALOADENECTOMY	0.8809	1
50	CLEFT LIP & PALATE REPAIR	0.8348	6
51	SINUS & MASTOID PROCEDURES AGE>17	1.3269	2
52	SINUS & MASTOID PROCEDURES AGE 0-17	0.4882	2
53	MISCELLANEOUS EAR, NOSE, MOUTH & THROAT PROCEDURES	0.9597	5
54	RHINOPLASTY	0.8711	76
55	T&A PROC, EXCEPT TONSILLECTOMY &/OR ADENOIDECTOMY ONLY, AGE>17	1.0428	12
56	T&A PROC, EXCEPT TONSILLECTOMY &/OR ADENOIDECTOMY ONLY, AGE 0-17	0.2772	45
57	TONSILLECTOMY &/OR ADENOIDECTOMY ONLY, AGE>17	0.8082	2
58	TONSILLECTOMY &/OR ADENOIDECTOMY ONLY, AGE 0-17	0.2110	12

Table 2-17 *(Continued)*

DRG	DRG TITLE	WEIGHTS	DISCHARGES
59	MYRINGOTOMY W TUBE INSERTION AGE>17	1.2867	0
60	MYRINGOTOMY W TUBE INSERTION AGE 0-17	0.2989	1
61	OTHER EAR, NOSE, MOUTH & THROAT O.R. PROCEDURES	1.3983	17
62	EAR, NOSE, MOUTH & THROAT MALIGNANCY	1.1663	3
63	DYSEQUILIBRIUM	0.5991	7
64	EPISTAXIS	0.5958	0
65	EPIGLOTTITIS	0.7725	1
66	OTITIS MEDIA & URI AGE>17 W CC	0.6611	0
67	OTITIS MEDIA & URI AGE>17 W/O CC	0.4850	0
68	OTITIS MEDIA & URI AGE 0-17	0.4210	0
69	LARYNGOTRACHEITIS	0.7524	0
70	NASAL TRAUMA & DEFORMITY	0.7449	14
71	OTHER EAR, NOSE, MOUTH & THROAT DIAGNOSES AGE>17	0.8527	13
72	OTHER EAR, NOSE, MOUTH & THROAT DIAGNOSES AGE 0-17	0.3398	15
73	MAJOR CHEST PROCEDURES	3.0732	117
74	OTHER RESP SYSTEM O.R. PROCEDURES W CC	2.8830	89
75	OTHER RESP SYSTEM O.R. PROCEDURES W/O CC	1.1857	57
76	PULMONARY EMBOLISM	1.2427	14
77	RESPIRATORY INFECTIONS & INFLAMMATIONS AGE>17 W CC	1.6238	115
78	RESPIRATORY INFECTIONS & INFLAMMATIONS AGE>17 W/O CC	0.8947	157
79	RESPIRATORY INFECTIONS & INFLAMMATIONS AGE 0-17	1.5383	17
80	RESPIRATORY NEOPLASMS	1.3936	134
81	MAJOR CHEST TRAUMA W CC	0.9828	54
82	MAJOR CHEST TRAUMA W/O CC	0.5799	45
83	PLEURAL EFFUSION W CC	1.2405	100
84	PLEURAL EFFUSION W/O CC	0.6974	78
85	PULMONARY EDEMA & RESPIRATORY FAILURE	1.3654	47
86	CHRONIC OBSTRUCTIVE PULMONARY DISEASE	0.8778	275
87	SIMPLE PNEUMONIA & PLEURISY AGE>17 W CC	1.0320	154
88	SIMPLE PNEUMONIA & PLEURISY AGE>17 W/O CC	0.6104	112
89	SIMPLE PNEUMONIA & PLEURISY AGE 0-17	0.8124	15
90	INTERSTITIAL LUNG DISEASE W CC	1.1853	1
91	INTERSTITIAL LUNG DISEASE W/O CC	0.7150	2
92	PNEUMOTHORAX W CC	1.1354	6
93	PNEUMOTHORAX W/O CC	0.6035	1
94	BRONCHITIS & ASTHMA AGE>17 W CC	0.7303	214
95	BRONCHITIS & ASTHMA AGE>17 W/O CC	0.5364	187
96	BRONCHITIS & ASTHMA AGE 0-17	0.5560	21
97	RESPIRATORY SIGNS & SYMPTOMS W CC	0.7094	44
98	RESPIRATORY SIGNS & SYMPTOMS W/O CC	0.5382	52
99	OTHER RESPIRATORY SYSTEM DIAGNOSES W CC	0.8733	4
100	OTHER RESPIRATORY SYSTEM DIAGNOSES W/O CC	0.5402	7
101	HEART TRANSPLANT OR IMPLANT OF HEART ASSIST SYSTEM	18.5617	0
102	CARDIAC VALVE & OTH MAJOR CARDIOTHORACIC PROC W CARD CATH	8.2201	0

(Continued)

Table 2-17 *(Continued)*

DRG	DRG TITLE	WEIGHTS	DISCHARGES
103	CARDIAC VALVE & OTH MAJOR CARDIOTHORACIC PROC W/O CARD CATH	6.0192	0
104	CORONARY BYPASS W PTCA	7.0346	0
105	OTHER CARDIOTHORACIC PROCEDURES	5.8789	0
106	MAJOR CARDIOVASCULAR PROCEDURES W CC	3.8417	0
107	MAJOR CARDIOVASCULAR PROCEDURES W/O CC	2.4840	0
108	AMPUTATION FOR CIRC SYSTEM DISORDERS EXCEPT UPPER LIMB & TOE	3.1682	14
109	UPPER LIMB & TOE AMPUTATION FOR CIRC SYSTEM DISORDERS	1.7354	24
110	CARDIAC PACEMAKER REVISION EXCEPT DEVICE REPLACEMENT	1.3223	101
111	CARDIAC PACEMAKER DEVICE REPLACEMENT	1.6380	156
112	VEIN LIGATION & STRIPPING	1.3456	1
113	OTHER CIRCULATORY SYSTEM O.R. PROCEDURES	2.3853	65
114	CIRCULATORY DISORDERS W AMI & MAJOR COMP, DISCHARGED ALIVE	1.6136	115
115	CIRCULATORY DISORDERS W AMI W/O MAJOR COMP, DISCHARGED ALIVE	0.9847	156
116	CIRCULATORY DISORDERS W AMI, EXPIRED	1.5407	54
117	CIRCULATORY DISORDERS EXCEPT AMI, W CARD CATH & COMPLEX DIAG	1.4425	87
118	CIRCULATORY DISORDERS EXCEPT AMI, W CARD CATH W/O COMPLEX DIAG	1.0948	44
119	ACUTE & SUBACUTE ENDOCARDITIS	2.7440	2
120	HEART FAILURE & SHOCK	1.0345	276
121	DEEP VEIN THROMBOPHLEBITIS	0.6949	22
122	CARDIAC ARREST, UNEXPLAINED	1.0404	0
123	PERIPHERAL VASCULAR DISORDERS W CC	0.9425	33
124	PERIPHERAL VASCULAR DISORDERS W/O CC	0.5566	21
125	ATHEROSCLEROSIS W CC	0.6273	12
126	ATHEROSCLEROSIS W/O CC	0.5337	21
127	HYPERTENSION	0.6068	114
128	CARDIAC CONGENITAL & VALVULAR DISORDERS AGE>17 W CC	0.8917	12
129	CARDIAC CONGENITAL & VALVULAR DISORDERS AGE>17 W/O CC	0.6214	21
130	CARDIAC CONGENITAL & VALVULAR DISORDERS AGE 0-17	0.8288	99
131	CARDIAC ARRHYTHMIA & CONDUCTION DISORDERS W CC	0.8287	224
132	CARDIAC ARRHYTHMIA & CONDUCTION DISORDERS W/O CC	0.5227	155
133	ANGINA PECTORIS	0.5116	65
134	SYNCOPE & COLLAPSE W CC	0.7521	54
135	SYNCOPE & COLLAPSE W/O CC	0.5852	67
136	CHEST PAIN	0.5659	185
137	OTHER CIRCULATORY SYSTEM DIAGNOSES W CC	1.2761	119
138	OTHER CIRCULATORY SYSTEM DIAGNOSES W/O CC	0.5835	106
139	RECTAL RESECTION W CC	2.6621	2
140	RECTAL RESECTION W/O CC	1.4781	5

Table 2-17 *(Continued)*

DRG	DRG TITLE	WEIGHTS	DISCHARGES
141	MAJOR SMALL & LARGE BOWEL PROCEDURES W CC	3.4479	118
142	MAJOR SMALL & LARGE BOWEL PROCEDURES W/O CC	1.4324	226
143	PERITONEAL ADHESIOLYSIS W CC	2.8061	5
144	PERITONEAL ADHESIOLYSIS W/O CC	1.2641	4
145	MINOR SMALL & LARGE BOWEL PROCEDURES W CC	1.8783	194
146	MINOR SMALL & LARGE BOWEL PROCEDURES W/O CC	1.0821	186
147	STOMACH, ESOPHAGEAL & DUODENAL PROCEDURES AGE>17 W CC	4.0399	103
148	STOMACH, ESOPHAGEAL & DUODENAL PROCEDURES AGE>17 W/O CC	1.2889	87
149	STOMACH, ESOPHAGEAL & DUODENAL PROCEDURES AGE 0-17	0.8535	1
150	ANAL & STOMAL PROCEDURES W CC	1.3356	17
151	ANAL & STOMAL PROCEDURES W/O CC	0.6657	2
152	HERNIA PROCEDURES EXCEPT INGUINAL & FEMORAL AGE>17 W CC	1.4081	2
153	HERNIA PROCEDURES EXCEPT INGUINAL & FEMORAL AGE>17 W/O CC	0.8431	7
154	INGUINAL & FEMORAL HERNIA PROCEDURES AGE>17 W CC	1.1931	12
155	INGUINAL & FEMORAL HERNIA PROCEDURES AGE>17 W/O CC	0.6785	18
156	HERNIA PROCEDURES AGE 0-17	0.6723	1
157	APPENDECTOMY W COMPLICATED PRINCIPAL DIAG W CC	2.2476	204
158	APPENDECTOMY W COMPLICATED PRINCIPAL DIAG W/O CC	1.1868	191
159	APPENDECTOMY W/O COMPLICATED PRINCIPAL DIAG W CC	1.4521	44
160	APPENDECTOMY W/O COMPLICATED PRINCIPAL DIAG W/O CC	0.8929	12
161	MOUTH PROCEDURES W CC	1.2662	2
162	MOUTH PROCEDURES W/O CC	0.7297	5
163	OTHER DIGESTIVE SYSTEM O.R. PROCEDURES W CC	2.9612	4
164	OTHER DIGESTIVE SYSTEM O.R. PROCEDURES W/O CC	1.1905	51
165	DIGESTIVE MALIGNANCY W CC	1.4125	75
166	DIGESTIVE MALIGNANCY W/O CC	0.7443	53
167	G.I. HEMORRHAGE W CC	1.0060	142
168	G.I. HEMORRHAGE W/O CC	0.5646	44
169	COMPLICATED PEPTIC ULCER	1.1246	24
170	UNCOMPLICATED PEPTIC ULCER W CC	0.9166	12
171	UNCOMPLICATED PEPTIC ULCER W/O CC	0.7013	42
172	INFLAMMATORY BOWEL DISEASE	1.0911	17
173	G.I. OBSTRUCTION W CC	0.9784	62
174	G.I. OBSTRUCTION W/O CC	0.5614	56
175	ESOPHAGITIS, GASTROENT & MISC DIGEST DISORDERS AGE>17 W CC	0.8413	177
176	ESOPHAGITIS, GASTROENT & MISC DIGEST DISORDERS AGE>17 W/O CC	0.5848	150
177	ESOPHAGITIS, GASTROENT & MISC DIGEST DISORDERS AGE 0-17	0.5663	1
178	DENTAL & ORAL DIS EXCEPT EXTRACTIONS & RESTORATIONS, AGE>17	0.8702	0

(Continued)

Table 2-17   *(Continued)*

DRG	DRG TITLE	WEIGHTS	DISCHARGES
179	DENTAL & ORAL DIS EXCEPT EXTRACTIONS & RESTORATIONS, AGE 0-17	0.3253	0
180	DENTAL EXTRACTIONS & RESTORATIONS	0.8363	0
181	OTHER DIGESTIVE SYSTEM DIAGNOSES AGE>17 W CC	1.1290	12
182	OTHER DIGESTIVE SYSTEM DIAGNOSES AGE>17 W/O CC	0.6064	2
183	OTHER DIGESTIVE SYSTEM DIAGNOSES AGE 0-17	0.6179	1
184	PANCREAS, LIVER & SHUNT PROCEDURES W CC	3.9680	1
185	PANCREAS, LIVER & SHUNT PROCEDURES W/O CC	1.6793	1
186	BILIARY TRACT PROC EXCEPT ONLY CHOLECYST W OR W/O C.D.E. W CC	3.2818	5
187	BILIARY TRACT PROC EXCEPT ONLY CHOLECYST W OR W/O C.D.E. W/O CC	1.5748	6
188	CHOLECYSTECTOMY W C.D.E. W CC	3.0530	74
189	CHOLECYSTECTOMY W C.D.E. W/O CC	1.6031	23
190	CHOLECYSTECTOMY EXCEPT BY LAPAROSCOPE W/O C.D.E. W CC	2.5425	1
191	CHOLECYSTECTOMY EXCEPT BY LAPAROSCOPE W/O C.D.E. W/O CC	1.1604	2
192	HEPATOBILIARY DIAGNOSTIC PROCEDURE FOR MALIGNANCY	2.4073	4
193	HEPATOBILIARY DIAGNOSTIC PROCEDURE FOR NON-MALIGNANCY	2.7868	35
194	OTHER HEPATOBILIARY OR PANCREAS O.R. PROCEDURES	3.7339	1
195	CIRRHOSIS & ALCOHOLIC HEPATITIS	1.3318	2
196	MALIGNANCY OF HEPATOBILIARY SYSTEM OR PANCREAS	1.3552	4
197	DISORDERS OF PANCREAS EXCEPT MALIGNANCY	1.1249	1
198	DISORDERS OF LIVER EXCEPT MALIG, CIRR, ALC HEPA W CC	1.2059	26
199	DISORDERS OF LIVER EXCEPT MALIG, CIRR, ALC HEPA W/O CC	0.7292	21
200	DISORDERS OF THE BILIARY TRACT W CC	1.1746	12
201	DISORDERS OF THE BILIARY TRACT W/O CC	0.6895	1
202	HIP & FEMUR PROCEDURES EXCEPT MAJOR JOINT AGE>17 W CC	1.9059	165
203	HIP & FEMUR PROCEDURES EXCEPT MAJOR JOINT AGE>17 W/O CC	1.2690	123
204	HIP & FEMUR PROCEDURES EXCEPT MAJOR JOINT AGE 0-17	1.2877	0
205	AMPUTATION FOR MUSCULOSKELETAL SYSTEM & CONN TISSUE DISORDERS	2.0428	0
206	BIOPSIES OF MUSCULOSKELETAL SYSTEM & CONNECTIVE TISSUE	1.9131	3
207	WND DEBRID & SKN GRFT EXCEPT HAND, FOR MUSCSKELET & CONN TISS DIS	3.0596	7
208	LOWER EXTREM & HUMER PROC EXCEPT HIP, FOOT, FEMUR AGE>17 W CC	1.6648	2
209	LOWER EXTREM & HUMER PROC EXCEPT HIP, FOOT, FEMUR AGE>17 W/O CC	1.0443	4
210	LOWER EXTREM & HUMER PROC EXCEPT HIP, FOOT, FEMUR AGE 0-17	0.5913	3

Table 2-17 *(Continued)*

DRG	DRG TITLE	WEIGHTS	DISCHARGES
211	MAJOR SHOULDER/ELBOW PROC, OR OTHER UPPER EXTREMITY PROC W CC	1.1164	18
212	SHOULDER, ELBOW OR FOREARM PROC, EXC MAJOR JOINT PROC, W/O CC	0.8185	15
213	FOOT PROCEDURES	1.2251	1
214	SOFT TISSUE PROCEDURES W CC	1.5884	7
215	SOFT TISSUE PROCEDURES W/O CC	0.8311	12
216	MAJOR THUMB OR JOINT PROC, OR OTH HAND OR WRIST PROC W CC	1.1459	1
217	HAND OR WRIST PROC, EXCEPT MAJOR JOINT PROC, W/O CC	0.6976	2
218	LOCAL EXCISION & REMOVAL OF INT FIX DEVICES OF HIP & FEMUR	1.3174	54
219	ARTHROSCOPY	0.9702	1
220	OTHER MUSCULOSKELET SYS & CONN TISS O.R. PROC W CC	1.9184	34
221	OTHER MUSCULOSKELET SYS & CONN TISS O.R. PROC W/O CC	1.2219	45
222	FRACTURES OF FEMUR	0.7768	74
223	FRACTURES OF HIP & PELVIS	0.7407	54
224	SPRAINS, STRAINS, & DISLOCATIONS OF HIP, PELVIS & THIGH	0.6090	6
225	OSTEOMYELITIS	1.4401	1
226	PATHOLOGICAL FRACTURES & MUSCULOSKELETAL & CONN TISS MALIGNANCY	1.0767	15
227	CONNECTIVE TISSUE DISORDERS W CC	1.4051	2
228	CONNECTIVE TISSUE DISORDERS W/O CC	0.6629	2
229	SEPTIC ARTHRITIS	1.1504	0
230	MEDICAL BACK PROBLEMS	0.7658	98
231	BONE DISEASES & SPECIFIC ARTHROPATHIES W CC	0.7200	5
232	BONE DISEASES & SPECIFIC ARTHROPATHIES W/O CC	0.4583	4
233	NON-SPECIFIC ARTHROPATHIES	0.5932	1
234	SIGNS & SYMPTOMS OF MUSCULOSKELETAL SYSTEM & CONN TISSUE	0.5795	4
235	TENDONITIS, MYOSITIS & BURSITIS	0.8554	3
236	AFTERCARE, MUSCULOSKELETAL SYSTEM & CONNECTIVE TISSUE	0.7095	1
237	FX, SPRN, STRN & DISL OF FOREARM, HAND, FOOT AGE>17 W CC	0.6974	0
238	FX, SPRN, STRN & DISL OF FOREARM, HAND, FOOT AGE>17 W/O CC	0.4749	0
239	FX, SPRN, STRN & DISL OF FOREARM, HAND, FOOT AGE 0-17	0.2567	0
240	FX, SPRN, STRN & DISL OF UPARM, LOWLEG EX FOOT AGE>17 W CC	0.7747	0
241	FX, SPRN, STRN & DISL OF UPARM, LOWLEG EX FOOT AGE>17 W/O CC	0.4588	0
242	FX, SPRN, STRN & DISL OF UPARM, LOWLEG EX FOOT AGE 0-17	0.2990	0
243	OTHER MUSCULOSKELETAL SYSTEM & CONNECTIVE TISSUE DIAGNOSES	0.8509	18
244	TOTAL MASTECTOMY FOR MALIGNANCY W CC	0.8967	156

(Continued)

Table 2-17 *(Continued)*

DRG	DRG TITLE	WEIGHTS	DISCHARGES
245	TOTAL MASTECTOMY FOR MALIGNANCY W/O CC	0.7138	143
246	SUBTOTAL MASTECTOMY FOR MALIGNANCY W CC	0.9671	87
247	SUBTOTAL MASTECTOMY FOR MALIGNANCY W/O CC	0.7032	46
248	BREAST PROC FOR NON-MALIGNANCY EXCEPT BIOPSY & LOCAL EXCISION	0.9732	23
249	BREAST BIOPSY & LOCAL EXCISION FOR NON-MALIGNANCY	0.9766	12
250	SKIN GRAFT &/OR DEBRID FOR SKN ULCER OR CELLULITIS W CC	2.1130	42
251	SKIN GRAFT &/OR DEBRID FOR SKN ULCER OR CELLULITIS W/O CC	1.0635	14
252	SKIN GRAFT &/OR DEBRID EXCEPT FOR SKIN ULCER OR CELLULITIS W CC	1.6593	25
253	SKIN GRAFT &/OR DEBRID EXCEPT FOR SKIN ULCER OR CELLULITIS W/O CC	0.8637	47
254	PERIANAL & PILONIDAL PROCEDURES	0.8962	0
255	SKIN, SUBCUTANEOUS TISSUE & BREAST PLASTIC PROCEDURES	1.1326	14
256	OTHER SKIN, SUBCUT TISS & BREAST PROC W CC	1.8352	25
257	OTHER SKIN, SUBCUT TISS & BREAST PROC W/O CC	0.8313	45
258	SKIN ULCERS	1.0195	24
259	MAJOR SKIN DISORDERS W CC	0.9860	2
260	MAJOR SKIN DISORDERS W/O CC	0.5539	2
261	MALIGNANT BREAST DISORDERS W CC	1.1294	74
262	MALIGNANT BREAST DISORDERS W/O CC	0.5340	54
263	NON-MALIGNANT BREAST DISORDERS	0.6892	12
264	CELLULITIS AGE>17 W CC	0.8676	32
265	CELLULITIS AGE>17 W/O CC	0.5391	54
266	CELLULITIS AGE 0-17	0.7822	1
267	TRAUMA TO THE SKIN, SUBCUT TISS & BREAST AGE>17 W CC	0.7313	0
268	TRAUMA TO THE SKIN, SUBCUT TISS & BREAST AGE>17 W/O CC	0.4913	0
269	TRAUMA TO THE SKIN, SUBCUT TISS & BREAST AGE 0-17	0.2600	0
270	MINOR SKIN DISORDERS W CC	0.7423	0
271	MINOR SKIN DISORDERS W/O CC	0.4563	0
272	AMPUTAT OF LOWER LIMB FOR ENDOCRINE,NUTRIT,& METABOL DISORDERS	2.1831	41
273	ADRENAL & PITUITARY PROCEDURES	1.9390	0
274	SKIN GRAFTS & WOUND DEBRID FOR ENDOC, NUTRIT & METAB DISORDERS	1.9470	25
275	O.R. PROCEDURES FOR OBESITY	2.0384	62
276	PARATHYROID PROCEDURES	0.9315	1
277	THYROID PROCEDURES	0.8891	27
278	THYROGLOSSAL PROCEDURES	1.0877	0
279	OTHER ENDOCRINE, NUTRIT & METAB O.R. PROC W CC	2.6395	5
280	OTHER ENDOCRINE, NUTRIT & METAB O.R. PROC W/O CC	1.3472	4
281	DIABETES AGE>35	0.7652	178
282	DIABETES AGE 0-35	0.7267	46
283	NUTRITIONAL & MISC METABOLIC DISORDERS AGE>17 W CC	0.8187	74

Table 2-17 *(Continued)*

DRG	DRG TITLE	WEIGHTS	DISCHARGES
284	NUTRITIONAL & MISC METABOLIC DISORDERS AGE>17 W/O CC	0.4879	56
285	NUTRITIONAL & MISC METABOLIC DISORDERS AGE 0-17	0.5486	1
286	INBORN ERRORS OF METABOLISM	1.0329	0
287	ENDOCRINE DISORDERS W CC	1.0922	3
288	ENDOCRINE DISORDERS W/O CC	0.6118	5
289	KIDNEY TRANSPLANT	3.1679	0
290	KIDNEY,URETER & MAJOR BLADDER PROCEDURES FOR NEOPLASM	2.2183	57
291	KIDNEY,URETER & MAJOR BLADDER PROC FOR NON-NEOPL W CC	2.3761	45
292	KIDNEY,URETER & MAJOR BLADDER PROC FOR NON-NEOPL W/O CC	1.1595	54
293	PROSTATECTOMY W CC	1.2700	78
294	PROSTATECTOMY W/O CC	0.6202	52
295	MINOR BLADDER PROCEDURES W CC	1.6349	42
296	MINOR BLADDER PROCEDURES W/O CC	0.9085	12
297	TRANSURETHRAL PROCEDURES W CC	1.1898	106
298	TRANSURETHRAL PROCEDURES W/O CC	0.6432	123
299	URETHRAL PROCEDURES, AGE>17 W CC	1.1159	21
300	URETHRAL PROCEDURES, AGE>17 W/O CC	0.6783	1
301	URETHRAL PROCEDURES, AGE 0-17	0.5012	0
302	OTHER KIDNEY & URINARY TRACT O.R. PROCEDURES	2.0823	1
303	RENAL FAILURE	1.2692	98
304	ADMIT FOR RENAL DIALYSIS	0.7942	3
305	KIDNEY & URINARY TRACT NEOPLASMS W CC	1.1539	54
306	KIDNEY & URINARY TRACT NEOPLASMS W/O CC	0.6385	24
307	KIDNEY & URINARY TRACT INFECTIONS AGE>17 W CC	0.8658	117
308	KIDNEY & URINARY TRACT INFECTIONS AGE>17 W/O CC	0.5652	189
309	KIDNEY & URINARY TRACT INFECTIONS AGE 0-17	0.5498	4
310	URINARY STONES W CC, &/OR ESW LITHOTRIPSY	0.8214	75
311	URINARY STONES W/O CC	0.5050	24
312	KIDNEY & URINARY TRACT SIGNS & SYMPTOMS AGE>17 W CC	0.6436	2
313	KIDNEY & URINARY TRACT SIGNS & SYMPTOMS AGE>17 W/O CC	0.4391	4
314	KIDNEY & URINARY TRACT SIGNS & SYMPTOMS AGE 0-17	0.3748	5
315	URETHRAL STRICTURE AGE>17 W CC	0.7079	4
316	URETHRAL STRICTURE AGE>17 W/O CC	0.4701	6
317	URETHRAL STRICTURE AGE 0-17	0.3227	4
318	OTHER KIDNEY & URINARY TRACT DIAGNOSES AGE>17 W CC	1.0619	4
319	OTHER KIDNEY & URINARY TRACT DIAGNOSES AGE>17 W/O CC	0.6160	45
320	OTHER KIDNEY & URINARY TRACT DIAGNOSES AGE 0-17	0.9669	3
321	MAJOR MALE PELVIC PROCEDURES W CC	1.4368	18
322	MAJOR MALE PELVIC PROCEDURES W/O CC	1.1004	12
323	TRANSURETHRAL PROSTATECTOMY W CC	0.8425	68
324	TRANSURETHRAL PROSTATECTOMY W/O CC	0.5747	98
325	TESTES PROCEDURES, FOR MALIGNANCY	1.3772	14
326	TESTES PROCEDURES, NON-MALIGNANCY AGE>17	1.1866	22

(Continued)

Table 2-17 *(Continued)*

DRG	DRG TITLE	WEIGHTS	DISCHARGES
327	TESTES PROCEDURES, NON-MALIGNANCY AGE 0-17	0.2868	4
328	PENIS PROCEDURES	1.2622	7
329	CIRCUMCISION AGE>17	0.8737	0
330	CIRCUMCISION AGE 0-17	0.1559	0
331	OTHER MALE REPRODUCTIVE SYSTEM O.R. PROCEDURES FOR MALIGNANCY	1.2475	6
332	OTHER MALE REPRODUCTIVE SYSTEM O.R. PROC EXCEPT FOR MALIGNANCY	1.1472	4
333	MALIGNANCY, MALE REPRODUCTIVE SYSTEM, W CC	1.0441	12
334	MALIGNANCY, MALE REPRODUCTIVE SYSTEM, W/O CC	0.6104	5
335	BENIGN PROSTATIC HYPERTROPHY W CC	0.7188	66
336	BENIGN PROSTATIC HYPERTROPHY W/O CC	0.4210	54
337	INFLAMMATION OF THE MALE REPRODUCTIVE SYSTEM	0.7289	4
338	STERILIZATION, MALE	0.2392	4
339	OTHER MALE REPRODUCTIVE SYSTEM DIAGNOSES	0.7360	1
340	PELVIC EVISCERATION, RADICAL HYSTERECTOMY & RADICAL VULVECTOMY	1.8504	19
341	UTERINE,ADNEXA PROC FOR NON-OVARIAN/ADNEXAL MALIG W CC	1.5135	5
342	UTERINE,ADNEXA PROC FOR NON-OVARIAN/ADNEXAL MALIG W/O CC	0.8824	15
343	FEMALE REPRODUCTIVE SYSTEM RECONSTRUCTIVE PROCEDURES	0.7428	21
344	UTERINE & ADNEXA PROC FOR OVARIAN OR ADNEXAL MALIGNANCY	2.2237	1
345	UTERINE & ADNEXA PROC FOR NON-MALIGNANCY W CC	1.1448	42
346	UTERINE & ADNEXA PROC FOR NON-MALIGNANCY W/O CC	0.7948	21
347	VAGINA, CERVIX & VULVA PROCEDURES	0.8582	
348	LAPAROSCOPY & INCISIONAL TUBAL INTERRUPTION	1.0847	5
349	ENDOSCOPIC TUBAL INTERRUPTION	0.3057	6
350	D&C, CONIZATION & RADIO-IMPLANT, FOR MALIGNANCY	0.9728	4
351	D&C, CONIZATION EXCEPT FOR MALIGNANCY	0.8709	3
352	OTHER FEMALE REPRODUCTIVE SYSTEM O.R. PROCEDURES	2.0408	1
353	MALIGNANCY, FEMALE REPRODUCTIVE SYSTEM W CC	1.2348	12
354	MALIGNANCY, FEMALE REPRODUCTIVE SYSTEM W/O CC	0.5728	12
355	INFECTIONS, FEMALE REPRODUCTIVE SYSTEM	1.1684	6
356	MENSTRUAL & OTHER FEMALE REPRODUCTIVE SYSTEM DISORDERS	0.6310	42
357	CESAREAN SECTION W CC	0.8974	72
358	CESAREAN SECTION W/O CC	0.6066	456
359	VAGINAL DELIVERY W COMPLICATING DIAGNOSES	0.5027	854
360	VAGINAL DELIVERY W/O COMPLICATING DIAGNOSES	0.3556	1065
361	VAGINAL DELIVERY W STERILIZATION &/OR D&C	0.6712	165
362	VAGINAL DELIVERY W O.R. PROC EXCEPT STERIL &/OR D&C	0.5837	6

Table 2-17 *(Continued)*

DRG	DRG TITLE	WEIGHTS	DISCHARGES
363	POSTPARTUM & POST ABORTION DIAGNOSES W/O O.R. PROCEDURE	0.5242	12
364	POSTPARTUM & POST ABORTION DIAGNOSES W O.R. PROCEDURE	1.6996	21
365	ECTOPIC PREGNANCY	0.7472	42
366	THREATENED ABORTION	0.3578	62
367	ABORTION W/O D&C	0.3925	1
368	ABORTION W D&C, ASPIRATION CURETTAGE OR HYSTEROTOMY	0.6034	6
369	FALSE LABOR	0.2070	45
370	OTHER ANTEPARTUM DIAGNOSES W MEDICAL COMPLICATIONS	0.5053	85
371	OTHER ANTEPARTUM DIAGNOSES W/O MEDICAL COMPLICATIONS	0.3225	92
372	NEONATES, DIED OR TRANSFERRED TO ANOTHER ACUTE CARE FACILITY	1.3930	362
373	EXTREME IMMATURITY OR RESPIRATORY DISTRESS SYNDROME, NEONATE	4.5935	89
374	PREMATURITY W MAJOR PROBLEMS	3.1372	24
375	PREMATURITY W/O MAJOR PROBLEMS	1.8929	55
376	FULL TERM NEONATE W MAJOR PROBLEMS	3.2226	41
377	NEONATE W OTHER SIGNIFICANT PROBLEMS	1.1406	2
378	NORMAL NEWBORN	0.1544	2101
379	SPLENECTOMY AGE>17	3.0459	25
380	SPLENECTOMY AGE 0-17	1.3645	3
381	OTHER O.R. PROCEDURES OF THE BLOOD AND BLOOD FORMING ORGANS	1.9109	1
382	RED BLOOD CELL DISORDERS AGE>17	0.8328	24
383	RED BLOOD CELL DISORDERS AGE 0-17	0.8323	1
384	COAGULATION DISORDERS	1.2986	3
385	RETICULOENDOTHELIAL & IMMUNITY DISORDERS W CC	1.2082	0
386	RETICULOENDOTHELIAL & IMMUNITY DISORDERS W/O CC	0.6674	0
387	LYMPHOMA & NON-ACUTE LEUKEMIA W OTHER O.R. PROC W CC	2.9678	1
388	LYMPHOMA & NON-ACUTE LEUKEMIA W OTHER O.R. PROC W/O CC	1.1810	56
389	LYMPHOMA & NON-ACUTE LEUKEMIA W CC	1.8432	45
390	LYMPHOMA & NON-ACUTE LEUKEMIA W/O CC	0.9265	5
391	ACUTE LEUKEMIA W/O MAJOR O.R. PROCEDURE AGE 0-17	1.9346	12
392	MYELOPROLIF DISORD OR POORLY DIFF NEOPL W MAJ O.R. PROC W CC	2.7897	5
393	MYELOPROLIF DISORD OR POORLY DIFF NEOPL W MAJ O.R. PROC W/O CC	1.2289	6
394	MYELOPROLIF DISORD OR POORLY DIFF NEOPL W OTHER O.R. PROC	2.2460	4
395	RADIOTHERAPY	1.2074	275
396	CHEMOTHERAPY W/O ACUTE LEUKEMIA AS SECONDARY DIAGNOSIS	1.1069	675

(Continued)

Table 2-17 *(Continued)*

DRG	DRG TITLE	WEIGHTS	DISCHARGES
397	HISTORY OF MALIGNANCY W/O ENDOSCOPY	0.3635	0
398	HISTORY OF MALIGNANCY W ENDOSCOPY	0.8451	14
399	OTHER MYELOPROLIF DIS OR POORLY DIFF NEOPL DIAG W CC	1.3048	2
400	OTHER MYELOPROLIF DIS OR POORLY DIFF NEOPL DIAG W/O CC	0.7788	4
401	O.R. PROCEDURE FOR INFECTIOUS & PARASITIC DISEASES	3.9890	0
402	SEPTICEMIA AGE>17	1.6774	117
403	SEPTICEMIA AGE 0-17	1.1689	41
404	POSTOPERATIVE & POST-TRAUMATIC INFECTIONS	1.0716	7
405	FEVER OF UNKNOWN ORIGIN AGE>17 W CC	0.8453	6
406	FEVER OF UNKNOWN ORIGIN AGE>17 W/O CC	0.6077	21
407	VIRAL ILLNESS AGE>17	0.7664	2
408	VIRAL ILLNESS & FEVER OF UNKNOWN ORIGIN AGE 0-17	0.6171	1
409	OTHER INFECTIOUS & PARASITIC DISEASES DIAGNOSES	1.9196	0
410	O.R. PROCEDURE W PRINCIPAL DIAGNOSES OF MENTAL ILLNESS	2.2773	0
411	ACUTE ADJUSTMENT REACTION & PSYCHOSOCIAL DYSFUNCTION	0.6191	0
412	DEPRESSIVE NEUROSES	0.4656	0
413	NEUROSES EXCEPT DEPRESSIVE	0.5135	0
414	DISORDERS OF PERSONALITY & IMPULSE CONTROL	0.6981	0
415	ORGANIC DISTURBANCES & MENTAL RETARDATION	0.7919	0
416	PSYCHOSES	0.6483	0
417	CHILDHOOD MENTAL DISORDERS	0.5178	0
418	OTHER MENTAL DISORDER DIAGNOSES	0.6282	0
419	ALCOHOL/DRUG ABUSE OR DEPENDENCE, LEFT AMA	0.2776	0
420	SKIN GRAFTS FOR INJURIES	1.9398	65
421	WOUND DEBRIDEMENTS FOR INJURIES	1.9457	14
422	HAND PROCEDURES FOR INJURIES	0.9382	25
423	OTHER O.R. PROCEDURES FOR INJURIES W CC	2.5660	56
424	OTHER O.R. PROCEDURES FOR INJURIES W/O CC	0.9943	10
425	TRAUMATIC INJURY AGE>17 W CC	0.7556	21
426	TRAUMATIC INJURY AGE>17 W/O CC	0.5033	32
427	TRAUMATIC INJURY AGE 0-17	0.2999	4
428	ALLERGIC REACTIONS AGE>17	0.5569	6
429	ALLERGIC REACTIONS AGE 0-17	0.0987	1
430	POISONING & TOXIC EFFECTS OF DRUGS AGE>17 W CC	0.8529	1
431	POISONING & TOXIC EFFECTS OF DRUGS AGE>17 W/O CC	0.4282	5
432	POISONING & TOXIC EFFECTS OF DRUGS AGE 0-17	0.2663	3
433	COMPLICATIONS OF TREATMENT W CC	1.0462	6
434	COMPLICATIONS OF TREATMENT W/O CC	0.5285	4
435	OTHER INJURY, POISONING & TOXIC EFFECT DIAG W CC	0.8141	1
436	OTHER INJURY, POISONING & TOXIC EFFECT DIAG W/O CC	0.4725	2
437	O.R. PROC W DIAGNOSES OF OTHER CONTACT W HEALTH SERVICES	1.3974	0
438	REHABILITATION	0.8700	0
439	SIGNS & SYMPTOMS W CC	0.6960	6

Table 2-17 *(Continued)*

DRG	DRG TITLE	WEIGHTS	DISCHARGES
440	SIGNS & SYMPTOMS W/O CC	0.5055	24
441	AFTERCARE W HISTORY OF MALIGNANCY AS SECONDARY DIAGNOSIS	0.6224	0
442	AFTERCARE W/O HISTORY OF MALIGNANCY AS SECONDARY DIAGNOSIS	0.7806	0
443	OTHER FACTORS INFLUENCING HEALTH STATUS	0.4803	0
444	EXTENSIVE O.R. PROCEDURE UNRELATED TO PRINCIPAL DIAGNOSIS	4.0031	85
445	PRINCIPAL DIAGNOSIS INVALID AS DISCHARGE DIAGNOSIS	0.0000	0
446	UNGROUPABLE	0.0000	0
447	BILATERAL OR MULTIPLE MAJOR JOINT PROCS OF LOWER EXTREMITY	3.1391	0
448	ACUTE LEUKEMIA W/O MAJOR O.R. PROCEDURE AGE>17	3.4231	6
449	RESPIRATORY SYSTEM DIAGNOSIS WITH VENTILATOR SUPPORT	3.6091	152
450	PROSTATIC O.R. PROCEDURE UNRELATED TO PRINCIPAL DIAGNOSIS	2.1822	6
451	NON-EXTENSIVE O.R. PROCEDURE UNRELATED TO PRINCIPAL DIAGNOSIS	2.0607	78
452	OTHER VASCULAR PROCEDURES W/O CC	1.4434	36
453	LIVER TRANSPLANT AND/OR INTESTINAL TRANSPLANT	8.9693	0
454	BONE MARROW TRANSPLANT	6.2321	0
455	TRACHEOSTOMY FOR FACE, MOUTH & NECK DIAGNOSES	3.3387	6
456	CRANIOTOMY FOR MULTIPLE SIGNIFICANT TRAUMA	5.1438	4
457	LIMB REATTACHMENT, HIP AND FEMUR PROC FOR MULTIPLE SIGNIFICANT TRA	3.4952	0
458	OTHER O.R. PROCEDURES FOR MULTIPLE SIGNIFICANT TRAUMA	4.7323	45
459	OTHER MULTIPLE SIGNIFICANT TRAUMA	1.9459	54
460	HIV W EXTENSIVE O.R. PROCEDURE	4.4353	6
461	HIV W MAJOR RELATED CONDITION	1.8058	2
462	HIV W OR W/O OTHER RELATED CONDITION	1.0639	4
463	MAJOR JOINT & LIMB REATTACHMENT PROCEDURES OF UPPER EXTREMITY	1.6780	0
464	CHEMOTHERAPY W ACUTE LEUKEMIA OR W USE OF HI DOSE CHEMOAGENT	3.5926	14
465	LAPAROSCOPIC CHOLECYSTECTOMY W/O C.D.E. W CC	1.8333	32
466	LAPAROSCOPIC CHOLECYSTECTOMY W/O C.D.E. W/O CC	1.0285	21
467	LUNG TRANSPLANT	8.5736	0
468	COMBINED ANTERIOR/POSTERIOR SPINAL FUSION	6.0932	12
469	SPINAL FUSION EXCEPT CERVICAL W CC	3.6224	32
470	SPINAL FUSION EXCEPT CERVICAL W/O CC	2.7791	62
471	BACK & NECK PROCEDURES EXCEPT SPINAL FUSION W CC	1.3831	189
472	BACK & NECK PROCEDURES EXCEPT SPINAL FUSION W/O CC	0.9046	204
473	KNEE PROCEDURES W PDX OF INFECTION W CC	2.6462	2
474	KNEE PROCEDURES W PDX OF INFECTION W/O CC	1.4462	3
475	KNEE PROCEDURES W/O PDX OF INFECTION	1.2038	6

(Continued)

Table 2-17 *(Continued)*

DRG	DRG TITLE	WEIGHTS	DISCHARGES
476	EXTEN. BURNS OR FULL THICKNESS BURN W/MV 96+HRS W/SKIN GFT	11.8018	0
477	EXTEN. BURNS OR FULL THICKNESS BURN W/MV 96+HRS W/O SKIN GFT	2.2953	0
478	FULL THICKNESS BURN W SKIN GRAFT OR INHAL INJ W CC OR SIG TRAUMA	4.0939	0
479	FULL THICKNESS BURN W SKIN GRFT OR INHAL INJ W/O CC OR SIG TRAUMA	1.7369	0
480	FULL THICKNESS BURN W/O SKIN GRFT OR INHAL INJ W CC OR SIG TRAUMA	1.2767	0
481	FULL THICKNESS BURN W/O SKIN GRFT OR INH INJ W/O CC OR SIG TRAUMA	0.8217	0
482	NON-EXTENSIVE BURNS W CC OR SIGNIFICANT TRAUMA	1.1817	0
483	NON-EXTENSIVE BURNS W/O CC OR SIGNIFICANT TRAUMA	0.7424	0
484	SIMULTANEOUS PANCREAS/KIDNEY TRANSPLANT	5.3660	0
485	PANCREAS TRANSPLANT	5.9669	0
486	CARDIAC DEFIBRILLATOR IMPLANT W/O CARDIAC CATH	5.5205	14
487	PERC CARDIO PROC W/O CORONARY ARTERY STENT OR AMI	1.6544	23
488	CERVICAL SPINAL FUSION W CC	2.4695	54
489	CERVICAL SPINAL FUSION W/O CC	1.6788	54
490	ALCOHOL/DRUG ABUSE OR DEPENDENCE W CC	0.6939	0
491	ALC/DRUG ABUSE OR DEPEND W REHABILITATION THERAPY W/O CC	0.4794	0
492	ALC/DRUG ABUSE OR DEPEND W/O REHABILITATION THERAPY W/O CC	0.3793	0
493	TRANSIENT ISCHEMIA	0.7288	75
494	OTHER HEART ASSIST SYSTEM IMPLANT	11.4282	25
495	INTRACRANIAL VASCULAR PROC W PDX HEMORRHAGE	7.0505	41
496	VENTRICULAR SHUNT PROCEDURES W CC	2.3160	3
497	VENTRICULAR SHUNT PROCEDURES W/O CC	1.2041	4
498	SPINAL PROCEDURES W CC	3.1279	51
499	SPINAL PROCEDURES W/O CC	1.4195	12
500	EXTRACRANIAL PROCEDURES W CC	1.5767	5
501	EXTRACRANIAL PROCEDURES W/O CC	1.0201	4
502	CARDIAC DEFIB IMPLANT W CARDIAC CATH W AMI/HF/SHOCK	7.9738	32
503	CARDIAC DEFIB IMPLANT W CARDIAC CATH W/O AMI/HF/SHOCK	6.9144	62
504	LOCAL EXCIS & REMOV OF INT FIX DEV EXCEPT HIP & FEMUR W CC	1.8360	42
505	LOCAL EXCIS & REMOV OF INT FIX DEV EXCEPT HIP & FEMUR W/O CC	0.9833	52
506	LYMPHOMA & LEUKEMIA W MAJOR OR PROCEDURE W CC	3.2782	12
507	LYMPHOMA & LEUKEMIA W MAJOR OR PROCEDURE W/O CC	1.1940	54
508	ECMO OR TRACH W MV 96+HRS OR PDX EXC FACE, MOUTH & NECK W MAJ O.R.	19.8038	24

Table 2-17   *(Continued)*

DRG	DRG TITLE	WEIGHTS	DISCHARGES
509	TRACH W MV 96+HRS OR PDX EXC FACE, MOUTH & NECK W/O MAJ O.R.	12.8719	7
510	CRANIOTOMY W/IMPLANT OF CHEMO AGENT OR ACUTE COMPLX CNS PDX	4.4184	1
511	MAJOR JOINT REPLACEMENT OR REATTACHMENT OF LOWER EXTREMITY	1.9643	12
512	REVISION OF HIP OR KNEE REPLACEMENT	2.4827	17
513	SPINAL FUSION EXC CERV WITH CURVATURE OF THE SPINE OR MALIG	5.0739	21
514	CORONARY BYPASS W CARDIAC CATH W MAJOR CV DX	6.1948	0
515	CORONARY BYPASS W CARDIAC CATH W/O MAJOR CV DX	4.7198	0
516	CORONARY BYPASS W/O CARDIAC CATH W MAJOR CV DX	5.0980	0
517	CORONARY BYPASS W/O CARDIAC CATH W/O MAJOR CV DX	3.6151	0
518	PERMANENT CARDIAC PACEMAKER IMPL W MAJ CV DX OR AICD LEAD OR GNRTR	3.1007	65
519	OTHER PERMANENT CARDIAC PACEMAKER IMPLANT W/O MAJOR CV DX	2.0996	41
520	OTHER VASCULAR PROCEDURES W CC W MAJOR CV DX	3.0957	55
521	OTHER VASCULAR PROCEDURES W CC W/O MAJOR CV DX	2.0721	63
522	PERCUTANEOUS CARDIOVASCULAR PROC W MAJOR CV DX	2.4315	6
523	PERCUTANEOUS CARDIOVASC PROC W NON-DRUG-ELUTING STENT W/O MAJ CV DX	1.9132	12
524	PERCUTANEOUS CARDIOVASCULAR PROC W DRUG-ELUTING STENT W MAJOR CV DX	2.8717	56
525	PERCUTANEOUS CARDIOVASCULAR PROC W DRUG-ELUTING STENT W/O MAJ CV DX	2.2108	54
526	ACUTE ISCHEMIC STROKE WITH USE OF THROMBOLYTIC AGENT	2.2473	12
527	**TOTAL DISCHARGES**		22,247

CASE 2-32

Case Mix Index (CMI) Analysis

You have been asked to speak at the local health information management program on the CMI. The instructor has asked you to talk about the CMI in general and then to discuss your facility's data to keep the dry information interesting. You think that it is a good idea, because when you were in school, you preferred real-world examples. You decide to take it a step further and walk the students through your calculations, so they understand that process as well. Continue using the data provided in Table 2-17 to calculate the CMI.

What does the CMI tell you about the facility?

What would you need to do to increase your CMI? Include facility and HIM-related activities.

CASE 2-33

Medicare Provider Analysis and Review (MEDPAR) Data Analysis

Based on the data in Tables 2-18 and 2-19, identify/answer the following:

- The top 20 DRGs by number of discharges
- The top 10 DRGs by patient days
- The highest 5 DRGs by ALOS
- What state is the most efficient based on ALOS?
- What state is the most efficient based on cost of stay?
- How can MEDPAR be used by a hospital?

Table 2-18 *Medicare Provider Analysis and Review (MEDPAR) Data 2003 by Diagnosis-Related Group Short Stay Inpatient by State*

Centers for Medicare and Medicaid Services
100% MEDPAR Inpatient Hospital Fiscal Year 2003, 6/04 Update
Short Stay Inpatient by State

State	Total Charges	Covered Charges	Medicare Reimbursement	Total Days	Number of Discharges	Average Total Days
ALABAMA	$6,416,561,403	$6,376,255,484	$1,739,671,113	1,594,312	294,850	5.4
ALASKA	$288,106,450	$277,321,974	$120,305,527	67,826	11,398	6.0
ARIZONA	$4,178,939,882	$4,154,555,455	$1,202,376,919	821,577	165,231	5.0
ARKANSAS	$3,038,670,848	$3,019,694,729	$1,019,945,287	984,602	170,421	5.8
CALIFORNIA	$36,412,016,996	$35,993,315,579	$8,325,469,263	5,069,193	836,444	6.1
COLORADO	$2,582,844,001	$2,567,883,634	$812,049,029	543,483	109,879	4.9
CONNECTICUT	$3,083,849,020	$3,065,222,735	$1,446,085,710	921,407	154,460	6.0
DELAWARE	$646,612,564	$642,344,326	$304,053,095	253,198	38,216	6.6
WASH. D.C.	$1,167,001,937	$1,153,448,017	$439,385,661	267,540	39,151	6.8
FLORIDA	$25,706,772,089	$25,550,742,319	$6,321,318,465	5,211,650	899,404	5.8
GEORGIA	$6,869,954,038	$6,826,742,743	$2,456,125,859	1,991,992	342,392	5.8
HAWAII	$692,771,899	$673,772,759	$219,252,150	195,729	26,302	7.4
IDAHO	$602,223,883	$600,958,968	$260,868,573	187,843	40,738	4.6
ILLINOIS	$13,602,965,323	$13,504,911,405	$4,338,401,957	3,394,914	607,561	5.6
INDIANA	$5,108,870,833	$5,086,414,348	$2,027,798,313	1,706,900	303,404	5.6
IOWA	$2,301,487,211	$2,287,690,068	$890,554,905	775,366	148,591	5.2
KANSAS	$2,571,736,968	$2,560,848,898	$847,472,436	699,564	131,412	5.3
KENTUCKY	$4,284,476,992	$4,263,389,438	$1,604,911,996	1,407,762	255,264	5.5
LOUISIANA	$5,627,755,763	$5,570,302,771	$1,708,760,974	1,547,550	253,774	6.1
MAINE	$1,087,404,258	$1,082,209,438	$451,839,283	365,569	67,401	5.4
MARYLAND	$2,577,198,033	$2,555,563,694	$2,199,435,496	1,345,779	251,754	5.3
MASSACHU-SETTS	$4,998,491,441	$4,929,164,860	$2,458,503,701	1,637,847	291,062	5.6
MICHIGAN	$9,526,204,118	$9,474,063,461	$4,208,420,181	2,926,420	506,259	5.8
MINNESOTA	$4,111,652,729	$4,088,163,193	$1,573,589,556	1,017,084	208,364	4.9
MISSISSIPPI	$3,248,195,351	$3,233,322,714	$1,062,874,681	1,152,338	183,965	6.3
MISSOURI	$6,685,702,385	$6,643,052,069	$2,251,930,792	1,816,419	320,454	5.7
MONTANA	$583,026,415	$582,048,476	$258,718,188	192,520	40,952	4.7
NEBRASKA	$1,692,343,764	$1,683,604,420	$570,042,977	387,556	71,577	5.4
NEVADA	$2,128,374,175	$2,111,162,417	$468,633,282	353,667	57,345	6.2
NEW HAMPSHIRE	$890,189,492	$882,718,146	$381,213,456	271,610	46,304	5.9
NEW JERSEY	$21,236,987,868	$20,970,954,003	$3,902,933,850	2,890,303	404,035	7.2
NEW MEXICO	$922,847,462	$918,000,095	$343,190,717	261,792	51,533	5.1
NEW YORK	$19,696,237,785	$19,347,015,673	$8,059,214,390	5,933,251	780,893	7.6
NORTH CAROLINA	$7,224,136,034	$7,186,460,243	$3,005,355,694	2,501,344	431,441	5.8
NORTH DAKOTA	$530,804,119	$527,712,406	$250,309,723	182,184	34,645	5.3
OHIO	$10,417,593,388	$10,367,795,206	$4,009,360,017	3,096,228	565,314	5.5

Table 2-18   *(Continued)*

Centers for Medicare and Medicaid Services
100% MEDPAR Inpatient Hospital Fiscal Year 2003, 6/04 Update
Short Stay Inpatient by State

State	Total Charges	Covered Charges	Medicare Reimbursement	Total Days	Number of Discharges	Average Total Days
OKLAHOMA	$3,346,755,657	$3,332,971,698	$1,176,876,717	1,047,061	187,913	5.6
OREGON	$1,704,294,585	$1,697,304,500	$757,587,628	471,332	102,182	4.6
PUERTO RICO	$1,012,340,904	$1,001,377,119	$388,416,225	952,724	134,979	7.1
RHODE ISLAND	$754,524,382	$747,600,267	$309,294,356	232,286	38,506	6.0
SOUTH CAROLINA	$5,032,603,685	$5,012,674,579	$1,554,695,703	1,355,379	218,775	6.2
SOUTH DAKOTA	$699,581,011	$697,574,351	$268,660,072	218,176	42,626	5.1
TENNESSEE	$6,943,392,279	$6,908,794,236	$2,365,038,485	2,040,610	348,700	5.9
TEXAS	$22,316,838,067	$22,121,438,362	$6,372,643,897	5,071,757	868,784	5.8
UTAH	$982,864,007	$979,958,531	$421,161,893	271,398	57,928	4.7
VERMONT	$326,743,664	$323,195,314	$183,579,894	126,825	22,690	5.6
VIRGIN ISLANDS	$24,259,689	$23,763,419	$9,870,252	15,670	1,641	9.5
VIRGINIA	$6,248,299,036	$6,203,231,157	$2,130,328,480	1,846,749	315,181	5.9
WASHINGTON	$3,199,633,821	$3,179,263,174	$1,411,620,782	820,705	167,102	4.9
WEST VIRGINIA	$1,754,457,566	$1,747,213,122	$767,443,818	736,513	131,953	5.6
WISCONSIN	$4,399,848,381	$4,383,608,273	$1,738,470,646	1,273,282	244,100	5.2
WYOMING	$250,862,852	$250,782,214	$102,973,104	77,686	16,416	4.7
UNKNOWN	$15,928,610	$15,729,931	$11,643,853	13,109	2,061	6.4
TOTAL LINE	$300,194,347,235	$297,677,999,538	$96,636,077,829	74,443,350	12,698,388	5.9

Extracted from http://www.cms.hhs.gov/MedicareFeeforSvcPartsAB/Downloads/DRGstate03.pdf.

Table 2-19 *Medicare Provider Analysis and Review (MEDPAR) Inpatient National Data by Short Stay Inpatient Diagnosis-Related Groups (DRGs)*

Centers for Medicare and Medicaid Services
100% MEDPAR Inpatient Hospital National Data for Fiscal Year 2003 6/04 Update
Short Stay Inpatient Diagnosis Related Groups
Blank cells represent ten or less discharges in order to conform to CMS guidelines, zero means no discharges, therefore, sum of columns will not equal total.

DRG	Total Charges	Covered Charges	Medicare Reimbursement	Total Days	Number of Discharges	Average Total Days
001	$2,070,225,086	$2,058,048,914	$742,001,883	349,386	33,031	10.6
002	452,655,611	449,477,510	146,824,565	61,611	13,528	4.6
003	0	0	0	0	0	0.0
004	297,806,132	295,567,799	94,300,816	51,721	7,170	7.2
005	1,999,974,999	1,993,480,644	623,968,451	274,901	94,895	2.9
006	4,868,776	4,844,977	1,463,202	1,293	371	3.5
007	687,000,396	681,435,303	223,550,026	150,227	15,364	9.8
008	105,053,919	104,603,809	30,119,501	10,722	3,899	2.7
009	43,226,627	42,907,414	15,342,287	13,129	1,955	6.7
010	394,876,154	392,042,598	127,450,269	121,652	19,440	6.3
011	50,156,657	49,805,823	14,516,754	13,463	3,456	3.9
012	1,285,225,742	1,273,508,686	465,012,734	643,301	81,349	7.9
013	102,492,448	101,505,054	28,656,394	36,496	7,232	5.0
014	4,956,031,087	4,933,559,378	1,515,805,190	1,434,042	244,047	5.9
015	1,252,133,932	1,246,272,246	378,498,704	400,518	84,050	4.8
016	220,466,769	219,110,412	68,110,962	67,972	10,929	6.2
017	32,495,901	32,121,579	8,159,795	9,162	2,852	3.2
018	509,311,338	500,901,229	147,990,644	168,973	31,226	5.4
019	104,040,842	103,436,312	28,001,656	31,409	8,858	3.5
020	303,426,050	301,050,060	102,287,581	67,488	6,649	10.2
021	56,588,881	56,299,783	17,531,047	14,734	2,207	6.7
022	59,065,012	58,624,070	15,793,788	16,411	3,203	5.1
023	184,515,675	182,300,796	54,719,745	58,631	13,693	4.3
024	1,025,472,686	1,015,305,621	308,115,855	295,465	61,536	4.8
025	298,995,739	296,563,077	79,512,716	90,432	28,724	3.1
026	395,078	380,583	144,974	112	36	3.1
027	123,481,117	122,944,869	37,821,709	26,143	5,098	5.1
028	369,409,765	367,135,077	117,022,105	98,238	16,212	6.1
029	73,056,636	72,373,470	19,834,428	20,738	5,933	3.5
030	0	0	0	0	0	0.0
031	74,710,775	73,901,940	18,696,861	18,918	4,748	4.0
032	20,384,435	20,089,300	3,973,773	5,139	2,013	2.6
033	0	0	0	0	0	0.0
034	426,177,621	422,812,752	132,961,274	127,802	25,752	5.0
035	87,488,015	86,740,578	23,963,895	25,863	8,036	3.2
036	19,476,082	19,350,837	5,463,417	2,568	1,626	1.6
037	29,815,704	29,773,684	8,578,436	5,504	1,392	4.0
038	684,671	684,194	183,656	177	78	2.3

Table 2-19 *(Continued)*

Centers for Medicare and Medicaid Services
100% MEDPAR Inpatient Hospital National Data for Fiscal Year 2003 6/04 Update
Short Stay Inpatient Diagnosis Related Groups
Blank cells represent ten or less discharges in order to conform to CMS guidelines, zero means no discharges, therefore, sum of columns will not equal total.

DRG	Total Charges	Covered Charges	Medicare Reimbursement	Total Days	Number of Discharges	Average Total Days
039	6,599,432	6,433,082	1,779,605	1,239	559	2.2
042	17,008,198	16,803,497	4,407,300	3,521	1,257	2.8
043	1,428,026	1,417,772	286,028	433	126	3.4
044	15,130,996	14,969,127	4,167,393	6,247	1,260	5.0
045	34,461,787	34,271,289	9,127,981	9,093	2,861	3.2
046	46,631,760	46,400,037	13,487,001	15,437	3,617	4.3
047	13,209,149	13,128,518	3,223,497	4,567	1,419	3.2
048	0	0	0	0	0	0.0
049	78,748,908	78,555,806	25,996,569	11,502	2,472	4.7
050	34,466,155	34,389,854	9,236,460	4,539	2,329	1.9
051	3,262,208	3,253,468	1,086,519	686	239	2.9
052	2,358,783	2,356,892	741,283	385	176	2.2
053	49,032,089	48,782,614	14,671,465	8,278	2,293	3.6
054	0	0	0	0	0	0.0
055	24,079,109	23,838,162	7,575,549	4,329	1,500	2.9
056	7,355,055	7,155,590	2,185,199	1,314	478	2.7
057	12,662,114	12,521,765	3,552,246	2,817	731	3.9
058	0	0	0	0	0	0.0
059	1,214,716	1,214,368	380,005	305	121	2.5
060	0	0	0	0	0	0.0
061	7,008,317	7,003,782	2,070,866	1,536	263	5.8
062	0	0	0	0	0	0.0
063	69,263,833	68,548,247	22,696,190	12,474	2,815	4.4
064	77,009,612	76,669,942	25,881,196	22,080	3,343	6.6
065	397,249,216	395,248,046	92,761,029	115,367	41,186	2.8
066	76,960,904	76,542,987	19,943,482	24,586	7,943	3.1
067	5,603,243	5,502,921	1,374,640	1,450	409	3.5
068	96,821,280	95,969,754	26,585,157	33,492	8,947	3.7
069	24,324,091	24,031,435	5,933,582	8,837	3,006	2.9
070	223,188	200,544	61,980	75	26	2.9
071	593,213	577,661	181,909	240	67	3.6
072	15,001,961	14,809,653	4,042,696	4,395	1,231	3.6
073	109,825,931	109,064,638	30,718,756	35,878	8,014	4.5
074	0	0	0	0	0	0.0
075	2,233,510,454	2,221,145,916	772,509,575	439,946	44,814	9.8
076	2,180,514,265	2,152,078,362	747,832,739	511,574	46,635	11.0
077	47,794,391	47,665,734	14,242,106	11,154	2,377	4.7
078	857,332,549	852,879,692	272,525,147	277,782	43,316	6.4
079	4,454,453,889	4,411,162,300	1,426,232,647	1,450,637	174,044	8.3

(Continued)

Table 2-19 *(Continued)*

Centers for Medicare and Medicaid Services
100% MEDPAR Inpatient Hospital National Data for Fiscal Year 2003 6/04 Update
Short Stay Inpatient Diagnosis Related Groups
Blank cells represent ten or less discharges in order to conform to CMS guidelines, zero means no discharges, therefore, sum of columns will not equal total.

DRG	Total Charges	Covered Charges	Medicare Reimbursement	Total Days	Number of Discharges	Average Total Days
080	108,674,895	108,135,337	32,250,169	42,877	7,981	5.4
081	0	0	0	0	0	0.0
082	1,474,330,730	1,466,206,345	470,758,469	450,459	66,637	6.8
083	110,850,963	110,066,797	29,444,867	37,856	7,072	5.4
084	13,963,580	13,807,369	2,690,918	4,848	1,531	3.2
085	447,240,017	444,464,835	138,155,418	143,645	22,722	6.3
086	23,589,506	23,433,957	6,901,264	7,503	2,083	3.6
087	1,411,294,558	1,393,945,561	442,554,434	432,278	67,457	6.4
088	5,669,182,255	5,630,698,366	1,625,123,716	1,983,852	399,007	5.0
089	8,561,664,390	8,513,117,352	2,527,415,468	2,986,606	522,560	5.7
090	427,676,932	425,112,444	110,709,056	171,076	44,283	3.9
091	653,709	653,617	224,788	197	51	3.9
092	322,101,850	319,944,867	100,799,821	104,114	16,753	6.2
093	19,357,048	19,263,180	5,491,068	6,643	1,679	4.0
094	243,718,001	242,041,978	72,938,740	82,303	13,332	6.2
095	15,935,061	15,793,723	3,962,530	5,987	1,625	3.7
096	604,281,371	599,063,311	165,235,232	226,963	51,335	4.4
097	228,188,313	226,270,509	58,391,401	90,052	26,337	3.4
098	181,615	179,595	50,718	49	16	3.1
099	253,816,054	251,385,398	69,855,552	69,561	22,018	3.2
100	66,787,121	66,247,856	16,457,618	16,399	7,677	2.1
101	332,061,162	328,229,858	95,020,362	101,560	23,383	4.3
102	50,232,784	49,814,036	12,420,228	14,280	5,596	2.6
103	238,124,402	225,167,604	89,507,830	24,172	576	42.0
104	2,812,901,928	2,800,836,501	1,015,051,283	307,509	20,986	14.7
105	3,000,146,529	2,989,366,194	1,050,390,719	306,555	30,794	10.0
106	413,146,371	411,504,092	141,581,372	39,508	3,506	11.3
107	6,861,175,704	6,838,549,763	2,271,233,244	831,079	78,781	10.5
108	621,064,789	617,621,682	227,768,870	67,693	7,081	9.6
109	3,523,581,852	3,511,857,610	1,162,973,262	424,242	54,767	7.7
110	3,618,552,533	3,603,573,074	1,285,704,776	482,701	55,797	8.7
111	377,461,378	376,461,126	117,735,954	34,944	9,490	3.7
112	0	0	0	0	0	0.0
113	1,813,758,271	1,794,604,998	590,551,038	488,231	38,825	12.6
114	242,447,928	239,273,404	76,628,448	73,569	8,441	8.7
115	1,286,178,560	1,281,351,976	408,158,826	153,221	21,918	7.0
116	4,437,990,955	4,425,986,841	1,379,205,305	510,509	118,019	4.3
117	110,457,056	109,054,827	35,061,202	21,220	4,903	4.3
118	232,506,664	231,908,775	67,510,264	25,408	8,420	3.0

Table 2-19 *(Continued)*

Centers for Medicare and Medicaid Services
100% MEDPAR Inpatient Hospital National Data for Fiscal Year 2003 6/04 Update
Short Stay Inpatient Diagnosis Related Groups
Blank cells represent ten or less discharges in order to conform to CMS guidelines, zero means no discharges, therefore, sum of columns will not equal total.

DRG	Total Charges	Covered Charges	Medicare Reimbursement	Total Days	Number of Discharges	Average Total Days
119	26,922,178	26,822,118	7,798,257	5,977	1,113	5.4
120	1,457,681,158	1,436,839,348	479,232,874	330,494	37,191	8.9
121	4,036,958,379	4,019,320,405	1,267,412,717	1,030,865	165,004	6.2
122	1,084,690,837	1,079,474,688	325,510,709	244,457	71,205	3.4
123	921,416,923	917,057,437	296,281,354	171,488	36,443	4.7
124	3,160,190,703	3,143,807,450	947,423,734	597,800	134,960	4.4
125	1,671,137,453	1,661,010,594	465,062,135	259,415	93,629	2.8
126	240,574,587	237,331,935	83,662,506	63,595	5,640	11.3
127	11,533,957,976	11,466,411,393	3,403,949,561	3,608,040	697,071	5.2
128	73,198,266	72,786,658	19,557,455	33,893	6,222	5.4
129	67,100,339	66,330,365	21,074,078	10,730	4,021	2.7
130	1,401,441,885	1,390,562,876	426,300,776	508,416	91,188	5.6
131	234,075,017	232,826,081	62,415,581	102,421	25,896	4.0
132	1,313,842,534	1,304,180,664	367,378,406	372,549	129,579	2.9
133	70,259,937	69,487,048	18,858,668	17,629	7,679	2.3
134	423,449,591	420,020,359	106,337,609	135,722	42,968	3.2
135	117,970,729	117,236,272	35,855,903	34,418	7,608	4.5
136	10,989,822	10,928,320	2,866,297	2,954	1,110	2.7
137	0	0	0	0	0	0.0
138	2,768,567,747	2,756,303,830	784,657,727	817,176	205,966	4.0
139	691,415,125	688,576,250	166,837,375	203,780	82,663	2.5
140	379,327,682	376,276,291	96,202,240	115,432	46,261	2.5
141	1,433,602,647	1,426,717,150	386,003,753	404,735	115,328	3.5
142	518,032,395	515,695,809	126,007,311	134,138	52,940	2.5
143	2,261,680,173	2,240,475,481	549,422,138	521,746	247,641	2.1
144	2,043,056,006	2,001,875,424	617,456,019	555,693	97,999	5.7
145	65,382,567	64,731,696	17,745,039	17,554	6,762	2.6
146	470,852,439	469,416,002	158,485,255	111,148	11,052	10.1
147	66,829,242	66,491,104	20,585,025	16,586	2,742	6.0
148	7,481,447,845	7,435,815,815	2,623,430,383	1,677,147	137,260	12.2
149	463,282,855	461,563,114	145,637,682	123,313	20,213	6.1
150	982,873,662	977,996,593	334,362,985	245,326	22,299	11.0
151	110,815,081	110,110,026	33,089,489	28,897	5,347	5.4
152	149,560,572	147,894,459	49,739,697	39,054	4,873	8.0
153	38,856,950	38,617,553	12,166,123	11,116	2,167	5.1
154	1,943,924,191	1,932,254,653	714,370,099	385,647	28,950	13.3
155	138,523,484	137,959,883	41,497,280	27,211	6,571	4.1
156	0	0	0	0	0	0.0
157	176,384,705	174,957,278	53,162,184	47,148	8,377	5.6

(Continued)

Table 2-19 *(Continued)*

Centers for Medicare and Medicaid Services
100% MEDPAR Inpatient Hospital National Data for Fiscal Year 2003 6/04 Update
Short Stay Inpatient Diagnosis Related Groups
Blank cells represent ten or less discharges in order to conform to CMS guidelines, zero means no discharges,
therefore, sum of columns will not equal total.

DRG	Total Charges	Covered Charges	Medicare Reimbursement	Total Days	Number of Discharges	Average Total Days
158	44,372,019	44,192,743	10,928,947	11,019	4,181	2.6
159	421,343,846	419,757,281	125,419,267	96,843	18,921	5.1
160	160,783,162	160,068,595	41,539,793	32,805	12,150	2.7
161	204,594,496	203,575,255	58,394,166	46,942	10,771	4.4
162	64,112,553	63,869,122	15,173,045	12,120	5,995	2.0
163	0	0	0	0	0	0.0
164	213,347,921	212,522,357	67,006,360	48,212	5,860	8.2
165	46,678,709	46,398,727	13,823,252	10,658	2,478	4.3
166	105,239,755	104,811,822	31,234,780	21,078	4,530	4.7
167	62,721,775	62,283,100	16,827,064	10,210	4,417	2.3
168	34,173,830	33,820,984	11,382,631	7,421	1,590	4.7
169	11,740,001	11,632,593	3,245,973	2,233	888	2.5
170	821,517,164	811,788,422	282,748,347	186,497	17,229	10.8
171	28,679,929	28,396,244	8,291,466	6,310	1,483	4.3
172	764,382,985	760,136,493	240,989,703	228,588	32,720	7.0
173	33,112,143	32,862,414	9,874,337	9,744	2,653	3.7
174	4,238,704,907	4,214,219,586	1,236,043,597	1,240,432	260,960	4.8
175	314,314,526	312,590,107	76,326,752	98,909	34,128	2.9
176	237,806,582	236,522,538	69,947,685	69,476	13,149	5.3
177	131,147,762	130,284,056	36,613,188	40,213	8,812	4.6
178	35,281,280	35,091,733	9,245,040	10,024	3,260	3.1
179	253,089,951	250,829,954	73,620,110	84,051	14,190	5.9
180	1,460,114,745	1,448,736,218	419,872,687	502,150	93,577	5.4
181	235,477,631	234,187,406	56,995,025	89,996	26,782	3.4
182	3,858,312,366	3,828,153,922	1,070,810,286	1,291,491	294,294	4.4
183	846,537,568	840,623,084	208,279,653	264,965	91,571	2.9
184	683,114	668,097	168,490	213	66	3.2
185	88,683,081	88,105,760	26,174,665	27,310	5,830	4.7
186	0	0	0	0	0	0.0
187	10,633,657	10,409,280	3,342,457	3,293	767	4.3
188	1,640,834,304	1,619,839,639	503,019,404	494,865	89,211	5.5
189	128,458,136	127,734,050	33,499,215	40,268	13,197	3.1
190	887,033	846,394	364,998	338	78	4.3
191	730,288,361	725,067,040	286,204,175	136,373	10,323	13.2
192	43,414,362	43,195,862	14,436,579	8,191	1,448	5.7
193	253,359,589	252,278,454	87,894,980	56,295	4,459	12.6
194	14,407,812	14,344,255	4,583,585	3,625	551	6.6
195	173,931,540	173,186,442	58,212,475	38,329	3,769	10.2
196	20,068,901	20,009,489	6,070,882	4,503	823	5.5

Table 2-19 *(Continued)*

Centers for Medicare and Medicaid Services
100% MEDPAR Inpatient Hospital National Data for Fiscal Year 2003 6/04 Update
Short Stay Inpatient Diagnosis Related Groups
Blank cells represent ten or less discharges in order to conform to CMS guidelines, zero means no discharges,
therefore, sum of columns will not equal total.

DRG	Total Charges	Covered Charges	Medicare Reimbursement	Total Days	Number of Discharges	Average Total Days
197	738,730,719	734,412,218	237,175,926	165,555	18,169	9.1
198	92,427,561	92,045,946	27,022,144	21,990	4,975	4.4
199	62,505,272	61,775,981	22,408,009	15,075	1,611	9.4
200	45,636,207	44,800,442	16,820,669	9,657	965	10.0
201	169,621,730	167,863,918	62,708,677	37,291	2,648	14.1
202	592,056,337	587,309,444	182,688,399	163,628	26,146	6.3
203	729,500,500	725,154,806	228,711,548	211,481	31,870	6.6
204	1,309,744,956	1,294,939,124	410,863,297	402,646	70,683	5.7
205	649,564,851	642,257,493	204,068,755	189,586	31,409	6.0
206	25,585,965	25,409,693	6,873,304	7,946	2,078	3.8
207	670,416,429	667,343,170	197,351,352	184,802	35,162	5.3
208	112,739,414	112,244,945	28,646,649	29,626	10,152	2.9
209	13,501,104,807	13,460,409,879	4,194,142,863	2,036,260	429,483	4.7
210	3,701,075,457	3,686,873,305	1,142,745,495	867,984	127,031	6.8
211	574,012,209	572,273,411	169,716,057	137,711	28,744	4.8
212	0	0	0	0	0	0.0
213	329,020,889	324,224,434	108,767,633	93,703	10,333	9.1
214	0	0	0	0	0	0.0
215	0	0	0	0	0	0.0
216	410,642,403	408,199,380	148,303,284	86,923	12,999	6.7
217	937,898,005	920,117,251	330,293,131	238,764	18,174	13.1
218	702,058,145	698,334,139	206,905,126	150,247	27,331	5.5
219	356,757,508	355,230,110	97,668,281	68,743	21,740	3.2
220	0	0	0	0	0	0.0
221	0	0	0	0	0	0.0
222	0	0	0	0	0	0.0
223	237,910,480	236,817,199	62,740,914	42,689	13,874	3.1
224	147,245,889	146,546,479	37,336,387	22,410	11,760	1.9
225	124,851,977	124,075,023	34,856,025	33,684	6,433	5.2
226	170,308,549	169,259,671	54,741,340	43,027	6,652	6.5
227	72,582,553	72,048,704	19,316,836	14,183	5,269	2.7
228	51,886,876	51,517,528	14,922,651	11,254	2,700	4.2
229	14,542,253	14,474,349	3,569,240	2,974	1,178	2.5
230	53,353,230	53,065,494	15,671,680	13,707	2,412	5.7
231	334,451,310	330,979,744	100,526,813	71,270	14,085	5.1
232	12,564,462	12,372,521	3,609,520	2,196	773	2.8
233	330,998,460	329,306,714	115,188,407	77,832	10,274	7.6
234	95,453,163	94,978,718	29,598,343	16,782	4,992	3.4
235	62,556,386	62,176,836	19,062,156	25,723	5,241	4.9

(Continued)

Table 2-19 *(Continued)*

Centers for Medicare and Medicaid Services
100% MEDPAR Inpatient Hospital National Data for Fiscal Year 2003 6/04 Update
Short Stay Inpatient Diagnosis Related Groups
Blank cells represent ten or less discharges in order to conform to CMS guidelines, zero means no discharges,
therefore, sum of columns will not equal total.

DRG	Total Charges	Covered Charges	Medicare Reimbursement	Total Days	Number of Discharges	Average Total Days
236	536,142,821	533,595,906	156,616,281	220,489	44,342	5.0
237	18,967,116	18,802,942	4,947,037	7,378	1,919	3.8
238	223,456,663	218,218,828	70,854,876	83,197	9,710	8.6
239	776,019,144	771,902,369	228,161,832	282,967	45,523	6.2
240	289,355,953	285,640,249	93,648,666	84,829	12,725	6.7
241	34,453,631	33,984,591	9,435,740	11,470	3,036	3.8
242	53,739,529	53,316,724	15,987,081	19,289	2,805	6.9
243	1,269,125,630	1,260,591,452	343,511,603	480,065	102,336	4.7
244	223,842,296	222,352,877	75,706,740	94,488	18,202	5.2
245	62,106,828	61,791,965	21,863,088	29,421	7,188	4.1
246	19,615,712	19,436,045	6,638,333	8,518	1,788	4.8
247	207,567,918	205,468,722	55,519,122	73,509	21,805	3.4
248	204,378,570	202,939,253	59,214,454	70,837	14,687	4.8
249	170,438,363	168,574,790	53,656,727	59,149	14,331	4.1
250	45,753,097	45,429,395	12,517,456	15,998	3,981	4.0
251	19,096,072	19,017,684	4,420,452	6,749	2,375	2.8
252	0	0	0	0	0	0.0
253	301,959,233	300,122,596	82,409,141	112,683	23,830	4.7
254	83,353,790	82,418,535	19,551,532	34,849	10,955	3.2
255	0	0	0	0	0	0.0
256	98,390,143	96,265,243	28,990,608	36,640	7,110	5.2
257	212,164,925	211,580,167	58,263,419	39,023	14,548	2.7
258	151,653,950	151,013,466	38,439,621	23,878	13,325	1.8
259	51,658,181	51,428,353	13,893,216	9,070	3,222	2.8
260	41,373,831	41,213,993	10,247,440	5,143	3,698	1.4
261	27,453,835	26,837,446	7,481,816	3,573	1,686	2.1
262	10,105,885	10,042,749	2,763,328	3,020	642	4.7
263	898,230,994	872,216,265	291,833,092	293,842	25,890	11.3
264	72,119,993	70,320,381	21,768,018	26,057	4,011	6.5
265	115,229,559	113,170,781	37,676,533	28,131	4,204	6.7
266	39,665,387	39,479,507	11,008,109	8,479	2,631	3.2
267	3,614,174	3,603,075	1,256,242	1,082	240	4.5
268	20,372,683	19,671,956	5,381,147	3,471	968	3.6
269	303,971,262	300,040,878	95,930,762	89,157	10,402	8.6
270	40,125,364	39,521,374	10,470,911	10,762	2,890	3.7
271	352,995,711	345,370,778	106,203,124	144,811	20,429	7.1
272	103,132,549	102,069,511	32,175,287	34,897	5,910	5.9
273	14,047,218	13,892,546	3,526,267	5,091	1,366	3.7
274	43,292,256	43,062,824	14,288,105	14,602	2,322	6.3

Table 2-19 *(Continued)*

Centers for Medicare and Medicaid Services
100% MEDPAR Inpatient Hospital National Data for Fiscal Year 2003 6/04 Update
Short Stay Inpatient Diagnosis Related Groups
Blank cells represent ten or less discharges in order to conform to CMS guidelines, zero means no discharges, therefore, sum of columns will not equal total.

DRG	Total Charges	Covered Charges	Medicare Reimbursement	Total Days	Number of Discharges	Average Total Days
275	1,938,891	1,932,892	520,982	597	187	3.2
276	16,992,378	16,719,658	4,418,783	6,578	1,390	4.7
277	1,575,479,710	1,562,362,932	448,590,978	621,588	110,115	5.6
278	299,380,984	297,374,782	74,778,226	138,724	33,518	4.1
279	0	0	0	0	0	0.0
280	224,762,779	222,964,648	59,573,919	77,211	18,861	4.1
281	61,016,282	60,615,770	13,250,022	21,470	7,473	2.9
282	0	0	0	0	0	0.0
283	79,774,377	79,024,451	22,613,344	29,201	6,217	4.7
284	13,886,148	13,776,700	3,549,805	5,703	1,891	3.0
285	248,483,663	245,547,373	79,269,556	74,720	7,213	10.4
286	91,025,734	90,601,126	32,001,765	14,813	2,668	5.6
287	208,159,686	204,396,565	67,241,211	65,397	6,494	10.1
288	311,681,456	309,024,853	99,937,558	39,257	8,678	4.5
289	112,079,985	111,419,195	33,012,076	17,979	6,841	2.6
290	156,251,561	155,667,453	43,108,867	22,561	10,478	2.2
291	872,856	871,645	213,487	108	71	1.5
292	322,698,777	316,987,726	108,755,630	71,758	7,009	10.2
293	8,198,928	8,048,698	2,179,276	1,633	350	4.7
294	1,287,455,704	1,273,665,602	366,024,269	441,205	99,955	4.4
295	53,213,668	50,824,993	15,574,712	15,495	4,048	3.8
296	3,543,066,819	3,517,758,688	1,074,384,568	1,278,648	263,025	4.9
297	384,774,955	382,300,189	98,430,901	150,927	48,023	3.1
298	1,368,228	1,332,375	354,434	444	119	3.7
299	21,811,282	20,065,105	6,683,181	7,572	1,442	5.3
300	359,356,900	357,147,323	110,608,537	118,303	19,832	6.0
301	42,395,652	42,147,946	11,504,077	13,537	3,895	3.5
302	973,840,943	959,396,922	200,261,791	76,418	9,325	8.2
303	934,933,190	930,997,606	321,976,983	184,980	23,839	7.8
304	548,104,241	543,205,251	186,625,114	116,475	13,493	8.6
305	61,940,844	61,436,321	18,498,421	10,485	3,139	3.3
306	144,088,056	143,341,347	43,889,615	38,034	7,078	5.4
307	19,026,943	18,960,025	4,910,680	3,992	1,940	2.1
308	195,367,709	194,088,598	64,579,813	44,896	7,516	6.0
309	57,934,605	57,728,395	15,699,789	7,960	3,918	2.0
310	489,345,668	486,345,079	140,924,157	113,737	25,870	4.4
311	70,779,725	70,431,458	18,084,324	12,723	7,048	1.8
312	27,725,490	27,573,002	8,329,536	7,125	1,542	4.6
313	6,561,306	6,530,096	1,758,746	1,238	563	2.2

(Continued)

Table 2-19 *(Continued)*

Centers for Medicare and Medicaid Services
100% MEDPAR Inpatient Hospital National Data for Fiscal Year 2003 6/04 Update
Short Stay Inpatient Diagnosis Related Groups
Blank cells represent ten or less discharges in order to conform to CMS guidelines, zero means no discharges, therefore, sum of columns will not equal total.

DRG	Total Charges	Covered Charges	Medicare Reimbursement	Total Days	Number of Discharges	Average Total Days
314	0	0	0	0	0	0.0
315	1,278,219,745	1,262,039,136	427,082,267	249,150	36,391	6.8
316	3,199,237,156	3,172,579,698	1,052,309,870	975,712	151,840	6.4
317	33,622,687	33,147,844	8,548,968	8,270	2,532	3.3
318	116,694,625	116,171,285	37,124,988	35,019	6,006	5.8
319	4,775,072	4,723,458	1,293,769	1,207	436	2.8
320	2,970,632,086	2,945,832,711	858,923,339	1,099,893	212,354	5.2
321	286,871,915	285,238,125	74,011,454	115,274	31,590	3.6
322	736,092	731,806	231,813	260	70	3.7
323	274,584,563	273,121,309	73,092,977	65,596	20,778	3.2
324	48,255,198	47,823,530	10,121,721	11,866	6,302	1.9
325	105,872,373	105,031,523	29,995,596	36,899	9,736	3.8
326	20,274,510	20,079,300	5,187,850	7,459	2,809	2.7
327	0	0	0	0	0	0.0
328	7,791,264	7,714,399	2,334,397	2,326	683	3.4
329	507,872	507,787	151,649	145	65	2.2
330	0	0	0	0	0	0.0
331	967,455,849	954,688,043	299,446,220	301,260	54,256	5.6
332	48,877,365	48,418,431	13,644,701	15,543	4,766	3.3
333	5,613,767	5,505,682	1,613,038	1,501	286	5.2
334	245,336,569	243,952,230	75,600,443	46,827	10,529	4.4
335	228,520,393	226,975,951	62,674,624	36,887	12,790	2.9
336	459,746,967	458,305,413	132,636,464	111,728	33,494	3.3
337	246,250,494	245,009,296	63,024,133	52,439	26,570	2.0
338	14,002,490	13,961,124	4,302,004	4,046	719	5.6
339	29,053,762	28,958,216	8,162,274	7,700	1,452	5.3
340	0	0	0	0	0	0.0
341	78,920,660	78,140,592	22,258,613	10,789	3,666	2.9
342	8,010,232	7,965,891	2,204,029	2,041	635	3.2
343	0	0	0	0	0	0.0
344	68,242,747	67,904,507	20,097,910	7,904	3,169	2.5
345	26,929,586	26,795,054	8,243,809	6,636	1,359	4.9
346	83,037,177	82,552,946	24,221,294	27,824	4,614	6.0
347	2,692,194	2,683,918	793,817	814	288	2.8
348	40,623,726	40,441,627	11,169,836	13,790	3,394	4.1
349	4,054,945	4,019,255	854,762	1,360	543	2.5
350	86,214,334	85,427,405	22,627,160	32,154	7,105	4.5
351	0	0	0	0	0	0.0
352	14,378,633	14,175,544	3,847,428	4,554	1,090	4.2

Table 2-19 *(Continued)*

Centers for Medicare and Medicaid Services
100% MEDPAR Inpatient Hospital National Data for Fiscal Year 2003 6/04 Update
Short Stay Inpatient Diagnosis Related Groups
Blank cells represent ten or less discharges in order to conform to CMS guidelines, zero means no discharges,
therefore, sum of columns will not equal total.

DRG	Total Charges	Covered Charges	Medicare Reimbursement	Total Days	Number of Discharges	Average Total Days
353	96,761,503	96,516,294	31,814,665	17,837	2,743	6.5
354	200,017,369	199,466,023	64,841,186	44,619	7,636	5.8
355	80,701,602	80,320,651	22,719,413	16,977	5,371	3.2
356	297,264,557	296,003,074	78,657,294	51,117	25,508	2.0
357	217,509,157	216,823,965	76,312,695	47,593	5,761	8.3
358	407,185,346	405,538,171	122,791,253	87,651	21,392	4.1
359	386,073,465	384,654,814	102,403,274	75,793	30,239	2.5
360	220,108,513	219,065,496	61,733,023	42,101	15,652	2.7
361	5,486,472	5,405,521	1,555,034	1,060	298	3.6
362	0	0	0	0	0	0.0
363	42,193,796	42,003,182	11,807,729	9,632	2,511	3.8
364	25,267,626	25,102,044	6,502,202	6,513	1,477	4.4
365	59,350,011	58,191,390	18,747,671	13,521	1,709	7.9
366	100,185,561	99,732,080	32,972,829	32,283	4,806	6.7
367	4,667,945	4,626,044	1,431,753	1,580	485	3.3
368	78,216,860	77,501,376	24,647,708	26,709	3,932	6.8
369	38,347,343	38,090,513	9,845,232	11,814	3,606	3.3
370	33,480,198	33,025,305	10,050,907	9,266	1,681	5.5
371	21,703,220	21,378,094	5,870,971	7,189	2,063	3.5
372	11,306,232	11,183,480	3,458,948	3,902	1,103	3.5
373	29,057,177	28,723,817	6,734,799	10,508	4,648	2.3
374	1,473,331	1,323,289	418,925	433	132	3.3
375	0	0	0	0	0	0.0
376	4,133,114	4,047,933	1,116,910	1,782	371	4.8
377	1,100,823	1,052,770	429,631	276	58	4.8
378	2,561,576	2,541,069	717,106	418	192	2.2
379	2,874,866	2,859,821	731,136	1,316	446	3.0
380	611,689	520,536	128,555	179	96	1.9
381	2,511,703	2,450,206	546,873	445	207	2.1
382	131,290	117,042	17,434	60	30	2.0
383	24,949,072	24,487,332	7,743,003	11,466	2,610	4.4
384	721,798	715,497	237,488	288	142	2.0
385	0	0	0	0	0	0.0
386	0	0	0	0	0	0.0
387	0	0	0	0	0	0.0
388	0	0	0	0	0	0.0
389	0	0	0	0	0	0.0
390	199,943	196,048	48,784	49	11	4.5
391	0	0	0	0	0	0.0

(Continued)

Table 2-19 *(Continued)*

Centers for Medicare and Medicaid Services
100% MEDPAR Inpatient Hospital National Data for Fiscal Year 2003 6/04 Update
Short Stay Inpatient Diagnosis Related Groups
Blank cells represent ten or less discharges in order to conform to CMS guidelines, zero means no discharges, therefore, sum of columns will not equal total.

DRG	Total Charges	Covered Charges	Medicare Reimbursement	Total Days	Number of Discharges	Average Total Days
392	115,479,014	114,735,070	38,842,021	20,418	2,169	9.4
393	0	0	0	0	0	0.0
394	87,713,538	86,235,024	28,148,506	19,089	2,656	7.2
395	1,541,488,955	1,485,327,864	433,092,195	485,796	112,386	4.3
396	565,109	564,941	135,537	111	11	10.1
397	435,186,904	431,103,577	147,078,784	99,807	19,515	5.1
398	378,869,246	376,569,750	124,900,357	108,099	18,306	5.9
399	18,182,132	18,004,394	5,288,878	5,496	1,690	3.3
400	306,019,899	304,020,510	107,354,498	60,716	6,707	9.1
401	297,246,178	295,098,712	98,588,933	69,014	6,006	11.5
402	28,405,880	28,225,957	8,168,042	6,133	1,503	4.1
403	977,218,607	970,935,290	322,330,100	258,461	32,480	8.0
404	64,274,196	63,922,486	18,728,533	17,278	4,207	4.1
405	0	0	0	0	0	0.0
406	120,925,280	120,142,251	42,219,994	24,212	2,504	9.7
407	13,483,992	13,361,688	4,268,596	2,623	631	4.2
408	82,442,426	81,880,203	27,362,867	18,286	2,215	8.3
409	49,729,166	49,520,298	15,948,583	12,604	2,082	6.1
410	585,397,444	581,719,226	185,016,114	119,584	30,053	4.0
411	0	0	0	0	0	0.0
412	215,389	187,970	20,516	23	15	1.5
413	130,828,592	130,124,122	41,015,322	41,384	5,684	7.3
414	6,648,705	6,548,382	2,083,446	2,354	606	3.9
415	2,871,536,417	2,811,695,129	1,031,699,448	661,057	46,843	14.1
416	5,526,166,904	5,456,001,174	1,756,261,145	1,559,295	212,062	7.4
417	1,108,749	1,081,756	240,115	179	30	6.0
418	494,381,925	489,535,491	156,866,361	172,923	27,835	6.2
419	247,369,072	244,194,845	72,064,219	78,239	17,020	4.6
420	28,652,692	28,454,640	7,501,288	9,687	2,951	3.3
421	140,863,770	139,802,112	34,822,585	45,273	10,750	4.2
422	895,573	879,536	279,751	229	71	3.2
423	251,976,682	248,759,689	84,188,255	68,753	8,481	8.1
424	98,348,884	94,765,328	29,530,233	39,335	2,455	16.0
425	225,036,997	223,025,704	69,594,368	93,760	19,861	4.7
426	180,033,345	175,968,552	64,274,414	115,645	17,647	6.6
427	52,325,436	50,876,619	19,098,955	35,154	5,792	6.1
428	44,087,658	41,101,045	14,970,839	29,058	3,165	9.2
429	988,659,519	975,901,829	379,932,058	597,637	62,943	9.5
430	5,613,991,345	5,434,829,853	1,992,036,455	3,662,396	339,818	10.8

Table 2-19 *(Continued)*

Centers for Medicare and Medicaid Services
100% MEDPAR Inpatient Hospital National Data for Fiscal Year 2003 6/04 Update
Short Stay Inpatient Diagnosis Related Groups
Blank cells represent ten or less discharges in order to conform to CMS guidelines, zero means no discharges, therefore, sum of columns will not equal total.

DRG	Total Charges	Covered Charges	Medicare Reimbursement	Total Days	Number of Discharges	Average Total Days
431	18,506,034	17,785,181	6,899,518	13,117	1,425	9.2
432	6,451,842	6,397,178	2,276,977	3,493	542	6.4
433	33,374,731	31,848,343	8,312,450	18,459	6,252	3.0
434	0	0	0	0	0	0.0
435	0	0	0	0	0	0.0
436	0	0	0	0	0	0.0
437	0	0	0	0	0	0.0
438	0	0	0	0	0	0.0
439	56,574,792	54,404,122	18,386,940	14,691	1,709	8.6
440	187,756,395	184,473,422	66,848,033	53,267	5,964	8.9
441	10,565,810	10,459,988	3,263,391	2,214	720	3.1
442	734,534,036	722,481,010	247,821,484	155,245	17,659	8.8
443	61,703,630	61,391,957	19,094,815	12,755	3,735	3.4
444	77,453,735	76,618,550	21,144,910	25,586	6,123	4.2
445	21,254,757	21,056,325	4,799,352	7,093	2,487	2.9
446	0	0	0	0	0	0.0
447	59,149,618	58,923,024	14,145,500	16,598	6,458	2.6
448	0	0	0	0	0	0.0
449	514,205,113	508,972,426	148,532,623	135,226	36,376	3.7
450	54,785,768	54,353,174	12,839,013	15,844	7,816	2.0
451	0	0	0	0	0	0.0
452	480,868,975	473,832,876	152,893,232	137,024	27,635	5.0
453	48,518,024	48,079,375	13,288,856	15,913	5,630	2.8
454	62,891,316	61,652,342	18,143,533	18,776	4,372	4.3
455	8,242,495	8,076,706	1,832,538	2,400	990	2.4
456	0	0	0	0	0	0.0
457	0	0	0	0	0	0.0
458	0	0	0	0	0	0.0
459	0	0	0	0	0	0.0
460	0	0	0	0	0	0.0
461	303,037,539	298,240,765	107,420,671	94,315	9,459	10.0
462	6,900,205,949	6,861,280,910	3,755,779,201	3,632,223	309,700	11.7
463	347,748,070	345,366,648	102,922,579	125,567	29,950	4.2
464	65,053,463	64,431,450	17,137,191	24,444	7,779	3.1
465	2,462,621	2,439,472	868,231	725	225	3.2
466	23,611,172	23,117,909	9,491,563	9,035	1,970	4.6
467	13,661,752	12,813,750	4,353,451	4,578	1,342	3.4
468	3,332,401,550	3,292,700,828	1,144,688,411	686,117	54,423	12.6
469	0	0	0	0	0	0.0

(Continued)

Table 2-19 *(Continued)*

Centers for Medicare and Medicaid Services
100% MEDPAR Inpatient Hospital National Data for Fiscal Year 2003 6/04 Update
Short Stay Inpatient Diagnosis Related Groups
Blank cells represent ten or less discharges in order to conform to CMS guidelines, zero means no discharges,
therefore, sum of columns will not equal total.

DRG	Total Charges	Covered Charges	Medicare Reimbursement	Total Days	Number of Discharges	Average Total Days
470	0	0	0	0	0	0.0
471	698,698,379	694,990,094	223,013,397	76,383	14,478	5.3
472	0	0	0	0	0	0.0
473	542,167,302	535,225,364	203,329,136	115,018	8,876	13.0
474	0	0	0	0	0	0.0
475	6,690,233,099	6,556,382,952	2,316,973,104	1,245,866	111,885	11.1
476	119,984,688	119,504,462	39,164,775	35,042	3,251	10.8
477	803,545,056	793,711,771	256,626,287	208,006	25,635	8.1
478	4,432,319,240	4,403,795,427	1,446,790,803	806,494	110,942	7.3
479	556,183,249	554,322,563	164,369,223	72,841	23,932	3.0
480	228,662,179	226,601,658	82,443,433	17,007	988	17.2
481	147,893,847	143,324,607	59,038,957	25,196	1,117	22.6
482	319,066,940	316,653,678	122,322,288	64,409	5,455	11.8
483	12,138,030,684	11,922,741,160	4,689,212,879	1,773,111	45,925	38.6
484	38,958,579	37,799,991	14,500,971	5,478	424	12.9
485	185,959,468	184,632,928	59,441,544	33,542	3,411	9.8
486	206,188,854	204,594,020	68,193,406	30,784	2,445	12.6
487	152,537,243	151,399,193	45,837,360	33,717	4,521	7.5
488	78,179,273	77,161,400	28,904,503	14,100	819	17.2
489	479,031,204	472,196,963	173,658,122	116,683	14,032	8.3
490	105,495,456	103,591,477	34,171,154	28,265	5,330	5.3
491	470,620,316	469,016,299	140,778,718	57,815	17,380	3.3
492	249,560,696	247,936,934	97,374,666	55,089	3,669	15.0
493	1,766,831,023	1,761,055,563	537,766,122	372,551	61,558	6.1
494	435,925,883	434,226,195	119,033,956	72,643	27,412	2.7
495	66,447,571	63,628,305	20,666,689	5,070	300	16.9
496	397,103,865	395,132,641	144,386,899	34,937	4,620	7.6
497	1,465,803,477	1,459,571,837	460,239,220	161,323	25,794	6.3
498	727,793,098	724,220,084	206,935,127	68,466	17,337	3.9
499	883,798,762	880,362,093	262,926,759	167,553	37,661	4.4
500	779,376,822	775,658,405	210,740,870	119,070	51,208	2.3
501	119,617,858	118,434,986	40,824,666	28,512	2,842	10.0
502	16,187,131	16,158,198	5,183,257	4,269	712	6.0
503	119,105,400	118,547,674	34,086,784	22,768	6,018	3.8
504	35,726,095	35,397,386	15,147,699	4,225	135	31.3
505	4,581,408	4,573,225	2,532,808	607	169	3.6
506	90,881,136	90,453,553	37,197,225	17,341	1,048	16.5
507	12,498,583	12,450,103	3,948,079	3,118	331	9.4
508	15,753,462	15,692,022	5,551,828	4,806	656	7.3

Table 2-19 *(Continued)*

Centers for Medicare and Medicaid Services
100% MEDPAR Inpatient Hospital National Data for Fiscal Year 2003 6/04 Update
Short Stay Inpatient Diagnosis Related Groups
Blank cells represent ten or less discharges in order to conform to CMS guidelines, zero means no discharges, therefore, sum of columns will not equal total.

DRG	Total Charges	Covered Charges	Medicare Reimbursement	Total Days	Number of Discharges	Average Total Days
509	2,100,921	2,099,445	861,202	790	169	4.7
510	42,588,348	42,226,264	13,893,932	12,179	1,786	6.8
511	8,793,464	8,648,232	2,433,384	2,618	642	4.1
512	109,656,621	107,839,921	21,833,204	7,715	558	13.8
513	23,987,007	23,799,100	7,545,758	1,919	194	9.9
514	3,930,311,306	3,907,164,526	1,293,586,563	229,753	35,544	6.5
515	1,190,513,660	1,184,333,338	378,018,970	62,630	13,235	4.7
516	3,432,001,571	3,417,910,401	1,113,226,629	372,450	80,330	4.6
517	6,183,200,313	6,161,675,085	1,963,599,329	456,539	182,769	2.5
518	1,449,806,075	1,441,191,810	446,356,462	170,916	49,032	3.5
519	372,496,234	371,230,025	115,888,281	44,736	9,677	4.6
520	361,473,433	359,894,867	96,158,925	27,765	13,886	2.0
521	452,883,781	446,459,896	145,430,428	230,052	38,748	5.9
522	64,091,440	62,986,135	22,371,256	66,380	6,859	9.7
523	158,223,059	153,657,068	48,722,334	95,403	21,574	4.4
524	1,470,007,117	1,463,050,738	386,015,200	407,911	124,455	3.3
525	101,546,500	99,184,546	38,057,137	8,366	429	19.5
526	549,382,238	546,570,249	182,606,069	48,265	11,253	4.3
527	1,864,628,988	1,855,932,172	630,406,416	103,726	49,051	2.1
TOTAL LINE	$300,194,347,235	$297,677,999,538	$96,636,077,829	74,443,350	12,698,388	5.9

Extracted from http://www.cms.hhs.gov/MedicareFeeforSvcPartsAB/Downloads/DRG03.pdf.

CASE 2-34

Explanation of Benefits (EOB)

As patient advocate, you frequently receive questions regarding bills. A patient called today and asked for you to explain a form that she received from her insurance company. She said the form was called an Explanation of Benefits. She said that it provided the following information:

Provider: Dr. Theodore Simmons
Date: 11/11/06
Type of service: Office visit
Amount submitted: $82.00
Amount allowed: $74.00
Coinsurance: $14.80
Deductible: $300.00
Copay: $20.00

How would you explain what an Explanation of Benefits form is?

How would you explain the difference between the amount submitted and the amount allowed?

After you explain the amount allowed to her, she gets irate and exclaims, "How dare Dr. Simmons overcharge me by $8.00!" She then said that she was going to call his office and give him a piece of her mind.

How will you respond to this?

CASE 2-35

Qualification for Insurance

You are working with a new graduate who relates that she never did understand the various types of insurance and who they typically insure. She asks you to help her understand. Review the patients described in Table 2-20. Explain to her which one of these insurance plans they are most likely enrolled in:

- Medicare
- Medicaid
- Commercial Insurance
- TRICARE
- worker's compensation

Table 2-20 *Patient Situations and Probable Insurer*

Patient Situation and Probable Insurer	
Patient	Probable Insurer
A 72-year-old male with diabetes	
A 45-year-old female with end-stage renal disease (ESRD)	
A newborn born to mother on Medicaid	
A 24-year-old female who works at Metro Hospital who was admitted for delivery	
A 33-year-old single mother who makes $8,000.00 per year	
A 26-year-old construction worker who fell off a ladder and broke his arm at work	
A 54-year-old male with urticaria; his wife is military	
A 64-year-old female with clinical depression; her husband is a coal miner	

CASE 2-36

Medicare Part D

You are a patient advocate. A patient comes to you with questions regarding Medicare Part D. You are not familiar with all of the pertinent details on this new program, so you go to http://www.medicare.gov to learn more information. (Accessed December 12, 2006, at http://www.medicare.gov/pdphome.asp.)

The patient is currently spending $250.00 per month on prescription drugs, on a total of four drugs.

Would you recommend she enroll in Medicare Part D? Why or why not?

CASE 2-37

Medicare Coverage

Identify whether Medicare A, Medicare B, Medicare C, or Medicare D covers each of the services in Table 2-21.

Table 2-21 *Medicare Services*

Service	Medicare Part
Prescriptions	
Physician office visit	
Hospice	
Eye examination	
Lab tests	
Physical therapy	
Long-term care hospitalization	
Inpatient hospitalization	
Dental services	
Same-day surgery hospital charges (OP surgery)	
Durable medical equipment	

CASE 2-38

Local Care Determination (LCD)

You are a compliance coordinator. Part of your job is to assist the admissions clerk in determining if Medicare will cover services ordered or if an advanced beneficiary notice needs to be given. You are developing a table for the admission clerks to cross-reference when admitting patients. To accomplish this, you must look up your state local care determination (LCD) for each procedure identified in Table 2-22; fill in the table with the information you find. LCDs can be found on the Internet at http://www.cms.hhs.gov.
(Accessed December 11, 2006 at http://www.cms.hhs.gov/mcd/search.asp?clickon=search.)

Table 2-22 *Local Care Determination (LCD)*

Local Care Determination (LCD)				
Procedure	Will Medicare Cover?	Limitations (Summarize)	Last Date Reviewed	LCD Number
Blepharoplasty				
Debridement of mycotic nails				
Flu vaccine				
Sleep testing				
Blood glucose testing				

Note: Some of the procedures may have multiple LCDs. If one is Blue Cross/Blue Shield, use that one. If there are multiple LCDs and none of them are Blue Cross/Blue Shield, use the first one in the list. Use only final LCDs.

CASE 2-39

National Coverage Determination (NCD)

You are a compliance coordinator. Part of your job is to assist the admissions clerk in determining if Medicare will cover services ordered or if an advanced beneficiary notice needs to be given. You are developing a table for the admission clerks to cross-reference when admitting patients. To accomplish this, you need to look up the national coverage determination (NCD) for each procedure identified in Table 2-23 and fill in the rest of the table. NCDs can be found on the Internet at http://www.cms.hhs.gov.
(Accessed December 11, 2006, at http://www.cms.hhs.gov/mcd/search.asp?clickon=search.)

Table 2-23 *National Coverage Determination (NCD) Table*

Procedure	Covered by Medicare?	Any Limitations	Implementation Date	NCD Section
Removal actinic keratosis				
Decubitus ulcer treatment				
Tubal ligation or other sterilization procedure				
PET scan				
Continuous positive airway pressure (CPAP) for obstructive sleep apnea				

Calculating Medicare Inpatient Psychiatric Reimbursement

Your facility is considering opening an inpatient psychiatric unit. As part of the cost-benefit analysis, you have been given case studies and are asked to calculate the reimbursement you would receive if you used the Medicare Inpatient Psychiatric reimbursement system. This is a very complicated reimbursement system, so you will need some help with the calculations.

You can locate the most recent the Inpatient Psychiatric Facility Prospective Payment System (IPF PPS) payment calculator at http://www/cms/hhs.gov.
(Accessed December 11, 2006, at http://www.cms.hhs.gov/InpatientPsychFacilPPS/04_tools.asp.)

(You can also go to IPF PPS Payment Calculator - RY 2007 [Excel Zipped, 101KB], accessed January 6, 2007, to retrieve the calculator.)

Determine the reimbursement for the discharges shown in Tables 2-24 through 2-28. Many of the fields have a drop-down box. You may not see the button to click until you have selected the cell in the Microsoft Excel spreadsheet.

Table 2-24 *Case 1: Calculating Medicare Inpatient Psychiatric Reimbursement*

Case 1: Calculating Medicare Inpatient Psychiatric Reimbursement	
DRG	12
Electroconvulsive shock therapy (ECTs)	2
LOS	24
Age	88
Geographic location	Rural
Emergency department	No
Residents	0
Wage area	Washington
Blended year	3
Federal payment	

Table 2-25 *Case 2: Calculating Medicare Inpatient Psychiatric Reimbursement*

Case 2: Calculating Medicare Inpatient Psychiatric Reimbursement	
DRG	23
ECTs	0
LOS	12
Age	42
Geographic location	rural
Emergency department	No
Residents	0
Wage area	Alabama
Blended year	2
Federal payment	

Table 2-26 *Case 3: Calculating Medicare Inpatient Psychiatric Reimbursement*

Case 3: Calculating Medicare Inpatient Psychiatric Reimbursement	
DRG	424
ECTs	4
LOS	7
Age	72
Geographic location	Urban
Emergency department	Yes
Residents	0
Wage area	Hawaii
Comorbidity	Cardiac complication
Blended year	1
Federal payment	

Table 2-27 *Case 4: Calculating Medicare Inpatient Psychiatric Reimbursement*

Case 4: Calculating Medicare Inpatient Psychiatric Reimbursement	
DRG	521
ECTs	12
LOS	5
Age	68
Geographic location	Urban
Emergency department	Yes
Residents	0
Wage area	New York
Blended year	3
Federal payment	

Table 2-28 *Case 5: Calculating Medicare Inpatient Psychiatric Reimbursement*

Case 5: Calculating Medicare Inpatient Psychiatric Reimbursement	
DRG	523
ECTs	3
LOS	8
Age	66
Geographic location	Rural
Emergency department	No
Residents	0
Wage area	Alaska
Comorbidity	
Blended year	2
Federal payment	

CASE 2-41

Medical Necessity

Part of your job is reviewing the denial letters that the hospital receives. After review of the denial letter and the patient's medical record, you determine if an appeal is warranted. If an appeal is warranted, you are responsible for ensuring that the appeal is processed in a timely manner. In today's mail, you received the letter shown in Figure 2-11 from your QIO.

If the denial stands, your hospital stands to lose a DRG payment of $4,324.44. How would you handle this denial?

Sarah James   May 12, 2006
HIM Director
Pinehurst Hospital
100 Hospital Drive
Pinehurst, MS 32488

Re: Thomas Avery   Beneficiary number: 123456789A
                                                        Encounter number: 1234567

Dear Ms. James:

The above mentioned claim has been denied. The reason for denial is:

• Lack of medical necessity

If you disagree with this decision, you have 10 days from the date of this letter to respond. Rebuttals must be received within 14 days of the date on this letter.

Submit all rebuttals to:

  Peer Review
  Delaware QIO
  123 Elm Street
  Dover, DE 54555

Sincerely,
Peer Review Services

Figure 2-11 *Denial Letter*

CASE 2-42

Calculating Commercial Insurance Reimbursement

You work for a billing service. You have been assigned the duty of calculating what the patient owes and what the insurance company owes, so that you can determine what revenue to expect for these services. You have the charge and the usual, customary, and reasonable (UCR) amount. The reimbursement will be calculated on the 80/20 distribution. Also, the deductibles for each of these patients have been met. Under this insurance plan, $20.00 copays are due for physician office visits but not for other services. Use the data in Table 2-29 to calculate the coinsurance, amount insurance will pay, and how much the patient owes.

Table 2-29 *Calculating Commercial Insurance Reimbursement*

Calculating Commercial Insurance Reimbursement					
Service	Charge	Usual, Customary, and Reasonable	Copay	Coinsurance	Insurance Pays
Physician Visit	$120.00	$120.00			
Physical Therapy	$150.00	$97.00			
X-ray	$76.00	$43.00			
MRI	$1,245.00	$1,047.00			
Physician Visit	$65.00	$70.00			
Physician Visit	$75.00	$70.00			

Ambulatory Payment Classification (APC)

A student, Julio, from the local Health Information Management Program (bachelor degree), is working on a clinical assignment at your facility. The assignment that you gave Julio required that he do some calculation of your ambulatory payment classification (APC) reimbursement, working with the other coders.

He went back to his workstation to begin but returned about 30 minutes later. He was at a complete loss. Julio knew the basics of the APC system, for example, that it was a hospital outpatient reimbursement system for Medicare and that a patient could have multiple APCs, but he was having trouble with the details that he needed to know for the project—especially the concept of discounting. So you decided to give Julio an additional assignment to help prepare him for the clinical assignment.

You provide Julio with a list of APCs to investigate. He is to identify the status indicator for the APC and determine if discounting applies to the APC. He goes to the CMS website (www.cms.gov) to research the APCs in Table 2-30.

For each APC in Table 2-30, identify the status indicator for the APC and indicate if discounting applies to the APC.

Table 2-30   *Ambulatory Payment Classification (APCs) with the Status Indicator and Discounting Status*

Ambulatory Payment Classification (APC) with the Status Indicator and Discounting Status		
APC	Status Indicator	Subject to Discounting
0001		
0077		
0171		
0236		
0429		
0617		
0891		
1011		
1555		
1820		

CASE 2-44

Discharged Not Final Billed (DNFB) Reduction

You are the coding supervisor with a DNFB report that is staying significantly over the limit that administration desires. You have been given the mandate to determine what needs to be done to significantly reduce the amount of claims not billed and bring the DNFB down. Your CFO is expecting immediate results.

Table 2-31 shows a portion the Discharged Not Final Billed Report and is representative of the entire report.

Where would you begin to give your CFO the quick fix that he wants?

What problems can you identify that got you into this situation?

What are some possible solutions for these problems?

Table 2-31 *Discharged Not Final Billed Report*

Discharged Not Final Billed Report			
Account Number	Discharge Date	Total Charges	Reason
1234567	2/7/06	$23,456.87	02
1234569	2/7/06	$12,564.88	02
1235712	2/12/06	$2,458.99	01
1238932	3/6/06	$1,345.77	01
1239999	3/12/06	$57,764.22	06
1305790	4/17/06	$39,652.13	05
1317267	5/15/06	$23,731.80	03
1419000	7/16/06	$2,653.44	02
1489001	8/15/06	$5,457.39	01
1506389	10/13/06	$7,987.33	01
1521111	10/31/06	$9,564.44	01
1529387	11/2/06	$10,536.63	01
1679835	12/16/06	$8.745.19	02

Legend:

01 Missing Codes
02 Missing Discharge Disposition
03 Missing Admitting Diagnosis
04 Billers Hold
05 Other—HIM
06 Other—Business Office

SECTION THREE

Statistics and Quality Improvement

CASE 3-1

Inpatient Service Days

As a HIM manager of a small county hospital, you oversee the statistical reporting. You are in the process of cross-training a back-up HI clerk II. You are showing her how to calculate the inpatient service days.

The hospital daily census reports show that the inpatient census at midnight was 67. Two patients were admitted yesterday morning. One of these patients admitted died 2 hours later; the second patient was discharged and transferred to another facility yesterday afternoon.

What would the inpatient service days for yesterday be?

CASE 3-2

Average Daily Census

You have been given an external report from Navaho Hospital administration requesting completion of a couple of statistical fields. Navaho Hospital has 275 adult beds, 30 pediatric beds, and 40 bassinets. Last year's (a non–leap year) inpatient service days were as shown in Table 3-1.

Table 3-1 *Navaho Hospital Inservice Patient Days for Year*

Navaho Hospital Inpatient Service Days for Year	
Type of Service	Number of Patients
Adult	75,860
Pediatric	7,100
Newborn	11,800

What was the average daily census of adults and children for the year? (Round to a whole number.)

What was the average daily census of newborns for the year? (Round to a whole number.)

CASE 3-3

Length of Stay (LOS)

As the education coordinator for HIM services, you have noted errors in the calculated length of stays (LOS) written on the discharge record facesheets by the new chart analyst. Your goal is to provide further training to him in calculating healthcare statistics to help alleviate this problem.

Discharge record MR# 010362 is of a patient who was admitted to the hospital on March 24 and discharged on April 9.

The second discharge record, MR# 120431, is of a patient admitted on the morning of July 12 who subsequently died at 11:10 p.m. on the same day.

Calculate the length of stay for each of these two patients.

CASE 3-4

Average Length of Stay (ALOS)

South Houston General Hospital has 500 beds and 55 bassinets. As the HIM manager, you report monthly statistical data of hospital operations to administration and departmental managers. Use the statistics reported in Table 3-2 for February (a non–leap year) to calculate the following statistics.

What is February's average length of stay for adults and children? (Round to 1 decimal place.)

What is February's average daily census for adults and children? (Round to a whole number.)

What is February's average length of stay for newborns? (Round to 1 decimal place.)

What is February's average daily census for newborns? (Round to a whole number.)

Table 3-2 *South Houston General Hospital Inpatient Service Days*

South Houston General Hospital
Inpatient Activity
February

Inpatient Service Days	Number of Patients
Adult and pediatric	12,345
Newborn	553
Discharges:	
Adult and pediatric	1,351
Newborn	93
Discharge days:	
Adult and pediatric	9,457
Newborn	231

CASE **3-5**

Percentage of Occupancy for Month

Royal Palm Hospital has 500 beds and 55 bassinets. As the HIM manager, you report monthly statistical data of hospital operations to administration and departmental managers. Use the information in Table 3-3 to calculate the percentage of occupancy for adults and pediatrics in the month of March. (Round to whole number.)

Table 3-3 *Royal Palm Hospital Inpatient Service Days*

Inpatient Activity	
March 2007	
Inpatient Service Days	Number of Patients
Adult and pediatric	12,345
Newborn	565
Discharges:	
Adult and pediatric	1,351
Newborn	77
Discharge days:	
Adult and pediatric	9,457
Newborn	231

Percentage of Occupancy for Year

Table 3-4 shows the statistics for bed count and inpatient service days that Manatee Bay Health Center reported for last year (a non–leap year). The hospital chief operations officer (COO) is meeting with the board of directors next Tuesday for a quarterly meeting. He asked you to figure the hospital's occupancy ratio for the past year. You have been given the statistics in Table 3-4 to calculate the annual percentage of occupancy for the past year's operations.

Table 3-4 *Manatee Bay Health Center Hospital Bed Count and Inpatient Service Days*

Manatee Bay Health Center Hospital Bed Count and Inpatient Service Days		
Time Period	Bed Count	Inpatient Service Days
January 1–May 31	200	28,690
June 1–October 15	250	27,400
October 16–December 31	275	19,250

CASE 3-7

Consultation Rate

Canyon Medical, a tertiary-care hospital, is participating in answering an external questionnaire requesting statistical information.

The hospital statistical data reported for the 300-bed hospital last year reflects:

20,932 discharges
136,651 discharge days
3,699 consultations performed

The chief medical officer (CMO) has requested that you calculate the consultation rate rounded to 1 decimal place.

CASE 3-8

Nosocomial and Community-Acquired Infection Rate

You are a HIM manager at Blue Glacier Hospital. You are responsible for reporting hospital monthly statistics. The hospital reports 1,652 discharges for September, and the infection control report documents that there were 21 nosocomial infections and 27 community-acquired infections for the same month.

You need to calculate both the nosocomial and community-acquired infection rates (rounded to 2 decimal places) and report them to the hospital Quality Improvement (QI) Council.

CASE 3-9

Incidence Rate

The incidence of bird flu has been a concern on the coast. As the HIM manager of the Washington County health department, you have been asked to report the month's cases. Twelve new cases of bird flu occurred during the month of August. There were 4,000 people in the community who were at risk.

Calculate the incidence rate for the month.

Comparative Health Data: Hospital Mortality Statistics

Bob and Pat are trying to decide where to spend their retirement. They have narrowed the field to four retirement centers. Their decision will be based largely upon the quality of care offered at the hospitals local to each of the retirement communities. They are researching the closest vicinity hospital to each of the retirement centers, and they want to know each hospital's mortality rate.

Use the statistics listed in Table 3-5 to calculate the gross mortality rate (rounded to 1 decimal place) for each retirement center.

Table 3-5 *Hospital Mortality Statistics*

| Hospital Mortality Statistics | | | |
Hospital Name	Discharged Patients	Inpatient Deaths	Mortality Rates
Northern Sea Breeze	223	23	
Great Plains City	418	28	
Rocky Mount Center	215	32	
South Beach Cove	319	29	

Based on this data, where will Bob and Pat choose to live? Explain why.

Which is the least desired? Explain why.

CASE 3-11

Joint Commission Hospital Quality Check

You are a health information practitioner, and personal issues require you and your family to relocate for your spouse's job transfer. As you seek hospital employment opportunities for yourself, you research Joint Commission accreditation status of the area hospitals.

Select three hospitals closest to your affiliated school to research. For help in selecting the hospitals, visit http://www.jointcommission.org and search under the Quality Check icon.

Develop a critique of each of your chosen hospital's most current surveys. Comment on significant areas of achievement and/or deficiency. Include the date of the most recent hospital survey and accreditation decision awarded.

Sparrow Hospital – Accredited
last survey 11/30/07
extensive list of services
patient safety goel implemented

Eaton Rapids Medical Center
Accredited
last survey – 12/13/05
had previous surveys that
needed improvement to get accredation
+ these were done because they
were fully accredited at last
surveys

Clinton Memorial Hospital
Accredited
last survey – 6/16/06
Performance similar to other local
hospitals
Numerous services offered.

CASE 3-12

Nursing Home Comparative Data

You have an aging loved one who needs skilled nursing care on a daily basis, and the inevitable time has come for nursing home placement. So that you may visit on a weekly basis, you want a nursing home within close proximity of your residence.

Research the quality of at least three nursing homes within your geographic region, comparing the outcomes of the "quality measures." Utilize the Centers for Medicare and Medicaid Services (CMS) nursing home database, which can be accessed by going to http://www.medicare.gov and clicking the Compare Nursing Homes in Your Area link, then clicking the Resources and Download Databases tabs.

(Accessed December 13, 2006, at http://www.medicare.gov/NHCompare/Static/Related/Download DB.asp? dest=NAV|Home|Resources|DownloadDatabase#TabTop.)

Complete the search parameters to locate nursing homes within your geographical area and execute to deliver outcomes data on each nursing home.

Build a table of the quality measures and demonstrate the percentage that each nursing home shows in meeting the outcomes measurement.

Based on your comparison, which would be your top choice to place your loved one?

CASE 3-13

Clinical Quality Improvement in Long-Term Care (LTC)

As a health information consultant of nursing homes, you need to acquire data on common characteristics (e.g., diagnosis and activities of daily living [ADL]) of the nursing home resident age 65 or older.

Perform a qualitative analysis using the Centers for Disease Control database for national statistics. What are at least 10 characteristics of the 1985 nursing home resident you determine from the nursing home government report?

Access the website at http://www.cdc.gov/nchs/ to research the data from the National Health Survey report titled "Vital and Health Statistics: Effects of the Prospective Payment System on Nursing Homes."
(Accessed December 13, 2006, at http://www.cdc.gov/nchs/data/series/sr_13/sr13_098.pdf.)

Relative Risk Comparison

As a data collection specialist at the National Institutes of Health (NIH), you have been involved in a research study conducted over the past year. The study found that liver cancer rates per 100,000 males among cigarette smokers to nonsmokers, in a major urban U.S. city, were 48.0 to 25.4, respectively.

In view of this data, what would be the relative risk of males in developing liver cancer, for smokers compared to nonsmokers? (Round to 2 decimal places.)

CASE 3-15

Determining Appropriate Formulas: Ratios

You are helping the nursing department write evaluation criteria for an upcoming quality improvement study. You need to determine appropriate formulas for ratios and set data collection time frames.

One important aspect of care is the documentation of education of patients. Specifically, the nursing department would like to assess its documentation compliance in education on colostomy care for patients receiving new colostomies.

You will help them decide what factors would be used for the numerator and denominator of the equation to gather their information.

Calculating Obstetrics (OB) Statistics

You are the HIM manager overseeing the state requirement for birth certificate reporting. Table 3-6 reflects the OB unit discharges for the month of January.

Calculate the monthly obstetric cesarean section rate and the neonatal death rate for January. (Round to 2 decimal places.)

Table 3-6   *January Discharge Data for the Obstetric Unit*

		Obstetric Unit Newborn Discharge Data January	
MR #	Deliveries	Cesarean Section Delivery Indicated (Y)	Neonatal Death (Y)
001	1-1-07	Y	
002	1-1-07		
003	1-2-07	Y	
004	1-3-07		
005	1-3-07		
006	1-4-07		
007	1-4-07		
008	1-5-07		
009	1-6-07		
010	1-7-07	Y	
011	1-7-07		
012	1-8-07		
013	1-9-07	Y	Y
014	1-9-07	Y	
015	1-10-07		
016	1-12-07		
017	1-13-07	Y	
018	1-13-07		

Table 3-6 *(Continued)*

		Obstetric Unit Newborn Discharge Data January	
MR #	Deliveries	Cesarean Section Delivery Indicated (Y)	Neonatal Death (Y)
019	1-14-07		
020	1-14-07		
021	1-15-07		
022	1-15-07	Y	
023	1-15-07		
024	1-16-07		
025	1-16-07		
026	1-17-07	Y	
027	1-17-07		
028	1-18-07		
029	1-18-07		
030	1-20-07		
031	1-21-07		
032	1-22-07		
033	1-22-07		
034	1-23-07		
035	1-24-07	Y	
036	1-24-07		
037	1-26-07		
038	1-27-07		
039	1-28-07	Y	
040	1-28-07		
041	1-29-07		
042	1-29-07		
043	1-30-07	Y	
044	1-31-07	Y	
045	1-31-07	Y	

Research Cesarean Section Trend

As a data specialist in the research department at the medical center, you are investigating the prevalence of cesarean section rates. Dr. Jenkins chairs the surgical committee and has been asked to research and compare statistics that include first births, repeat births, and vaginal births after previous cesarean delivery (VBAC) in low-risk pregnancies.

Public data is accessible through the Centers for Disease Control on the table entitled "Live births by method of delivery and rates of cesarean delivery and vaginal birth after previous cesarean delivery, by race and Hispanic origin of mother: United States, 1989–2004," at the CDC website: http://www.cdc.gov/nchs. (Accessed December 13, 2006, at http://www.cdc.gov/nchs/data/nvsr/nvsr55/nvsr55_01.pdf.)

Dr. Jenkins has asked you to review the national data comparing the years 1994, 1999, and 2004 from Table 28.

Create a table containing the findings for 1994, 1999, and 2004 for all races. Then create a graph that shows these results.

CASE 3-18

Hospital Statistics Spreadsheet

The HIM department of Jenkins County Hospital is responsible for reporting monthly statistics to administration, utilizing discharge data from the prior month. Jenkins County is a rural hospital with limited automation for reporting statistics. As the HIM director of this small-town hospital, you need to develop a discharge analysis spreadsheet to simplify calculations at month's end. Table 3-7 presents data from the daily census on each discharge during the month of January and Table 3-8 provides a key to discharge services.

Complete the requested monthly statistics report presented in Table 3-9.

Create a spreadsheet for posting the discharges. Utilize this electronic spreadsheet to build formulas and calculate the requested monthly statistics for January.

Table 3-7 *Jenkins County Hospital January Discharge Analysis Data*

		Jenkins County Hospital Discharge Analysis Data January		
MR #	Admit Date	Discharge Date	Discharge Service	Indicate Death
001	12-29-06	1-1-07	Med	
002	12-28-06	1-1-07	Med	
003	12-28-06	1-2-07	Sur	
004	12-28-06	1-3-07	Orth	
005	1-1-07	1-3-07	Med	
006	1-1-07	1-4-07	Neur	
007	1-1-07	1-4-07	Sur	
008	1-3-07	1-5-07	OB/Gyn	

(Continued)

Table 3-7   *(Continued)*

		Jenkins County Hospital Discharge Analysis Data January		
MR #	Admit Date	Discharge Date	Discharge Service	Indicate Death
009	1-1-07	1-6-07	Orth	
010	1-4-07	1-7-07	Med	
011	12-31-06	1-7-07	Sur	
012	12-30-06	1-8-07	Med	
013	1-6-07	1-9-07	Med	
014	12-27-06	1-9-07	Neur	
015	1-7-07	1-10-07	Sur	
016	1-7-07	1-12-07	Orth	
017	1-10-07	1-13-07	OB/Gyn	
018	1-11-07	1-13-07	Sur	
019	1-10-07	1-14-07	OB/Gyn	
020	1-13-07	1-14-07	Med	Died
021	1-10-07	1-15-07	Med	
022	1-8-07	1-15-07	Orth	
023	1-11-07	1-15-07	Sur	
024	1-13-07	1-16-07	Neur	
025	1-12-07	1-16-07	Med	
026	1-8-07	1-17-07	Orth	
027	1-10-07	1-17-07	Sur	
028	1-15-07	1-18-07	Neur	
029	1-15-07	1-18-07	OB/Gyn	
030	1-15-07	1-20-07	Med	
031	1-18-07	1-21-07	Orth	Died
032	1-18-07	1-22-07	Neur	
033	1-14-07	1-22-07	Med	
034	1-17-07	1-23-07	Sur	
035	1-21-07	1-24-07	OB/Gyn	
036	1-19-07	1-24-07	Med	
037	1-10-07	1-26-07	Sur	Died
038	1-23-07	1-27-07	Sur	
039	1-21-07	1-28-07	Med	
040	1-17-07	1-28-07	Orth	
041	1-24-07	1-29-07	OB/Gyn	
042	1-23-07	1-29-07	Neur	
043	1-25-07	1-30-07	Sur	
044	1-27-07	1-31-07	Med	
045	1-28-07	1-31-07	Orth	

Table 3-8 *Key to Discharge Services*

Key to Discharge Services	
Med	Medicine
Sur	Surgery
Orth	Orthopedic
Neur	Neurology
OB/Gyn	Obstetrics & Gynecology

Table 3-9 *Requested Monthly Statistics to Report*

Requested Monthly Statistics to Report	
Statistics Requested	**Statistics Reported for Month**
1. Total # Discharges 45	
2. LOS (for each patient)	(calculate on spreadsheet for each discharged patient)
3. Total LOS (for all patients)	
4. ALOS (for all patients) (round to 2 decimal places)	
5. Gross Death Rate 3	
6. Net Death Rate 3	

6.02

Benchmarks for Leading Causes of Death

The QI Committee is reviewing mortality data for the hospital in comparison to national mortality data. The QI coordinator will need to present a graph on the top 10 causes of death for the hospital. As HIM director, you have been asked to prepare a graph showing the top 10 causes of death in the United States for year 2003 to present at the next committee meeting.

To gather the information, you will need to utilize data the National Center for Health Statistics (NCHS) published on major causes of death in 2003, accessed on their website: http://www.cdc.gov/nchs.

Use Table 2, "Percentage of total deaths, death rates, age-adjusted death rates for 2003, percentage change in age-adjusted death rates from 2002 to 2003 and ratio of age-adjusted death rates by race and sex for the 15 leading causes of death for the total population in 2003: United States," to determine the top 10 causes of death for 2003.
(Accessed December 14, 2006, at http://www.cdc.gov/nchs/data/hestat/finaldeaths03_tables.pdf#2.)

Create a table to report the top 10 causes of death for the year 2003.

Develop a bar graph depicting the top 10 causes of death.

CASE **3-20**

Mortality Incidence in Alzheimer's and Memory-Impaired Patients

You work for NIH as a data specialist. You have been chosen to work on a mortality research project. Some data needs to be gathered for a meeting to discuss a new project on the aging population. Historical data on patients diagnosed with Alzheimer's disease is needed.

Retrieve data from "Vital and Health Statistics: National Mortality Followback Survey: 1986 Summary United States," which can be accessed on the NCHS website: http://cdc.gov/nchs.

Review Table 43, "Number and percent distribution of decedents by whether decedent ever was diagnosed by a physician as having Alzheimer's disease, chronic brain syndrome, dementia, senility, or any other serious memory impairment, according to sex, race, and age: United States, 1986," located on page 119 of the document. (Accessed December 14, 2006, at http://www.cdc.gov/nchs/data/series/sr_20/sr20_019.pdf.)

Utilizing data given in Table 43, develop a pie chart reflecting the mortality incidence that occurred in 1986 for both sexes by racial category of white, black, or other in U.S. patients diagnosed with Alzheimer's disease or other serious memory impairment.

Principal Diagnoses for U.S. Hospitalizations

The research department at your facility is conducting a study on principal diagnoses of U.S. hospitalizations for the year 2002. You are the data specialist instructed to gather statistics on stays in U.S. hospitals by principal diagnoses. This information can be obtained from the Agency for Healthcare Research and Quality (AHRQ) national statistics database at http://www.ahrq.gov ("HCUP Fact Book No. 6: Hospitalization in the United States, 2002").
(Accessed December 14, 2006, a: http://www.ahrq.gov/data/hcup/factbk6/factbk6d.htm.)

Choose four of the major groups presented in the following list or from the table on the website (Appendix: 2002. Statistics on Stays in U.S. Hospitals, Principal Diagnosis).

- Infectious and Parasitic Diseases
- Neoplasms (Cancer, Carcinoma-In-Situ, Benign Tumors)
- Endocrine, Nutritional, and Metabolic Diseases and Immunity Disorders
- Diseases of the Blood and Blood-Forming Organs
- Mental Disorders
- Diseases of the Nervous System and Sense Organs
- Diseases of the Circulatory System

Develop a bar graph or pie chart to show the incidence of principal diagnosis that occurs for each of your four chosen body systems.

CASE 3-22

Diagnosis-Related Groups (DRGs) and Revenue

Rocky Top Hospital collected the data displayed in Table 3-10 concerning their four highest volume DRGs.

Table 3-10 *Rocky Top Hospital's Highest Volume DRGs*

Rocky Top Hospital Highest Volume DRGs							
DRG A		DRG B		DRG C		DRG D	
CMS WEIGHT	NUMBER PATIENTS WITH THIS DRG	CMS WEIGHT	NUMBER PATIENTS WITH THIS DRG	CMS WEIGHT	NUMBER PATIENTS WITH THIS DRG	CMS WEIGHT	NUMBER PATIENTS WITH THIS DRG
2.0230	323	0.9870	489	1.9250	402	1.2430	386

Which of the DRGs listed in Table 3-10 generated the most revenue for Rocky Top Hospital?

CMS has increased the weight for DRG A by 14% and for DRG B by 20%. The weight for DRG D was decreased by 10%. Given these DRG weight changes, which DRG generated the most revenue for Rocky Top Hospital?

CASE 3-23

DRG 110 versus DRG 111 Cost Analysis (DRG version 10)

As a health information consultant, you need some financial data on cardiovascular procedures. Visit AHRQ's website: http://www.ahrq.gov.

Access the national statistics database that reports patients by DRG from 1994 discharges.

(Accessed December 16, 2006, at http://www.hcup-us.ahrq.gov/reports/natstats.jsp.)

Utilizing the historical DRG data given in the table, what are the financial implications in cost between DRG 111, Major cardiovascular procedures without cc, compared to DRG 110, Major cardiovascular procedures with cc, if 10% more of the discharges had complications or comorbidity conditions diagnosed?

CASE 3-24

Calculating Physician Service Statistics

You are on the Chargemaster Committee at Pike's Peak Clinic. An annual review of services and charges is being conducted for necessary revisions. Table 3-11 shows some statistics reported on the physicians' services at Pike's Peak Clinic last Tuesday.

Table 3-11 *Pike's Peak Clinic Physician Services Statistics for Tuesday*

	Pike's Peak Clinic Physician Service Statistics for Tuesday		
PHYSICIAN	SERVICE A	SERVICE B	SERVICE C
Truba	10	18	14
Wooley	14	22	9
Howe	18	5	6
Masters	12	20	7

It takes twice as long to perform Service C, so the physicians are proposing that Service C should count as two services for the purpose of calculating workload.

If Service C counts twice as much as Service A or Service B, which physician provided the most services on Tuesday?

Determining the Percentage of Patients with Unacceptable Waiting Time

You serve as the operations manager as well as HIM director at a community health clinic. Customer service indicators are tracked on an ongoing basis at your community health clinic. Currently, you are reviewing the data relative to wait times for patients to see their physician.

Use the information in Table 3-12 to calculate the average percentage of patients for the entire year who were delayed longer than an acceptable amount of waiting time. The sample size for each month's data is 100 (round to 1 decimal place).

Table 3-12 *Percent of Patients with Unacceptable Waiting Time*

Percent of Patients with Unacceptable Waiting Time	
Month	Percent of Patients with Unacceptable Waiting Time
January	5%
February	4%
March	3%
April	5%
May	3%
June	10%
July	5%
August	2%
September	1%
October	2%
November	1%
December	3%

CASE 3-26

Systems Analysis of Health Information Management (HIM) Function from Clinical Experience

In your clinical experience, you will be rotating through various services performed within health information management. There are common functions that you will observe and participate in during your clinical experience.

Perform a systems analysis of a selected function (system) within a hospital health information management department. If necessary, interview the area staff to acquire a more thorough knowledge of the process. Select a function of one of the following systems for analysis:

- Record Assembly and Analysis (quantitative analysis and incomplete record control)
- Filing and/or Storage and Retrieval of Patient Record
- Preparation of Record for Image Scanning and Indexing
- Processing a Request for Patient Records in ROI (release of information)
- Processing Record Completion from Time of Admission to after Discharge

Develop a flowchart. You may choose to use Microsoft Word software, which has a flowchart application, in completing your flowchart. (You may want to visit the Microsoft Office website at http://office.microsoft.com/training to search for tips or training material on flowcharting.)

A written procedure of the process should accompany your flowchart.

Clinical Quality Improvement Literature Research

Perform a literature search on clinical quality management (clinical quality improvement or clinical performance improvement) for articles presenting actual clinical QI studies performed in a healthcare facility. Select an article about a QI study performed to present and discuss the problem or process the study sought to improve. In your presentation, include as many of the following elements regarding the QI study performed:

- The problem or risk identified
- Why the topic was chosen to study
- Current method or process of performance
- Alternative methods of improvement considered
- Selected alternative to implement
- Implementation
- Monitoring or follow-up of the results

CASE 3-28

Quality Improvement (QI)/Performance Improvement (PI) Interview Project

As an HI student, contact a QI department at a healthcare facility to interview a staff representative of a QI/PI project performed by the facility. Identify what department/unit team members were represented (i.e., hospital, managed care organization, ambulatory surgery center) in the study performed within the facility. Obtain data regarding identification of the PI opportunity, findings, recommendations, and any follow-up made. The project will include a storyboard display and oral presentation reflecting the steps in the PI process.

Develop a storyboard display of QI/PI study project.

Present an oral presentation describing the QI/PI project conducted and overview, reflecting the mission, vision, customers and expectations, findings, and recommendations. The presentation should last approximately 10 minutes, and allow 5 maximum additional minutes for questions and answers.

SECTION FOUR

Healthcare Privacy, Confidentiality, Legal, and Ethical Issues

CASE 4-1

Notice of Privacy Practices (HIPAA)

The Health Insurance Portability and Accountability Act (HIPAA) Privacy Rule requires each covered entity to provide patients with a clear written explanation of how the covered entity may use and disclose their health information. The privacy rule gives specific content that must be included in a Notice of Privacy Practice.

Review the Notice of Privacy Practices shown in Figure 4-1.

What problems do you identify with this Notice of Privacy Practices?

Georgia State Hospital

Notice of Privacy Practices

THIS NOTICE DESCRIBES HOW INFORMATION ABOUT YOU MAY BE USED AND DISCLOSED AND HOW YOU CAN GET ACCESS TO THIS INFORMATION. PLEASE REVIEW IT CAREFULLY.

Although Georgia State Hospital has the responsibility of protecting your privacy, a healthcare facility may use your medical information to make treatment, payment, and healthcare operations decisions. Georgia State Hospital may also use your medical information without your consent as required by law. For any other usage, your written authorization is required. You may revoke your authorization at anytime prior to the actual release of the health information.

Georgia State Hospital may also use PHI to contact you with appointment reminders, treatment options, other services, and fund raising.

HIPAA gives you certain rights including:

- the right to request restrictions on the use of your PHI
- the right to confidential communications between you, your healthcare provider and the Hospital
- the right to review and obtain copies of PHI
- the right to obtain an accounting of disclosure once every five years
- the right to a copy of this notice upon request
- the right to file a privacy complaint
- the right to receive a copy of this notice electronically

Georgia State Hospital is required by law to protect the privacy of your PHI. This means that we cannot utilize your health information in anyway contrary to this notice. We are also responsible for providing you with our legal duties through the presentation of this document for your review.

Georgia State Hospital will conform to the guidelines outlined in this document as long as this document remains in effect. We do reserve the right to amend this form at any time. We will make any revised forms available to you via the website, when you return to our facility, or upon your written request. The new agreement will cover all PHI under the care of Georgia State Hospital.

If you believe that your privacy rights have been violated, you have the right to complain to either of the following:

Chief Privacy Officer
Georgia State Hospital
100 Main Street
Toccata, Georgia 12345
(706) 555-1212

Office for Civil Rights
U.S. Department of Health & Human Services
61 Forsyth Street, SW - Suite 3B70
Atlanta, GA 30323
(404) 562-7886; (404) 331-2867 (TDD)
(404) 562-7881 FAX

If you would like more information about your privacy rights, please contact the Chief Privacy Officer as described above. Georgia State Hospital cannot retaliate against you if you file a privacy complaint nor can we restrict any disclosures of your PHI.

Effective: 12/1/05

Figure 4-1 *Notice of Privacy Practices*

CASE 4-2

Accounting for Disclosure of Protected Health Information (PHI) Under the Health Insurance Portability and Accountability Act (HIPAA)

A request for an accounting of disclosure of PHI has been received. This request has been assigned to you to process. The patient, John Austin, had also requested an accounting for disclosure 14 months ago. His last visit was April 1, 2003. The routine charge for an accounting of disclosure is $150.00.

What HIPAA issues apply to this case study?

What information would you include?

How will you handle this situation?

Request for Accounting for Disclosure of Protected Health Information (PHI) (HIPAA)

A request has been received for an accounting of disclosure. See Table 4-1 for the list of the recorded disclosures of the PHI for this patient.

Evaluate each of the disclosures and determine if it should be included in the disclosure provided to the patient. Why should each one be included or not included?

Table 4-1 *Protected Health Information (PHI) Disclosures*

PHI Disclosures			
Released to	Date of Request	Authorized by	Evaluation
Attorney	3/7/05	Patient	
Attorney	3/2/05	TPO	
Physician	2/15/04	Patient	
Physician	1/13/04	TPO	
Blue Cross	2/11/03	TPO	
Patient	12/17/05	Patient	
Health Department	7/12/04	Law	
Subpoena	1/19/03	Law	
Researcher	12/28/03	Patient	
Prison official	11/19/03	Law	
Limited data set	6/10/06	Institutional Review Board	

CASE 4-4

Legal Issues in Accounting for Disclosure of Protected Health Information (PHI) to the Health Department (HIPAA)

George recently requested a copy of his accounting of disclosures. He is appalled to see that his diagnosis of syphilis was reported to the state health department 3 months ago. In this state, syphilis is a reportable disease. He comes to the hospital administrator's office demanding that the report be retracted. The administrator listens to George's complaints and then advises him that the appropriate action would be to file a privacy complaint. He files the complaint with the hospital and with the OIG.

What are George's legal rights?

What are the hospital's legal responsibilities?

What response would you expect from the hospital and the OIG?

Was this the best suggestion the administrator could have given the patient to pursue?

Patient Right to Amend Record (HIPAA)

Martha, a former patient at Talbotton Memorial Hospital, recently obtained a copy of her medical record. She saw on the discharge summary that her blood type was A+. It is actually B−.

Martha went to the ROI coordinator, showed her the Red Cross card documenting her true blood type, and asked the coordinator to change it.

The ROI coordinator refused, stating that the medical record is a legal document and cannot be changed. Martha was very angry by now.

She went to the HIM director who told her that the records can only be amended if her attorney obtains a court order.

Critique the responses to her request for changing the hospital's medical record.

CASE 4-6

Institutional Process for Patient Request to Amend Record (HIPAA)

You just had your first request for an amendment of the medical record. The process failed miserably. Lack of communication and documentation were identified as the root causes of the problem.

The request was not responded to in the appropriate time frame and the physician was not familiar with the process and did not know what to do. When the physician asked what to do, the HIM staff person coordinating the process could not explain it to him.

The privacy officer at the facility knew that they needed to fix the problem. The decision has been made to revise the existing form, to improve communication, and to update the process.

You have been given the responsibility of revising the Request for Amendment Form to ensure that the request by patient for amending the record is addressed and the process is documented appropriately.

How would you revise the form shown in Figure 4-2 to ensure that you are HIPAA compliant and have adequate communication via the form?

Include good form design principles.

Patient Request for Amendment to Health Record

Sherman Hospital
1123 Bay Drive
Sherman Utah, 84106

Patient Name_____   MRN: _____

Error: _____

_____

Decision: _____Revise   _____Do not revise

Signature_____   Date_____

Figure 4-2   *Internal Form for Patient Request for Amendment to Health Record*

CASE 4-7

Alteration of Patient Record

A patient was admitted to the hospital's ambulatory surgery unit for surgical removal of four impacted wisdom teeth. As required, a staff internist did a history and physical (H&P) examination prior to admission.

The dental surgeon removed the wisdom teeth and administered penicillin IM as a prophylactic. The patient had an immediate and violent reaction. After an extensive stay in the intensive care unit (ICU), the patient was discharged.

On routine discharge analysis, the HIM clerk found several deficiencies requiring physician completion. During this analysis of the record, the clerk observed that the H&P stated "no known allergies." As she was filing the ambulatory surgery record in the patient's file folder, she noticed that the previous encounter had ALLERGIC TO PENICILLIN stamped in red letters on the visit cover sheet. She placed the record in the incomplete chart area for completion.

When reanalyzing the chart a few days later, she saw that the H&P had been altered to read "patient denies any drug allergies." She took the record to the HIM director, who called the hospital attorney. The patient filed a malpractice suit a few months later.

What issues are involved?

What process could be implemented to prevent this from happening again?

Investigating Privacy Violations (HIPAA)

There have been several potential privacy incidents reported at your facility in the past week. Your job is to investigate these incidents to determine if they are truly privacy violations. If there are violations, decide what should be done.

Review each of the privacy incidents described in the following list. Determine which ones are privacy violations.

Identify the specific action(s) appropriate to address each of the situations.

A. Some alcohol and drug abuse records were inadvertently left accessible via the Internet. Fifty patients were affected.

B. A patient overheard a physician telling another patient's family that the cancer had spread to the surrounding lymph nodes. The physician was talking in a low voice in a corner of the hallway.

C. A hacker accessed the lab system. The hacker viewed multiple records.

D. A single form from a different patient was sent to the requesting patient.

E. A computer was not logged off and a visitor looked up his mother's PHI.

F. A monitor is turned toward the reception desk so that anyone who walks by can see it.

G. Patient complained that ex-wife looked at his record and told his girlfriend that he had human immunodeficiency virus (HIV).

CASE 4-9

Investigation of Breach of Privacy (HIPAA)

Margaret found herself facing a tough situation. Her babysitter called and cancelled 10 minutes before she needed to leave for work. She had a meeting with her manager that she could not miss. She brought her 12-year-old daughter, Molly, with her to work. Margaret sat Molly down in front of the computer in the office, telling her to play solitaire and surf the Internet until she returned. After the meeting, they went home.

Three days later, the chief privacy officer (CPO) confronted Margaret about her access of patient information. Several patients had received phone calls telling them that they had avian flu. The patients all panicked.

Margaret was the only user who had access to all of the patient accounts. She denied the accusations, but then realized that her daughter had had access to her computer. She relayed the story to her CPO.

What actions should be taken?

What could have been done to prevent this from happening?

Privacy Violation by Former Employee (HIPAA)

A patient has filed a privacy complaint with the physician office where you work. She says that her ex-sister-in-law, who works there, told her ex-husband that she was being treated for depression. Now he has taken her to court to challenge her custody of their children.

How would you investigate, if this was a paper record?

How would you investigate, if this was a computer record?

If you find evidence that the ex-sister-in-law did violate the privacy of the patient, what would you do?

If you found no evidence of any wrongdoings, what would you do?

CASE 4-11

Privacy and Security Training for New Staff (HIPAA)

You have been given the responsibility of providing HIPAA privacy training to new HIM staff when one is hired. The staff should receive HIPAA awareness training as part of the hospital new employee orientation.

Your training plan for the HIM Department staff is as follows:

- Timing of training:
  - Training should be implemented within 3 working days of working in the HIM department.
  - Training should be completed within 30 days of the employee's first day in the HIM department.
- Trainer: Assistant director of HIM or designee
- Method: Computer-assisted training and traditional classroom time.
- Handouts: None
- Records: Signature of attendees
- Retention of training records: Forever in employee file
- Testing: None
- Who should be included in training: All HIM staff
- Content:
  - Requesters should provide photo identification and written authorization.
  - Employees should not access charts that they do not have a business reason to access.
  - Send transcribed reports only to the physician(s) listed on the report.
  - There should be enough of an overview of functions of department so the employee knows who to refer people to when questions or requests arise.
  - Employees should log out of the computer when they leave.
  - Passwords should not be shared.
  - Physicians do not get access to PHI unless there is a treatment, payment, or healthcare operations (TPO) reason.
  - Hospital and departmental privacy policies are maintained by the secretary and are maintained in each functional area of the department for easy access.
  - Privacy problems in the department can be reported to your supervisor or the chief privacy officer.
  - PHI should only be released by authorized staff.

Is the content appropriate for HIM department new employee training?

Is this plan HIPAA compliant?

How can this plan be improved?

CASE 4-12

Release of Information (ROI) Staff Privacy and Health Insurance Portability and Accountability Act (HIPAA) Training Test

The staff of the release of information section frequently receives patient questions regarding the Notice of Privacy Practices and other HIPAA-related issues. The staff has to be well versed in patient rights and release of information regulations to answer these questions the patients ask.

The department supervisor has just developed a list of questions that will be used in training new ROI staff. The plan is to review each of the situations provided and have the new employee take a test. He or she will be instructed to place an X beside the situations that violate HIPAA.

Create an answer key for each of the questions presented in the new employee quiz shown in Figure 4-3 and give an explanation for your decision.

Privacy and HIPAA Training Quiz for Release of Information Staff

Instructions: Place an "X" beside the each of the following situations that violate HIPAA requirements.

_____a.   Marjorie just processed a request for PHI. It was dated 60 days ago.

_____b.   Mark, an HIM clerk, denied a request by Sarah, a patient, to obtain a copy of her pathology report from a hysterectomy.

_____c.   The authorization does not have a social security number on it, so the HIM Coordinator returned it stating that it does not meet HIPAA requirements.

_____d.   Natalie just requested a list of people who have reviewed her record. This is her second request of the year. The hospital is charging her $150.00.

_____e.   Bob just refused to sign the notice of privacy practice, but the hospital treated him anyway.

_____f.   The hospital received a request to amend a patient record. They refused to accept it.

_____g.   The hospital received a request to amend a patient record. They reviewed the request and denied the request.

_____h.   The request for an amendment of the medical record was processed in 28 days.

_____i.   The notice of privacy practices gives an example of treatment, payment, and healthcare operations.

Figure 4-3 *Release of Information (ROI) Staff Privacy and Health Insurance Portability and Accountability Act (HIPAA) Training Quiz*

CASE 4-13

Compliance with Privacy Training (HIPAA)

There has been no HIPAA privacy training since the April 14, 2003, implementation of HIPAA. The new CPO was horrified when she learned this. She immediately brought a committee together to develop a plan to get in compliance with the training requirements of HIPAA.

What needs to be done from a legal standpoint?

What needs to be done from training plan and management standpoint?

CASE 4-14

Privacy Plan Gap Analysis (HIPAA)

The CPO was walking around the hospital one day conducting a privacy gap analysis. He just happened to hear an admissions clerk tell a patient that she needed the patient to sign an acknowledgment of receipt of a Notice of Privacy Practices. The patient asked what the Notice of Privacy Practices was and why she needed to sign that she received it. The admissions clerk said, "I don't know what the Notice of Privacy Practices is. I was just told to provide it to each patient and have the patient sign the form." The admissions clerk also told the patient that she could not be seen by the physician unless she signed the acknowledgment of receipt of the Notice of Privacy Practices. The patient reluctantly signed the form.

The admissions clerk then asked the patient if she wanted to be in the directory. At the patient's questions regarding the directory, she is told that the directory is how family and friends find out what room you are staying in. The admissions clerk went on to say that the patient had to specifically list everyone whom she would like to be told what room she was in. If the patient chose not to be in the directory, then her presence in the facility and her room number would not be shared with anyone. The patient then agreed to be in the directory and provided the names of her children, their spouses, her grandchildren, and close friends.

He started investigating and got similar responses from other admissions clerks.

What HIPAA issues can you identify? How will you address these issues?

CASE 4-15

Security Measures for Access to Protected Health Information (HIPAA)

Your facility recently had a privacy violation.

Terry, a former employee, had been terminated 6 weeks ago. Apparently, Terry had a grudge against the hospital, so he went into the radiology information system, downloaded PHI, and then posted it on his personal website.

One of the current employees, Sean, who knew Terry, just happened to surf his website to see if it said what he was doing now. Sean saw an inflammatory story about the hospital and some PHI posted on Terry's website. Sean immediately reported the breach to the privacy and security officer.

What legal issues are involved?

What steps would this facility need to take during its investigation?

CASE 4-16

Access to Health Information for Treatment (HIPAA)

Lakeside Hospital takes patient privacy seriously. Their policy states that only healthcare professionals directly involved in the patient care should have access. They have had several incidents where a patient had an adverse outcome because the nurse who had access was at lunch and the nurse covering did not have all of the information that was required to provide care.

What options does the hospital have?

What would you recommend? Why?

CASE 4-17

Monitoring Regulations Affecting Healthcare (Federal Register)

You are responsible for identifying and monitoring the status of proposed regulations that may affect your organization. You are also responsible for submitting comments on these proposed regulations to the federal government when appropriate. Conduct a search of the recent issues of the *Federal Register* and review a proposed regulation that is related to healthcare. The *Federal Register* can be accessed at http://www.gpoaccess.gov/fr/. Regulations are sorted by agency. Examples of agencies that may have proposed regulations affecting healthcare are:

- Centers for Medicare and Medicaid Services
- Food and Drug Administration
- National Center for Health Statistics
- Centers for Disease Control

Complete the following:

- Name of the regulation:
- Regulation number:
- What agency has submitted this regulation?
- Summary of regulation:
- How does it apply to HIM?
- What changes would this regulation cause in healthcare and HIM?
- What comments would you submit to the agency proposing the regulation?
- What deadline is there for submitting comments?

Provide your instructor with a copy of the regulation, or an Internet link to this proposed regulation.

Monitoring Legislation Affecting Healthcare (Thomas)

In your job as government relations coordinator for the Southwestern Health Information Management Association, you are responsible for monitoring legislation under consideration in Congress. Your best tool is Thomas. Thomas is The Library of Congress search engine for the database of legislation under consideration in the U.S. Congress. You may locate Thomas at http://thomas.loc.gov/home/thomas.html.

CASE 4-19

Antidumping Regulations

Consolidated Omnibus Budget Reconciliation Act (COBRA) and the Emergency Medical Treatment and Labor Act (EMTLA)

St. Joseph's Hospital's emergency room is facing a busy night. They have a waiting room of people in various stages of need. There is everything from headaches, lacerations, and probable broken bones to fevers and GI upsets. The ER treatment rooms are full of patients with myocardial infarctions (MIs), possible strokes, and other life-threatening emergencies. Patients are experiencing a 3-hour wait. The hospital has asked ambulances to route patients to other hospitals when possible. Thirty minutes later a gun shot wound (GSW) patient walks into the hospital. The patient is bleeding profusely, but is alert and oriented times three. Pressure has already been applied to the wound. The patient's blood pressure is low. During triage, the patient is asked for basic demographic information and for a brief medical history. The patient is asked for an insurance card. The patient tells the triage nurse that he does not have insurance. Knowing that the patient is facing surgery, she talks to a physician and the decision is made to call an ambulance to take the patient to another facility.

Is this acceptable behavior?

Why or why not?

Responsibilities in Release of Information (ROI)

Margaret was the release of information supervisor. She overheard Susan explaining the content of the medical record to a patient. Specifically, Susan was explaining what the patient's diagnosis was and what the treatment usually was, and she was giving the patient advice on what she would do. Margaret was very concerned about Susan's actions, but decided to wait until the patient left to confront Susan.

Why would Margaret be concerned?

How would you have handled this situation? Why?

CASE 4-21

Release of Information and the "Legal Record"

Our facility has a hybrid medical record. We implemented an EHR 6 months ago. We store paper records in hard copy for 2 years. We store the microfilm for 50 years. We currently keep copies of records from other facilities in with our paper records. The radiology, lab, nurse's notes, orders, dictated reports, and pharmacy systems feed the EHR. Our physicians will not let us eliminate the hard copy record, so we print out everything in the EHR and file it in the chart. We received a subpoena for any and all records in a sensitive medical malpractice case. Since the case is so sensitive, we want to make sure that we provide the appropriate documentation. The patient has been to the facility multiple times beginning 30 years ago, with the most recent visit being 6 weeks ago.

What is the legal record for this patient?

How should the facility respond to the "any and all" statement?

Personal Rights to Healthcare Information

Jade is a 27-year-old Asian female admitted to the hospital 6 months ago with pancreatitis. It was determined during that admission that Jade had a pancreatic cancer as well. Jade was scheduled for radiation therapy and chemotherapy. Jade also has pain in her hips for which biopsy tests are being run to check for metastasis.

Jade is single, employed full time, and has her own apartment. Jade describes her family as being very close, with good relationships among all family members. These family members spend a lot of time at the hospital and have been involved in the decisions thus far. While Jade was recovering, the doctor came out and told the family that although he had to wait for pathology results to be sure, the biopsy looked cancerous to him.

The issue centers on Jade's parents requesting that Jade not be told that her biopsy was malignant. Their rationale is that Jade told them that she would not want to know if the test revealed a malignancy. Her parents feel that they are respecting her wishes. The oncologist believes that Jade is an adult and has the right to know and make her own decisions on her healthcare.

Should Jade be told?

Why or why not?

CASE 4-23

Authorization for Release of Information (ROI)

You are the ROI coordinator. You just received the following nine authorizations. Before you pull the charts, you will evaluate the authorizations to determine if they are valid.

Review these nine authorizations shown in Figures 4-4 through 4-12.

Determine if they are HIPAA compliant.

If they are not HIPAA compliant, identify any deficiencies.

AUTHORIZATION FOR RELEASE OF INFORMATION

Patient Name: Josiah Nix

DOB: 7-16-52

Social security number: 123-45-6789

Phone number: (478) 555-8153 and (478) 555-3630

Josiah Nix requests Mountaintop Health Care Center to disclose the following protected health
information to: Dr. Thomas Jones
                    123 Elm Street
                    Thomas, Georgia 12345

Information to be disclosed: Time period: November 5, 2004 to Present
                                   ER record, path report, x-ray, discharge summary

This authorization expires 60 days from the date of the signature below. I may revoke this authorization in
writing at any time by sending written notification to the Director of HIM. I understand that once the above
information is disclosed, it may be redisclosed by the recipient and the information may not be protected by
federal privacy laws or regulations. I understand that Mountaintop Health Care Center cannot condition
treatment on the patient's decision to sign this authorization.

Call when it is ready and I will pick up and take it to Dr. Jones.

*Josiah Nix*_____   *3/15/2006*_____

Signature of patient   Date

Figure 4-4   *Authorization for Release of Information Sample 1*

AUTHORIZATION FOR RELEASE OF INFORMATION

Patient Name: Josiah Nix

DOB: 7-16-52

Social security number: 123-45-6789

Phone number: (478) 555-8153 and (478) 555-3630

Josiah Nix requests Mountaintop Health Care Center to disclose the following protected health information to: Dr. Thomas Jones
                            123 Elm Street
                            Thomas, Georgia 12345

Information to be disclosed: Time period: November 5, 2004 to Present
                                ER record, path report, x-ray, discharge summary

This protected health information is being used or disclosed for the following purposes:

  Personal reasons

This authorization expires 60 days from the date of the signature below. I may revoke this authorization in writing at any time by sending written notification to the Director of HIM. I understand that once the above information is disclosed, it may be redisclosed by the recipient and the information may not be protected by federal privacy laws or regulations. Mountaintop Health Care Center cannot condition treatment on the patient's decision to sign this authorization.

Josiah Nix
_____

Signature of patient

Figure 4-5   *Authorization for Release of Information Sample 2*

AUTHORIZATION FOR RELEASE OF INFORMATION

Patient Name: Josiah Nix

DOB: 7-16-52

Social security number: 123-45-6789

Phone number: (478) 555-8153 and (478) 555-3630

Josiah Nix requests Mountaintop Health Care Center to disclose the following protected health information to: Dr. Jones

Information to be disclosed: Time period: November 5, 2004 to Present
                                ER record, path report, x-ray, discharge summary

This protected health information is being used or disclosed for the following purposes:

   Personal reasons

This authorization expires 60 days from the date of the signature below. I may revoke this authorization in writing at any time by sending written notification to the Director of HIM. I understand that once the above information is disclosed, it may be redisclosed by the recipient and the information may not be protected by federal privacy laws or regulations. I understand that Mountaintop Health Care Center cannot condition treatment on the patient's decision to sign this authorization.

Josiah Nix   *3/15/2006*
_____   _____

Signature of patient   Date

Figure 4-6 *Authorization for Release of Information Sample 3*

AUTHORIZATION FOR RELEASE OF INFORMATION

Patient Name: Josiah Nix

DOB: 7-16-52

Social security number: 123-45-6789

Phone number: (478) 555-8153 and (478) 555-3630

Josiah Nix requests Mountaintop Health Care Center to disclose the following protected health information to: Dr. Thomas Jones
123 Elm Street
Thomas, Georgia 12345

Information to be disclosed: Time period: November 5, 2004

This protected health information is being used or disclosed for the following purposes:

  Personal reasons

This authorization expires 60 days from the date of the signature below. I may revoke this authorization in writing at any time by sending written notification to the Director of HIM. I understand that once the above information is disclosed, it may be redisclosed by the recipient and the information may not be protected by federal privacy laws or regulations. I understand that Mountaintop Health Care Center cannot condition treatment on the patient's decision to sign this authorization.

Josiah Nix   *3/15/2006*
_____   _____

Signature of patient   Date

Figure 4-7   *Authorization for Release of Information Sample 4*

This authorizes General Hospital to release copy of my discharge summary and lab reports for my August hospitalization to Dr. John Doe. His address is:

1213 Main Street
Macon, GA 22255

My name is Jane S. Jones and my birth date is 11-2-54.

This release is valid for 60 days from the date signed.

Jane Jones

Figure 4-8   *Authorization for Release of Information Sample 5*

To Community Hospital Medical Record Department:

Please release a copy of my daughter's discharge summary from her April admission to me. Her name is Marsha Brodie and her date of birth is 10-21-1963.

Thank you.
Carolyn Brodie
123 Elm St.
Macon, GA 54695

This authorization is valid for 60 days from date signed.

Carolyn Brodie

Figure 4-9 *Authorization for Release of Information Sample 6*

To General Hospital Health Information Management Department:

Please release a copy of my daughter's prenatal records to me. Her name is Cindy Smith and her date of birth is 5-4-1987.

This authorization is valid for 60 days from date of signature. I understand that once the above information is disclosed, it may be redisclosed by the recipient and the information may not be protected by federal privacy laws or regulations. I understand that Mountaintop Health Care Center cannot condition treatment on the patient's decision to sign this authorization.

Thank you.

Naomi Johnson

Figure 4-10 *Authorization for Release of Information Sample 7*

This authorizes General Hospital to release copy of my discharge summary and lab reports for my August hospitalization to   Dr. John Doe. His address is:
1213 Main Street
Macon, GA 22255

My name is Jane S. Jones and my birth date is 11-2-54.

Jane Jones

Figure 4-11 *Authorization for Release of Information Sample 8*

This authorizes General Hospital to release copy of my discharge summary and lab reports for my August hospitalization to Dr. John Doe. His address is:

1213 Main Street
Macon, GA 22255

My name is Jane S. Jones and my birth date is 11-2-54.

This release is valid for 60 days from the date signed. I understand that once the above information is disclosed, it may be redisclosed by the recipient and the information may not be protected by federal privacy laws or regulations. I understand that Mountaintop Health Care Center cannot condition treatment on the patient's decision to sign this authorization.

Jane Jones

Figure 4-12 *Authorization for Release of Information Sample 9*

CASE 4-24

Processing a Request for Release of Information (ROI)

You are the ROI coordinator. You are having a busy day today. You are facing a variety of ROI situations. How should you handle the situations described below and what, if any, additional information would you need? If you would provide copies of the medical record, explain which forms (information) that you would provide. Include dates if appropriate.

a. A patient just called. The patient has an appointment at her doctor's office in 1 hour and wants copies of records to take to the office. The hospital has a policy that requires a 48-hour notice, except in medical emergencies. The patient did not specify what records she needs.

b. A patient has requested his charts to be sent to Disability Determination three times and they have not received them. Your records show that they have been sent twice. The patient is very upset.

c. An FBI agent shows up and flashes a badge at you. He demands that you release a patient's chart to him immediately.

d. Dr. Lawrence calls and requests a copy of the medical record on Stephanie Smith. The records show that Dr. Jones was the patient's physician. Dr. Jones and Dr. Lawrence are not partners.

e. You receive a subpoena requesting your presence in the court room. You do not want to appear, so you talk to the court clerk. The subpoena specifies all charts for a patient for the period of June 1998 to September 2001. The hospital has records for the period of April 1975 to present.

f. You receive a subpoena requesting the entire medical record for the 3/2/06 admission on Mary Taylor.

g. You receive a subpoena to appear in court and to bring a specific medical record. You are scheduled to testify tomorrow. How will you prepare? What guidelines will you follow in testifying?

h. You receive a subpoena for Mary Taylor's medical record. When the record is pulled and reviewed, you realized that she is HIV positive.

i. A patient requested a copy of all of his records today to take to his attorney. Your policy prohibits records to be released without a 24-hour notice, except for patient care. You explain the situation and he becomes extremely hostile.

j. A mother requests a discharge summary of her daughter's record (6/6/06 discharge). The daughter's record shows that she delivered a baby during this admission.

k. Dr. Smith requested his wife's medical record.

CASE 4-25

Reporting Communicable Diseases

One of the responsibilities of your job is to report communicable diseases.

Which of the diseases listed in Table 4-2 is classified as a reportable communicable disease by your state?

If the disease is reportable, how soon after diagnosis should it be reported?

Table 4-2 *Reportable Diseases*

Reportable Diseases		
Disease	Yes/Reporting deadline	No
Herpes zoster		
Cholera		
Hantavirus pulmonary syndrome		
Varicella		
Hepatitis A		
AIDS		
Cancer		
Gonorrhea		
Tetanus		
Rubella		
Malaria		
Poliomyelitis		
Whooping cough		
Diphtheria		
Mononucleosis		
Coxackie		
Pneumococcal septicemia		
Spirillum fever		
Whipple disease		
Influenza		
Streptococcal pneumoniae		

CASE 4-26

Disclosure of Information from a Psychiatric Record

Dr. Little is a psychiatrist. One of his patients threatened to harm his ex-wife. Dr. Little documented the following:

"Patient expresses anger against ex-wife and talked about how happy he would be if she were dead. He talked about how easy it would be to break into her house and kill her. I don't believe these threats are anything more than fantasies."

Two weeks later the patient is shown on the evening news as a murder suspect in the death of his ex-wife.

What legal principles apply?

CASE 4-27

Processing a Request for Information from an Attorney

You have just processed an attorney request for copies of records. There were 634 pages copied. Use the information in Table 4-3 to complete the invoice for this service (excluding postage). The following are some additional notes:

- Copies to healthcare providers for patient care are at no charge.
- First 10 copies to patients are free. The per-page fee applies after that. There is no retrieval fee.
- State law limits worker's comp to $0.25 per page.

For information on ROI, access the AHIMA Practice Brief Release of Information Reimbursement Laws and Regulations (Updated) on the AHIMA website: www.AHIMA.org.
(Accessed December 21, 2006, at http://library.ahima.org/xpedio/groups/public/documents/ahima/bok1_023132.hcsp?dDocName=bok1_023132.)

For a source of state-imposed fee schedules, access the website for the law offices of Thomas J. Lamb, PA, at http://www.lamblawoffice.com.
(Accessed December 21, 2006, at http://www.lamblawoffice.com/medical-records-copying-charges.html.)

Table 4-3 *Invoice for Retrieval Fees for Copies to Attorney*

Invoice for Retrieval Fees for Copies to Attorney			
Service	Charge (See notes below)	Quantity	Charges
Retrieval fee	$20.00		
Per page	$0.75 1–25 pages		
	$0.65 26–75 pages		
	$0.50 >75 pages		
Microfilm per page	$1.00		
Certification fee	$7.50		
Total charges (excluding postage)			

CASE 4-28

Processing a Request for Health Information from a Patient

You have just processed a patient request for information. There were 43 pages of hard copy and 39 pages of microfilm. Use the information in Table 4-4 and complete the invoice (excluding postage).

The following are some additional notes:

- Copies to healthcare providers for patient care: no charge.
- Copies to patients: first 10 copies are free. The per-page fee applies after that. There is no retrieval fee.
- State law limits worker's comp to $0.25 per page.

For information on ROI, access the AHIMA Practice Brief Release of Information Reimbursement Laws and Regulations (Updated) on the AHIMA website at www.AHIMA.org.

For a source of state-imposed fee schedules, access the website for the law offices of Thomas J. Lamb, PA, at http://www.lamblawoffice.com.
(Accessed December 21, 2006, at http://www.lamblawoffice.com/medical-records-copying-charges.html.)

Table 4-4 *Invoice for Retrieval Fees for Copies to Patient*

Invoice for Retrieval Fees for Copies to Patient			
Service	Charge (See notes below)	Quantity	Charges
Retrieval fee	$20.00	0	
Per page	$0.75 1–25 pages	25	
	$0.65 26–75 pages	8	
	$0.50 >75 pages	0	
Microfilm per page	$1.00	0	
Certification fee	$7.50	0	
Total charges			

Processing a Request for Certified Copy of Health Information

You have just processed a request for information. There were 423 pages of hard copy, 345 pages of microfilm copies. The authorization requests that the records be certified. Use the information in Table 4-5 and complete the invoice (excluding postage).

The following are some additional notes:

- Copies to healthcare providers for patient care: no charge.
- Copies to patients: first 10 copies are free. The per-page fee applies after that. There is no retrieval fee.
- State law limits worker's comp to $0.25 per page.

For information on ROI, access the AHIMA Practice Brief Release of Information Reimbursement Laws and Regulations (Updated) on the AHIMA website at www.AHIMA.org.

For a source of state-imposed fee schedules, access the website for the law offices of Thomas J. Lamb, PA, at http://www.lamblawoffice.com.
(Accessed December 21, 2006, at http://www.lamblawoffice.com/medical-records-copying-charges.html.)

Table 4-5 *Invoice for Retrieval Fees for Certified Copies*

Invoice for Retrieval Fees for Certified Copies			
Service	Charge (See notes below)	Quantity	Charges
Retrieval fee	$20.00	1	
Per page	$0.75 1–25 pages	25	
	$0.65 26–75 pages	50	
	$0.50 >75 pages	348	
Microfilm per page	$1.00	345	
Certification fee	$7.50	1	
Total charges (excluding postage)			

CASE 4-30

Processing a Request for Health Information for Worker's Compensation

You have just processed a worker's compensation request for information. There were 179 pages of hard copy. Use the information in Table 4-6 and complete the invoice excluding postage.

The following are some additional notes:

- Copies to healthcare providers for patient care: no charge.
- Copies to patients: first 10 copies are free. The per-page fee applies after that. There is no retrieval fee.
- State law limits worker's comp to $0.25 per page.

For information on ROI, access the AHIMA Practice Brief Release of Information Reimbursement Laws and Regulations (Updated) on the AHIMA website at www.AHIMA.org.

For a source of state-imposed fee schedules, access the website for the law offices of Thomas J. Lamb, PA, at http://www.lamblawoffice.com.
(Accessed December 21, 2006, at http://www.lamblawoffice.com/medical-records-copying-charges.html.)

Table 4-6 *Invoice for Retrieval Fees for Workers Compensation Request*

Invoice for Retrieval Fees for Workers Compensation Request			
Service	Charge (See notes below)	Quantity	Charges
Retrieval fee	$20.00		
Per page	$0.75 1–25 pages		
	$0.65 26–75 pages		
	$0.50 >75 pages		
Microfilm per page	$1.00		
Certification fee	$7.50		
Total charges (excluding postage)			

Valid Authorization for Requests for Release of Information (ROI)

You are the supervisor of release of information. You have hired a new graduate from the local HIT program. She will need extensive training. The first task is ensuring that she knows who should sign the authorization. To test her knowledge, you give her a stack of authorizations that you have received. Table 4-7 shows a summary of release of information requests that were received today. Who should sign the authorization? The age of majority in this state is 18.

Table 4-7 *Information Requests*

Information Requests	
Description of Patient	Who Should Sign Authorization and Why?
17-year-old with laceration	
14-year-old with gonorrhea	
26-year-old mentally retarded male	
43-year-old surgery patient	
83-year-old surgery patient	
63-year-old Alzheimer's patient	

CASE 4-32

Health Information Management (HIM) Department Process for Subpoenas for Release of Information (ROI)

The director received a phone call from the circuit court clerk earlier today. She immediately contacted the ROI section and called a mandatory meeting for that afternoon. She gave a synopsis of the phone call. She explained that the circuit court clerk was relaying a message from the judge. The message was, "If one more chart is late or does not contain the requested information, then someone is going to have to explain it to me in court! Then, if there is not a good reason, I will hold you in contempt of court!"

How should the director handle this?

Include quality improvement, training, and other issues, as appropriate.

Validate Subpoenas for Release of Information

You are the release of information coordinator and have been charged with processing all subpoenas received by the department. The first thing that you will need to do when you receive a subpoena from the appropriate authorities is to review it to ensure that the subpoena is valid.

Review the subpoenas shown in Figure 4-13 through Figure 4-16.

Determine if they are valid. If they are not valid, identify the deficiencies.

Subpoena

Issued by the United States District Court

Subpoena in a Civil Case: 12165486464   Thomas Smith vs. Jeff Jefferson

To: Custodian of Records
       General Hospital
       1551 Elm Street
       Macon, GA 22448

You are commanded to produce copies of any and all records regarding treatment for:
Linda Fields, DOB 11/5/52, dated April 11, 1998 or after.
These records are to be released to the Court Clerk by 9:00 a.m. May 5, 2007.

Requesting Attorney:
Sam Wallace, Attorney at Law
431 Main Street
Macon, GA 24886
(912)554-5548

Signed: *Sally Thompson,*

              Court Clerk

Figure 4-13   *Subpoena 1*

Subpoena

Issued by the United States District Court

Subpoena in a Civil Case Thomas Smith vs. Jeff Jefferson

To: Custodian of Records
General Hospital
1551 Elm Street
Macon, GA 22448

You are commanded to produce copies of any and all records regarding treatment for:
Linda Fields, DOB 11/5/52, dated April 11, 1998 or after.
These records are to be released to the Court Clerk by 9:00 a.m. May 5, 2007,

Requesting Attorney:
Sam Wallace, Attorney at Law
431 Main Street
Macon, GA 24886
(912)554-5548

Signed: *Sally Thompson*

Sally Thompson, Court Clerk

Figure 4-14 *Subpoena 2*

Subpoena

Issued by the United States District Court

Subpoena in a Civil Case: 12165486464

To: Custodian of Records
        General Hospital
        1551 Elm Street
        Macon, GA 22448

You are commanded to produce copies of any and all records regarding treatment for Linda Fields, DOB 11/5/52, dated April 11, 1998 or after.

Requesting Attorney:
Sam Wallace, Attorney at Law
431 Main Street
Macon, GA 24886
(912)554-5548

Signed: *Sally Thompson*

Sally Thompson, Court Clerk

Figure 4-15   *Subpoena 3*

Subpoena

Subpoena in a Civil Case: 12165486464 Thomas Smith vs. Jeff Jefferson

To: Custodian of Records
        General Hospital
        1551 Elm Street
        Macon, GA 22448

You are commanded to produce copies of any and all records regarding treatment for Linda Fields, DOB 11/5/52, dated April 11, 1998 or after.
These records are to be released to the Court Clerk by 9:00 a.m. May 5, 2006.

Requesting Attorney:
Sam Wallace, Attorney at Law
431 Main Street
Macon, GA 24886
(912)554-5548

Signed: *Sally Thompson*

Sally Thompson, Court Clerk

Figure 4-16 *Subpoena 4*

CASE 4-34

Quality and Performance Improvement in Release of Information (ROI) Turnaround Time

Your ROI area is having some problems with quality and turnaround times. You have been given the responsibility of determining how you will solve the problems. Your options are:

- Hire consultant to come in and clean it up.
- Clean it up yourself.
- Outsource the services to a copy service.

What are the benefits and disadvantages of each?

What facts would you want to make your decision?

What is your bias? Why?

Planning for a New Release of Information (ROI) Department

You have been hired as the director of HIM for a new 75-bed hospital. As part of planning the HIM department, your current task is to plan for the development of the ROI desk. Expectations are that you will average 5 requests per day for medical information during the first 6 months, and after that you expect 15 requests per day.

What needs to be done to get the release of information function operational by the time the hospital opens in 6 months?

These tasks include but are not limited to:

- Policy and procedure
- Equipment required
- Training
- Forms
- Information systems
- Management systems

You are not expected to conduct the development, just the planning. Be specific in developing your plan. For example, list all of the policies and procedures that must be written, forms that must be designed, and the like.

CASE 4-36

Choosing a Personal Health Record (PHR)

You have had a variety of illnesses, hospitalizations, and surgeries. Physicians who treat you include a primary care physician; an ear, nose, and throat specialist (ENT); a cardiologist; a nephrologist; a retinal specialist; a glaucoma specialist; a physiatrist; and a urologist. It seems that you are visiting the health information department frequently for copies of your health record for one physician or another. An HIM professional said that you could benefit from having a personal health record (PHR). You decided that you want to learn more about it.

Go to http://www.myphr.org website and review three of the web-based PHRs found there.

Use the following categories to conduct your investigation of the web-based PHRs:

- Back-up
- Robustness of content that can be entered
- Uptime
- Ease of use
- Expense
- Storage size
- Privacy and security

What benefits would you expect to encounter when you implement your PHI?

What other information might the patient want to know?

Updating the Retention and Destruction Policy for Healthcare Records

You work for a 575-bed acute care Level I research trauma center. This hospital is also a teaching hospital that is connected to a university. The medical center brings in multimillions of dollars in grants each year. This facility's maternity ward delivers the most babies in the city. They have an active heart surgery center.

There are 6 months of data in the new EHR. There are 2 years of paper on the shelf. The 2 years of paper records include the contents of the EHR, since administration does not trust the EHR yet. All older records are maintained on microfilm. You have just run out of storage space. Because of this, you have been asked to evaluate the current retention policy, which is to retain records forever.

What should the minimum retention policy be based on?

What are your options?

Which would you recommend? Why?

CASE 4-38

Evaluating Records for Destruction

You are conducting your annual purge of records. Based on your retention policy, charts are retained for 10 years after the last visit. It is your responsibility to determine which records should be destroyed.

Assume today's date is June 2, 2007. Which of the records in Table 4-8 should be destroyed?

Table 4-8   *Retention Decisions*

Retention Decisions		
Record Number	Dates of Service	Retention Decision
123456	12/6/95 4/16/92 4/16/91	
145321	1/14/00 3/6/92	
237621	7/6/98 9/1/96	
179341	2/25/05 7/16/97	
180072	10/19/93	

Developing a Documentation Destruction Plan

You have been given the responsibility of developing the documentation destruction plan for your facility. Your plan is as follows:

- The health center is dedicated to meeting the needs of its customers as well as complying with state and federal law.
- Patient information will be retained as per the criteria below:
  - MPI data will be retained 20 years.
  - Medical records will be retained for 5 years after the patient's last visit.
  - Registers and indices will be retained for 10 years.
  - Paper records will be destroyed by fire.

Critique the above plan.

Rewrite the plan so that it complies with federal laws (including HIPAA), your state laws, and recommended HIM practices. In your plan, correct any errors and make the necessary changes to make it meet the needs of not only the HIM department, but also the entire enterprise.

CASE 4-40

Informed Consent for Surgery

Fred is scheduled to have a laparoscopic appendectomy. Dr. Smith tells him that it needs to be done because the appendix is inflamed. Dr Smith then says that the nurse will give the patient a surgical consent to sign and that he will see the patient in surgery.

The physician goes to the unit records room and writes in the progress notes, "Patient has appendicitis. WBCs are elevated. Surgery in a.m. An informed consent was given."

Is this truly an informed consent?

Given the patient's diagnosis and treatment plan, what should the patient have been told?

Informed Consent Evaluation

Daphne Logan was admitted to the hospital and found to need a cholecystectomy. Dr. Tobias was scheduled to do the surgery at 6:00 a.m. the next morning. When Dr. Tobias left the hospital, he gave the nurses instructions to have the patient sign a surgical consent. He had already obtained the informed consent and documented it in the chart. About 10:00 p.m., a golfing friend called and invited him to play in a golf tournament the next morning. Another player had just cancelled out. Tee time was 7:00 a.m. Dr. Tobias agreed to play and then called his partner, Dr. Radner, who was on call to cover the surgery on Daphne. The next morning, Dr. Radner walked into the operating room after the patient had been anesthetized and announced that he was performing the surgery.

Is this appropriate?

CASE 4-42

Informed Consent: Legal and Ethical Issues

Tim was diagnosed with a cerebral aneurysm. The physician told Tim that he did this type of repair surgery all the time with good outcomes. He did not explain that the aneurysm was in the worst possible place and that there was a good possibility that Tim would end up being in a persistent vegetative state. He also did not explain that he could probably live for years without doing anything to the aneurysm. The patient agreed to the surgery.

The nurse was in the room during the physician visit and was very upset about the lack of information being presented to the patient. The nurse confronted the physician who told her to mind her own business.

What should the nurse do?

Ethics and Do Not Resuscitate (DNR) Orders

Wallace is a respiratory therapist. His patient, Maude, is 82 years old. She is conscious but on a ventilator. He sees from her old records that she is a do not resuscitate (DNR), but the physician orders full treatment, including resuscitation.

Wallace questions the physician. The physician thinks she has a chance to survive, so he wants to resuscitate her if needed.

Wallace is not comfortable with this. How should he proceed?

✓ with supervisor for advice on situation

✓ for Durable Power of ~~Attorney~~ Advance Directive; If present contact family member responsible for making decisions for patient.

Living will

CASE 4-44

Patient's Right to Refuse Treatment

Tina has been in a car wreck and has internal bleeding. In the ER, she tells the physician that she is a Jehovah's Witness and refuses blood transfusions. The physician tells her that she will die without the transfusions. She still refuses. There is no reason to believe the patient is mentally compromised.

The physician decides to try to save her life and rushes her to the OR. While the patient is under general anesthetic, the physician orders and gives four units of blood to the patient.

In the recovery room, the nurse, Tanya, is reviewing the record and sees the ER nurse's note about the refusal of blood. She saw that the patient was given blood and decides to talk to the physician.

The physician tells Tanya that his Hippocratic Oath would not allow him to stand by and watch the patient die when he could prevent it.

What should Tanya do?

Advanced Directives

As the HIM director, you have the responsibility for maintaining advanced directives. The facility's current policy states that the living wills and durable medical power of attorney will be maintained in the risk manager's office.

This policy designation was made so that the risk manager could ensure that the implementation of any advanced directive was handled appropriately. The risk management office is open from 8:00 a.m. to 5:00 p.m. Monday through Friday.

A former patient's estate has sued the hospital because the patient was resuscitated by the ER physician when he did not have knowledge of or access to the presence of the living will. The family's charge is that the patient suffered an additional 3 days because he was resuscitated, which was against the living will that he had signed.

The doctor said that he did what he was ethically bound to do.

What legal and ethical issues apply?

What could have been done differently to prevent this lawsuit?

CASE 4-46

Patient Self-Determination Act

You are the patient advocate for Dekalb Memorial Hospital. This is a newly created position. You have been in the position for only 2 months.

A patient was admitted to the hospital earlier today and was asked if she had an advanced directive. The admission clerk then continued to ask questions regarding the patient's choices in advanced directive. The patient did not understand the concept of advanced directives and became distraught.

The admissions clerk referred the patient to you for further discussion. When you arrived at the patient's room, she was still upset. The patient essentially knows nothing about advanced directives and doesn't understand why the hospital is "butting into her business."

What would you tell her about why the admissions clerk asked the questions?

How would you explain what advanced directives are and why they are important?

Duty to Report Unethical Behavior (Clayton Act)

Todd is the hospital administrator. He is good friends with Cliff, who is the hospital administrator at the hospital across town. They meet for dinner occasionally and play golf frequently. One day an assistant administrator, Karen, has dinner with them. During dinner, the men discuss prices and make plans to adjust some of their prices so that they will be more competitive. Karen is concerned because she knows that the OIG would call this price fixing.

She knows that she needs to do something, but what?

What risks does Karen take in reporting the incident?

CASE 4-48

Research Studies and Ethics

One of the physicians on staff is telling you about a study that he is doing on his patients. He hopes to have the study published and to receive a grant to expand his research. He offers to hire you to help him with the data collection during your off hours. You accept and begin helping him.

You start collecting data. When you access the file the next day, you realize that he has removed a number of patients from the study. You suspect that they were removed intentionally, but you cannot be sure. You put your suspicions aside and proceed with your work and add more patients to the database. A few days later more patients have been removed from the database.

When you do some investigation, you discover that the patients who were removed were sicker and/or had a poor outcome.

What should you do?

What issues are involved?

CASE 4-49

Identity Theft

Larry was having abdominal pains and went to the emergency room. When asked his name, he gave them his brother's name, Bob, because Bob had insurance and Larry did not. Larry's family was in on the conspiracy, but they accidentally called him Larry in front of the nurse, Sandra.

Sandra quizzed the family and they admitted the switch in identity, but they begged Sandra not to tell. They even offered her $200 to keep silent.

What should Sandra do?

CASE 4-50

Analyzing Incident Reporting Form Design

You have been given the responsibility of reviewing your facility's form for reporting incidents. There have been several cases where the hospital had to settle out of court because critical information had not been captured at the time of the incident. By the time some of the cases were filed, information that had not been documented was lost because the people involved could not clearly remember what happened at the time of the incident.

Critique the form in Figure 4-17 from both a forms design and the incident-reporting standpoint.

INCIDENT REPORT

Patient name: _____

Medical record number: _____   Date of incident: _____

Location of incident: _____Patient room #_____

                             _____Patient care area

                             _____Grounds

Equipment involved (include inventory tag number) _____

_____

Environmental issues contributing to event _____

_____

Witnesses: _____

Treatment required by patient: _____

Summary of event: _____

_____

_____

Signature of person completing form: _____

White copy to risk management   Goldenrod copy in patient's medical record

Figure 4-17 *Incident Report Form*

CASE 4-51

Employee Incident Reporting

One of your employees injured her knee when she fell off a ladder. There is a policy on the use of office equipment, including the ladder, but it is very general and essentially says that employees should be careful when using the ladder.

As her supervisor, how should you handle the situation?

How would you investigate?

What changes in policy might you want to consider?

Investigating an Incident

You have been given the responsibility of conducting the initial review of an incident report that arrived in the risk management department today. You will review the report and gather all of the information that the risk manager needs to decide what should be done.

Review the information from the completed incident report shown in Figure 4-18.

Based on the information, who is at fault?

Is there any contributory negligence attributable to other parties involved?

What could have been done to prevent the incident?

What further information would you want?

INCIDENT REPORT

Name: Molly Smith
Address: 5 Sun Rise Trail Marietta, AK 12347
Phone: 254-555-3217

Witnesses: Janet Sykes 123 Main Street Marietta, AK 12345 Phone: 254-555-1111

               Todd Byron 55 Elm Road Marietta, AK 12346 Phone: 254-555-2963

Incident Location: 2nd floor surgery waiting room

Conditions at time of incident: Floor was wet. The wet floor sign was in place.

Equipment involved: none

Description of incident:
Ms. Smith fell when walking across the wet floor of the surgery waiting room. The sign was in place as per policy. Mrs. Smith complains of ankle pain. She agrees to go to ER for exam. The exam shows mild sprain. She was discharged from ER. She went back to the surgery waiting room to wait for news of her husband's surgery. Witnesses said that patient was talking on the cell phone when she fell over a backpack that was sitting on the floor against a chair.

Figure 4-18   *Incident Report*

American Health Information Management Association (AHIMA) Code of Ethics

You have a learner in your department who asked you how you as an HIM professional can exhibit ethical behavior. You tell the learner about the AHIMA Code of Ethics and walk through each of the standards of the code.

Document how you as an HIM professional can comply with each standard.

Why is a code of ethics important?

What does the AHIMA Code of Ethics mean to you and your career?

Information Technology and Systems

System Conversion

Your facility is getting a new MPI. You are replacing an existing computerized MPI that no longer meets the needs of the organization. Most of the staff are excited about the new functionality that will be available. The problem you found is that there are some differences in the structure of the data fields between the two systems. Use Table 5-1 to review the differences between the two systems. Determine if the data in the old system needs to be converted. If any of the fields need to be converted, specify exactly what needs to be done. Precision is important, since the programmers will be using this information to write the conversion software code. If appropriate, provide examples to the programmers so that there will not be any confusion. Document your findings in the comments column in Table 5-1.

Table 5-1 *Field Analysis for System Conversion*

Field	Old System	New System	Comments
Date of Birth (DOB)	Mmddyyyy	Mmddyyyy	
Last Name	25 characters	30 characters	
First Name	20 characters	18 characters	
Service	Medical Newborn OB/Gyn Pediatrics Surgery	Cardiology Cardiovascular Surgery Dermatology Endocrinology Family Practice Gastroenterology General Surgery Gynecology Internal Medicine Neonatology Neurology Neurosurgery Newborn Obstetrics Oncology Orthopedics Pediatrics Pulmonary	
Patient Types	Inpatient ER Outpatient	Inpatient Cardiac Rehab ER Outpatient Surgery Outpatient	
Physician Number	4 digit	5 digit	
MRN	7 digit	10 digit	

Web Page Design

You are the information systems liaison for the HIM Department. You are a registered health information administrator (RHIA) with information systems experience, but you are not an expert web page designer so the pages will be simple. The HIM Department is constantly getting requests for the same information, so the HIM Director decided that basic information about the department should be provided on the hospital website and/ or intranet. This should cut down on the phone calls received in the department and improve customer service as well. The Director has told you to create three simple web pages for the HIM Department at Island Palms General Hospital. These pages should link together and include, at a minimum, the following content:

- Name of the hospital
- Name of department
- Hours of operation
- Picture of HIM Department and Director
- Services provided by HIM Department
- Phone numbers for services
- Health Information Management administration names and contact information
- Information on requesting information
- Location of department
- Information for physicians (pulling charts, research, incomplete charts, etc.)
- Other as appropriate

The Director also specified that the web pages should utilize:

- Hyperlinks
- Pictures
- Tables
- Background design
- Color font to accentuate key content
- Other tools as appropriate

The pages should all have the same look and feel, complementing each other in color, structure, and the like. They should not contain redundant information; however, the hospital and department name should be on each page as well as a link to the department home page and hospital home page. Make recommendations on whether these pages should be on the Internet or intranet.

CASE 5-3

Policy and Procedure Development

Write a policy and procedure on how to abstract a chart, which should include abstracting/verifying the following information: codes, discharge disposition, service, attending, date of surgery, and surgeon. Use proper policy and procedure formatting. Write this as if the reader knew nothing about the system or your policies and procedures, taking into consideration what you would want and need to know if you were using this system for the first time. Remember that policies and procedures should connect technology and the manual processes together. Assume that log-in instructions are spelled out in another policy and procedure.

Database Design

You are an RHIA who works in the information systems department. You have extensive HIM experience as well as information systems experience. You tend to get projects related to HIM, including data collection and reporting, and your next assignment is to create a data dictionary that will be used for data collection. Your HIM background kicks in when you see the data quality issues in the instructions that you are provided, which are given in Table 5-2. The requester has told you that the information collected in Table 5-2 will be used to create your new computerized MPI. Each row indicates one field; the format column tells how the data should be formatted and the number field is the number of characters the field should allow.

Analyze the information to find possible problems with the way the fields would be entered into the system. Make recommendations on how to improve the information, including missing data elements, inappropriate data elements, ways to build quality into the system, ways to improve data collection, and so on.

Table 5-2 *Field Properties*

Field	Format	Number of Characters
Name	FN MI LN (alpha)	25
Address	alpha	25
City, State, Zip	alphanumeric	25
Discharge Date	numeric	6
Admission Date	numeric	6
Discharge Disposition	01, 02, 03, 04, 05, 06, 07, 20	2
Service	alpha	3
Date of Birth	numeric	6
Race	b, w, h	2
Gender	m, f, u	1

CASE 5-5

Database Development

You are an HIM subject matter expert for a vendor who has just gotten into the Ambulatory EHR business. You have been assigned the responsibility of developing data entry screens for the programmer to use in the development of the system. Your instructions are to use Microsoft Access to develop three data entry computer screens for an EHR. You must use sound user interface principles. Each form should use different types of data entry skills and should build in data quality principles. In other words, you need to use different types of entry such as free text, radio buttons, check boxes, drop-down boxes, and the like. Because all of the screens will be part of the same EHR, they need to be the same colors, have the same look and feel, and so on. Each screen should contain at least eight data elements on it. All screens should have at least one drop-down box with data populated.

Write a narrative to describe each of the screens that you developed. In the narrative, answer the following questions:

1. What is the purpose of the screen?

2. Why is each data element important?

3. Why is the type of data entry appropriate?

4. How did you design data quality into the screen?

CASE 5-6

System Selection

Triad Hospital System comprises six hospitals. Corporate has asked their six HIM Directors to select the imaging system that will be used by all six of the hospitals. Three of the hospitals want Imaging Plus and three of the hospitals want HIM Imaging. No evaluation methods were established during the planning stage. The HIM Directors looked at demonstrations and the responses to the requests for proposals (RFPs) before voting; none of the Directors are willing to give way in their vote.

1. What evaluation criteria could have been in place to prevent this stalemate from occurring?

2. Who else should have been involved in the process?

3. What lessons should the facility learn about this experience?

CASE 5-7

System Life Cycle

You recently learned about the concept of system life cycle. You really do not understand what it is. You know that it has something to do with the different stages of the information system but you do not understand what those stages are and what would be included in the stages. Do some research to get the following information about system life cycle and write up your findings.

1. How can you tell what stage an information system is in?

2. Cite at least two specific examples of how information systems could fall into each of the categories.

3. What is the HIM role in each of the stages?

4. How can you plan for obsolescence?

Data Collection Questionnaire and Interview Questions for Systems Analysis

The HIM Director asked you, the Assistant Director, to represent the department on the Imaging System Steering Committee. At the first meeting, you were asked to develop a questionnaire and the interview questions that will be used to collect information from users about the functionality they need in an imaging system. You know how important this system is to the hospital and that administration is anxiously awaiting the findings, so you want to make sure that you use good form design principles and good questionnaire/interview design principles. You also want the questionnaire and interview questions to be comprehensive. Develop the questionnaire and the interview questions to be used.

CASE 5-9

Developing a Data Collection Plan for Systems Analysis

Your facility has decided to purchase an imaging system. You have just developed a survey instrument with interview questions to be used in determining the functional requirements of the system. Determine who should be included in the survey and interviews. Your facility has 1,800 employees and 500 physicians on medical staff. With your resources, there is no way that you can include everyone; however, you want to include as many people as possible, but you do not have a lot of time and personnel to do the data collection and analysis. You also want to include clinical and nonclinical users throughout the facility. At this time, you do not have to specify the number of surveys and interviews to conduct; the committee as a whole will make that decision.

1. Who should be interviewed (titles and/or categories of employees)?

2. Who should be administered a questionnaire (titles and/or categories of employees)?

3. Why did you choose these job titles?

4. How would you choose the specific individuals who should be included?

5. Would you recommend paper or web-based surveys?

CASE 5-10

Information System Project Steering Committee

The Information System Steering Committee in conjunction with administration has decided to implement a computerized physician order entry (CPOE) system. A separate committee is being created to control the implementation of the CPOE with the Information System Steering Committee providing guidance. As project manager, you have been given the responsibility for selecting the appropriate individuals—those with a vested interest in the CPOE—for inclusion on this committee.

1. What departments would you want represented on this committee?

2. Who should the committee report to?

3. How frequently would you recommend reporting to the Information System Steering Committee?

4. What responsibilities should the committee have?

5. What role would a trouble ticket play?

CASE 5-11

Developing a System Selection Plan

You are part of the five-member team responsible for selecting the new admission/discharge/transfer (ADT)/ MPI for your facility. You are replacing an existing MPI that no longer meets the needs of your organization. Even more important, in 18 months the MPI will no longer be supported by your vendor. The functional requirements and the request for proposal have been developed. The RFP is due back from the vendors in 1 week. Your facility wants to make the decision about which system to choose within 3 months. Your assignment is to evaluate the RFPs returned and to develop a plan to guide the team in the evaluation and selection of the final system. Your plan should answer these questions:

1. What process(es) will be used to evaluate systems?

2. How will you evaluate the RFPs?

3. Who will be involved in the process and in what roles?

4. Of all the evaluation methods used, which one do you believe should have the most impact on your decision? Why?

CASE 5-12

System Selection

Island Palms General Hospital has an existing ADT/MPI system that was implemented 20 years ago. It was developed in-house and all of the programmers have resigned or retired. It is cumbersome to manage and to update to meet the current needs of the hospital. Therefore the decision was made to purchase a new system.

An RFP was sent out to two vendors—System Patient Management, Inc., and System Patient Tracking, LLC. Key portions of the RFP have been summarized to allow for easy comparison. The responses to the functional requirements have also been provided.

Demonstrations were conducted at the hospital and both systems looked good. The master patient index (MPI) module is preferred on System Patient Management, and the ADT system is preferred on System Patient Tracking; however, both systems were received favorably. The committee went to see both systems in operation and liked both.

References were checked on both systems. The references for System Patient Tracking were glowing. The people all said that the system was good and the people were great to work with because they wanted their new company to succeed and to grow. The references on System Patient Management were excellent too. The only negative was that the company was too large and was sometimes slow to respond to what the company saw as minor problems.

The next release of System Patient Tracking is due out in 6 months and of System Patient Management is due out in 8 months. You expect to implement your system in 1 year.

The Committee has used Tables 5-3, 5-4, and 5-5 to summarize and compare the gathered information and is ready to vote on which system to purchase. Which one will it be and why?

Table 5-3 *System Comparison*

Topic	System Patient Management, Inc.	System Patient Tracking, LLC
Cost of interface	$35,000	$27,000
Cost of software licensing	$147,000	$127,000
Cost of hardware	$245,000	$254,000
Implementation costs	$45,000	$47,000
Other costs	$80,000	$80,000
Annual maintenance	$56,000	$48,000
Number systems in use in hospitals	452	8
Length of time in business	25 years	3 years
Stability of company	Good	Good

Table 5-4 *Response from System Patient Management, Inc., RFP for ADT/MPI System*

System Functions	Standard	Next Release	Not Available	Custom
Admit patient to ER	X			
Admit patient to inpatient status	X			
Admit patient to outpatient status	X			
Transfer patient from room to room	X			
Transfer patient from inpatient to outpatient	X			
Transfer patient from outpatient to inpatient	X			
Transfer patient from ER to inpatient status	X			
Discharge patient from ER	X			
Discharge patient from inpatient status	X			
Discharge patient from outpatient status	X			
Notify housekeeping when patient discharged		X		
Notify HIM when patient admitted		X		
Meets Uniform Hospital Discharge Data Set (UHDDS) requirements	X			
Meets HIPAA requirements		X		
Contains Joint Commission–required demographics	X			
Automated verification of insurance			X	
Graphical user interface (GUI) technology	X			
User friendly	X			
Delete patient from system	X			
Multiple levels of security	X			
Password protected	X			
Audit trail	X			
Biometric capable				X
Reads barcodes	X			
Edit demographics	X			
Edit insurance	X			
Allows for four insurances		X		

(Continued)

Table 5-4 *(Continued)*

System Functions	Standard	Next Release	Not Available	Custom
Prints standards reports at specified periods	X			
Ad hoc reporting	X			
Admission list	X			
Discharge list	X			
Transfer list	X			
Looks for potential duplicate medical records		X		
Quality edits built into system	X			
Oracle database			X	
Runs on Windows NT	X			
Enterprisewide ready		X		
Merge medical record numbers	X			
Allows for aliases	X			
Maintains old medical record numbers	X			
Maintains former names	X			
Allows at least 999 patient visits	X			
Data dictionary	X			
Three-character service field	X			
Allows housekeeping to notify admission that room is ready for patient	X			
Online no-bed list	X			
Sends out announcements to employees/staff	X			
Generates list of patients by physician	X			
Generates list of patients by unit	X			
Calculates census statistics	X			
Performs medical record number queries	X			
Performs patient name queries	X			

Table 5-5 *Response to System Patient Tracking, LLC, RFP for ADT/MPI*

Function	Standard	Next Release	Not Available	Custom
Admit patient to ER	X			
Admit patient to inpatient status	X			
Admit patient to outpatient status	X			
Transfer patient from room to room	X			
Transfer patient from inpatient to outpatient	X			
Transfer patient from outpatient to inpatient	X			
Transfer patient from ER to inpatient status	X			
Discharge patient from ER	X			
Discharge patient from inpatient status	X			
Discharge patient from outpatient status	X			
Notify housekeeping when patient discharged	X			

(Continued)

Table 5-5   *(Continued)*

Function	Standard	Next Release	Not Available	Custom
Notify HIM when patient admitted	X			
Meets UHDDS requirements	X			
Meets HIPAA requirements		X		
Contains Joint Commission–required demographics	X			
Automated verification of insurance				X
GUI technology	X			
User friendly	X			
Delete patient from system	X			
Multiple levels of security	X			
Password protected	X			
Audit trail	X			
Biometric capable		X		
Reads barcodes		X		
Edit demographics	X			
Edit insurance	X			
Allows for four insurances	X			
Prints standards reports at specified periods	X			
Ad hoc reporting	X			
Admission list	X			
Discharge list	X			
Transfer list	X			
Looks for potential duplicate medical records	X			
Quality edits built into system	X			
Oracle database	X			
Runs on Windows NT	X			
Enterprisewide ready	X			
Merge medical record numbers	X			
Allows for aliases		X		
Maintains old medical record numbers		X		
Maintains former names	X			
Allows at least 999 patient visits	X			
Data dictionary	X			
Three-character service field	X			
Allows housekeeping to notify admission that room is ready for patient	X			
Online no-bed list	X			
Sends out announcements to employees/staff	X			
Generates list of patients by physician	X			
Generates list of patients by unit	X			
Calculates census statistics	X			
Performs medical record number queries	X			
Performs patient name queries	X			

CASE 5-13

System Testing Plan

You are in the process of implementing a new Release of information system. You have an existing computerized release of information system, so the employees are comfortable with the technology—they just have to learn how to use the new one. As part of the implementation plan for the new ROI system, you will need to develop a testing plan that should include:

- Testing that needs to be conducted prior to implementation
- A minimum of six scenarios that you would encounter when using the system during testing
- List of resources needed to complete the testing
- What to do when a problem is identified
- How you will know the system is ready for implementation
- Who should be included in the testing plan

Workflow Technology

You started as the new Director of HIM last week. Your department began using workflow technology 6 weeks ago with a relatively new imaging system, which was implemented 1 year ago. With the implementation of workflow, the department started coding and analyzing charts online. Other tasks involved in the workflow are:

- Notifying risk management of issues identified
- Communications with physicians
- Communications with business office
- Communications with supervisor
- Routing charts that meet criteria to performance improvement

One of the first things that you noticed when you started work was the stress level of the coders—they are panicking. Upon questioning, you determine that they hate the new system. You also learn that they do not feel comfortable using the system, that they had only a short training period, and that they were not involved in the selection or implementation.

How would you proceed?

CASE 5-15

Developing a Workflow Plan

You just started as the new Director of HIM at a 200-bed hospital. This hospital is in the process of developing a new imaging system. One of the key benefits of this system is workflow technology. Charts will be routed to coding, analysis, documentation improvement, quality improvement, and risk management as appropriate. Make your recommendations for the system by answering the following questions:

1. Should we use push or pull technology? Why?

2. What specific tasks would you recommend being included?

3. What flow of these tasks would you recommend? Why?

4. What rules could you establish to route charts to each of the areas?

5. Why did you choose these rules? Include examples of rules for each of the areas.

6. As the director, what reports would you want to receive on a regular basis?

CASE 5-16

Goals of the Electronic Health Record (EHR)

Your facility, Good Samaritan Hospital, is implementing a new EHR. You are excited about the impact that the EHR will have on your organization. During the planning stage, the hospital developed goals that it would like to accomplish with this implementation. Administration has said that these goals are firm expectations for the team and the system. The goals of the system are to:

- reduce HIM staff.
- reduce time required to access health information.
- improve quality of care.
- decrease the number of duplicate and unnecessary tests.
- reduce the cost per case.

Critique the goals above.

How can they be improved?

How can you monitor to determine if you met the goals?

CASE 5-17

Order Entry/Results Reporting (OE/RR)

Your facility has made the decision to implement a new order entry/results reporting (OE/RR) system. The Steering Committee has to decide which of the following implementation strategies to utilize:

1. Implement the OE/RR on all units at the same time.
2. Implement the order entry system unit by unit.
3. Implement the results reporting system unit by unit.
4. Implement the order entry system on all units at the same time.
5. Implement the results reporting system on all units at the same time.

Which of the strategies would you choose to implement?

Justify your decision.

CASE 5-18

Normalization of Data Fields

You have recently been hired at Black Hills Medical Center to help with report generation. On your first day, you start investigating the databases that you will be working with. You see room for improvement in the first database that you look at—Human Resources. This does not include payroll. Normalize the data fields to allow for more flexibility in reporting. Identify gaps in data collected and present the results of your investigation in a table with one column for the original data fields and one column for the normalized data fields.

Data fields to consider are:

- Full name
- Address
- City, state, zip
- Phone
- Social security number
- Race
- Gender
- Degree/major
- Date of last evaluation
- Department
- Start date
- Credentials

Human Resource Database

You are the Director of the HIM Department. You constantly have to ask Human Resources for reports for your staff. Because of the frequency of these requests, you have asked for access to the Human Resources system, which provides you with access to all data, not just reports for your staff or no information at all. Because administration will not allow you to have access to all Human Resources data, however, you have decided to create your own minidatabase. This database will help you in many ways. The following are examples of how you will use this database:

- Track salaries
- Track open positions
- Track when performance evaluations are due
- Track anniversary dates
- Track birthdates
- Identify employees on probation

Use Microsoft Access to create the database. Design a data entry screen that utilizes good screen design. Populate the database with five test employees and generate two reports: a list of all employees by anniversary date and a list of employees on probation.

CASE 5-20

Tumor Registry System Questionnaire

You have been asked to develop the questionnaire that will be used to collect functional requirements for the new tumor registry system. This questionnaire will be sent to the Tumor Registrars and the Tumor Registry Supervisors and their customers, including the Cancer Committee, the Cancer Program Director, Oncologists, and the Vice President of Research. The questionnaire should use good design principles, be comprehensive, and should address accreditation, state cancer reporting, institutional needs, and user needs.

CASE 5-21

Bar Code Standards

You have been given the responsibility of developing the standards for using bar codes on medical record forms. Your facility plans to implement an EHR in 5 years and wants to take an intermediary step of purchasing an imaging system. They want to implement the imaging system in about 2 years. They believe imaging is an important step, since they want to stop microfilming and the images can be linked to the EHR. Because it will take a while to implement the imaging system, your facility has time to revise all medical record forms to add bar codes so that when the system is implemented, the time required to scan and index the records will be minimal and the quality of the indexing will be high.

What bar code format do you recommend? Why?

What other issues should you take into consideration?

CASE 5-22

Bar Code Policy

You have been given the responsibility of developing the standards for bar coding the forms that will be scanned into the new imaging system your facility is implementing in about a year. You have 6 months to have all of the forms redesigned to accommodate the bar code.

Review the Healthcare Information and Management Systems Society (HIMSS) *Implementation Guide for the Use of Bar Code Technology in Healthcare* at http://www.himss.org.
(Accessed December 6, 2006, at http://www.himss.org/content/files/Implementation_guide.pdf.)

Use the information there to develop your policy. The policy should be written in the policy and procedure format and should include specific guidelines that forms developers should follow.

CASE 5-23

Conversion of Admission Discharge Transfer (ADT) System

The service codes for your existing Admission Discharge Transfer System and the new system do not match. The old system uses a two-digit numeric code to indicate service, while the new system will accept up to a four-digit alphabetic code. The hospital has decided that it will use two- to four-digit codes depending on which are more user recognizable. Review the codes utilized by both systems, as shown in Tables 5-6 and 5-7, and develop a map that will be used by the programmers to convert the data from the old system to the new system.

Table 5-6 *Codes in Old ADT System*

Old System Code	Service Description
01	Medicine
02	Surgery
03	Obstetrics
04	Gynecology
05	Cardiology
06	Cardiovascular Surgery
07	Dermatology
08	Orthopedics
09	Endocrinology
10	Neonatology
11	Nephrology
12	Infectious Disease
13	Pulmonology
14	Gastroenterology
15	Otorhinolaryngology
16	Ophthalmology
17	Neurology
18	Neurosurgery
19	Trauma

Table 5-7 *Codes in New ADT System*

New System Code	Service Description
	Allergy
	Burn
	Cardiology
	Cardiovascular Surgery
	Dermatology
	Endocrinology
	Otorhinolaryngology
	Gastroenterology
	Gynecology
	Infectious Disease
	Neonatal
	Nephrology
	Neurology
	Neurosurgery
	Obstetrics
	Orthopedics
	Pulmonology

Admission Report Design

Your facility is about to implement a new hospital information system. The reports have been distributed to the members of the team for design. You have been given the responsibility of designing the admission report, which will come from the Hospital Information System and be used by multiple departments in identifying the patients who have been admitted to the hospital as an inpatient each day. You do not like the current report, so you are essentially developing a new one. It should include the appropriate data elements, date, title of report, time ran, and other data as needed.

What recommendations do you have for this report regarding:

- Print orientation
- Timing of printing
- Content of report
- Ad hoc versus standard report
- Who receives report
- Other

CASE 5-25

Choosing Software Packages

Technology Support is installing new computers throughout the HIM Department. The existing computers are slow and many freeze up several times a day. You receive an e-mail from the Supervisor of Technology Support relaying that Technology Support wants to install the same systems on all of the computers to make things easier. This is fine with you because that gives you flexibility in moving employees around the office. Technology Support is planning to load the following software packages on all of the computers:

- Chart locator system
- Hospital information system
- Financial information system
- Chart deficiency system
- Release of information system
- Encoder/grouper

You then read in the e-mail that Technology Support plans to install Microsoft Office only on the Secretary's and the Director's computers. You know that the facility has a site license for Microsoft Office, so expense is not the issue.

As director, how would you respond to the TS supervisor's plan for Microsoft Office?

What other systems would you request?

Should Microsoft Office be included for other HIM staff members? Be specific in what you would need Microsoft Office or other products to accomplish. Use specific HIM tasks that must be performed to justify the additions to this plan.

General Office Software

The staff in the HIM Department uses general office software just like any other office. The general software used includes spreadsheet, calendar/e-mail, word processor, database, and presentation applications. The management team uses these products the most.

Identify five ways that each of these general office software products can be used by the HIM staff.

CASE 5-27

Selecting an Internet-Based Personal Health Record (PHR)

You are a patient advocate. A patient of your facility has come to you and asked for advice in selecting an Internet-based Personal Health Record (PHR). She saw a physician talking on the news during the aftermath of Hurricane Katrina about how hard it was to treat patients without basic health information. The patient has not been able to get this out of her mind. She wants to ensure that her patient information is available if she finds herself or her family members in a similar situation.

Go to http://www.myphr.com to review three of the Internet-based PHRs that are available on the market.

Create a table for use in comparing the various functions of the PHRs. For each PHR reviewed, determine if you would recommend the product to the patient.

The patient asks which you would choose for your own PHR. What would you tell her?

Personal Health Record (PHR) Education

As the patient advocate at your facility, you have been asked to write a patient information sheet for the PHR your facility is rolling out. This is to be a one-page information sheet that defines the PHR, explains the benefits of the PHR, and tells about the PHR that your facility is offering. With the PHR, patients will have access to test results, key clinical findings, and secure e-mail to communicate with their doctors.

Write this information sheet. Keep in mind that this is being written for the patient to use.

CASE 5-29

Data Warehouse Development

Your facility is developing a data warehouse. You have been asked to determine which of your current systems should be included. You have also been asked to write a justification for each system, stating why or why not you would want to include it. The administrator has indicated that he plans to use the data warehouse for business and clinical data analysis. Complete this information for the current systems using Table 5-8.

Table 5-8 *System Justification*

System	Included Yes/No	Justification for Decision
Patient satisfaction		
ADT		
Lab information system		
Radiology information system		
Picture Archiving and Communication Systems (PACS)		
Nursing information system		
Fetal monitoring		
Financial information system		
ADT		
Human resources system		
Patient acuity system		
Chart deficiency system		
Quality indicator system		
Chart locator system		
Release of information system		

CASE 5-30

Data Tables

You have been given the responsibility of populating the deficiency and form types that will be used by your new chart deficiency system. The old system has such poor data quality that you are starting from scratch. In the current system, the deficiency type and form number have no logical meaning. For example, the form type of "X" means operative note and "P" is cancer staging form. You have been provided with the templates in Tables 5-9 and 5-10. Choose logical codes whenever possible.

Table 5-9 *Deficiency Type*

Deficiency Code	Deficiency Description

Table 5-10 *Form Type*

Form Code	Form Description

CASE 5-31

Electronic Forms Management System

Your facility wants to implement an EHR in about 5 years. Time and money are preventing you from doing it sooner. In the meantime, you want to get a better handle on your forms management. Currently you are still creating your forms. You are having the forms printed off by your local printing company in large bulk, and storing them in your materials management department. This is costly but effective. You tried just in time inventory, but this failed miserably because departments constantly failed to order supplies in advance. You are considering replacing the current method with an electronic forms management system. This system would allow you to design the forms, then store the files on a centralized server. When a patient is admitted, a packet of admission forms would be printed based on the patient type. Individual forms could also be printed on demand. The patient name and other identifying information would print out on the form.

1. What are the pros to implementing the forms management system?

2. What are the cons?

3. What departments would need to be involved in implementing the system?

4. Would you recommend doing this if you expect to implement an EHR in about 5 years? Why or why not?

CASE 5-32

Failure of an Electronic Health Record (EHR) System

Magnolia Hills Hospital implemented an EHR about a year ago. Your administrator decided to pull the plug on the project a week ago because of all the problems that you were experiencing. Physicians have refused to use the system. They made the nurses print out everything so they could review the patient's medical record. They would write orders on a piece of paper and ask the nurses to enter it into the order entry system. The few physicians who did try to use the system properly were still having problems using the system after a year. The system was down at least 2 hours a day. Many days the system was down for 4–5 hours. When the HIM Department printed out reports to satisfy release of information requests, what they received was more like screen prints than forms.

This system was the brain child of Dr. Anderson. He is a retired transplant surgeon whose name is on the new transplant center building. He and a small group of his cronies were the ones who picked and controlled the implementation of the system. There was no input from anyone else other than the information technology (IT) staff. The screens are cluttered, are difficult to use, and do not have data quality built in. The system does not meet Condition of Participation, state licensing, and HIPAA requirements.

The HIM Director, the physicians, nursing, and other staff learned about the system 3 weeks before implementation. The HIM Director was so angry at being left out of the loop that she took early retirement and left with only 2 days' notice. Physician's training was a demonstration at the quarterly medical staff meeting. Nursing and other staff were given 1 hour of training, which they learned about only 3 weeks prior to implementation when the new system was announced at a department head meeting. Since the implementation of the system, there has been a turnover in the hospital administrator position and a new HIM Director has been hired.

1. What failures can you identify from the history of the EHR implementation?

2. What should the hospital have done?

3. The hospital wants to salvage the system if they can. What should they do now to prepare to reimplement the system?

CASE 5-33

Preparation for an Electronic Health Record (EHR) System

An EHR is scheduled for implementation at Tres Rios Hospital in 3 years. The hospital is beginning to conduct the initial planning. They want to ensure that users are prepared for the changes that the EHR will bring to the facility. Not all of the staff and medical staff are excited about the implementation.

1. What change in management issues should be addressed?

2. What can you do to help prepare the medical staff and employees for the new system?

CASE 5-34

Employee Termination Procedure

Edward was terminated last week because of poor performance. He was constantly late or absent. Even when he was there, his productivity was low and the quality of his work was poor. Three days later, an audit trail review identified something strange. The information on 100 patients was deleted from the MPI, which is rare. If an MPI deletion does occur, there is typically one patient impacted. Further investigation revealed that someone using Edward's user name and password had been the person to delete the data. After this incident is turned over to the appropriate authorities to investigate, you turn your attention to ensuring that this does not happen again.

Write a policy and procedure for a termination procedure. Use sound policy and procedure rules and format.

CASE 5-35

Intranet Functionality

Your hospital has been discussing the possibility of an intranet for the past year. The Chief Information Officer (CIO) has asked you to create a list of functions that could be included in the intranet. It is to be used as a tool to get the discussions started. The only guidance that he gave you was that the intranet should be useful to staff, management, and the medical staff.

CASE 5-36

Evaluating Systems for Health Insurance Portability and Accountability Act (HIPAA) Compliance

You are the privacy and security officer for your facility; your background is HIM and you are an RHIA with a Certified in Healthcare Privacy and Security (CHPS) credential. You are part of a team that is reviewing the RFPs received from various EHR vendors. Your emphasis in the review is the privacy and security issues. You know that there are many requirements of HIPAA, some of which are policy related; however, many impact the functionality of information systems. You are in the process of reviewing the RFPs that were returned to you by various EHR vendors. One of the RFPs states that they are HIPAA compliant, so you decide to compare their product to the HIPAA security regulations to determine if this is true.

What functionality would you look for to support their claim?

CASE 5-37

Website Resources

Your HIM Director has asked you to identify 10 Internet websites that could be used by the HIM staff as resources in their job.

You are to provide the URL address and how the website can be used. Enter the information you have gathered into Table 5-11. One example is listed in the table to get you started.

Table 5-11 *Website Resources*

Name of Website	URL	How the Website Can Be Useful to the HIM Staff
Joint Commission	http://www.jointcommission.org	This website provides educational materials on the accreditation standards, general information on the Joint Commission and the accreditation. There are also videos and resources for purchase.

CASE 5-38

Entity Relationship Diagrams

You have been given the responsibility of leading the development of the entity relationship diagram for your data model. This is a work in progress. Thus far, the entities that have been identified are:

- Patient
- Physician
- Visit
- Test
- Encounter
- Consultant

Identify the attributes and primary key for each of the entities in Table 5-12.

Table 5-12 *Entities, Attributes, and Primary Key*

Entity	Attributes	Primary Key
Patient		
Physician		
Visit		
Test		
Encounter		
Consultant		

CASE 5-39

Identifying Relationships between Entities

Identify the relationship between each of the following entities in Table 5-13. Your choices are:

- One to one
- One to many
- Many to many

Table 5-13 *Entity Relationships*

Entities	Relationship
Patient and attending physician	
Patient and test	
Patient and consultant	
Patient and encounter	
Physician and service	

CASE 5-40

Quality Control of Scanning

You are implementing a new imaging system in about a month. As excited as you are about the new system, you are still concerned about the quality of scanned images. You are familiar with other facilities that implemented an imaging system and had serious quality problems. One of the facilities even ended up having to shut down their imaging system due to the problems. You want there to be a firm policy and procedure from the beginning to minimize system clean-up later.

What issues would you address in the policy and procedure regarding the quality control process?

Is there anything else that you can do to help ensure quality in the scanning process?

CASE 5-41

Contingency Planning

You work in a facility that was affected by Hurricane Katrina. You were more fortunate than most because only your basement was flooded. The problem is that your data center was in the basement. The data on the computers is completely lost because the computers were destroyed. Unfortunately, the back-up tapes were located in the room next to the data center and were also destroyed.

Fortunately, though, the HIM Department is on the second floor and the charts are intact. Although your lab, radiology, dictated reports, and nursing notes were electronic, the reports had been printed out and filed in the medical record. The HIM Director has been trying for a year to get the Information System Department to develop a contingency plan because she wants to stop filing the reports that are stored electronically. The IS staff had not recognized the need for the contingency plan, but Hurricane Katrina was the catalyst that convinced them.

What recommendations do you have to ensure that your facility would not lose everything if another category four hurricane hit the area?

CASE 5-42

Business Continuity Planning

Your facility does not have an EHR yet. In HIM, you have become dependent on computers to function. You still have paper records, but chart requests, release of information, transcription, dictation system, chart locator, MPI, and chart deficiencies are all computerized.

Write a policy that outlines how your department would operate if one or more of these systems went down for an extended period.

CASE 5-43

Audit Triggers

Since HIPAA was implemented, you have been drowning in your audit trail reviews. You have finally obtained permission from administration to develop and use triggers to help with the review. These triggers, although not eliminating review of the audit trail, can be used to identify potential problems much more quickly and easily than using a manual review. Now that you finally have approval, you have to develop the triggers to be used. Administration wants to review your proposed triggers before they are implemented.

Identify 10 triggers that you will present to administration for approval.

CASE 5-44

Password Management

Several managers have reported that they have concerns about how passwords are used in your facility.

Problems reported include:

- Passwords are being written down and placed near the computers. (For example, passwords have been taped to the bottom of phones.)
- Passwords are sometimes called across the nursing unit.
- Users do not log out when leaving a computer. Then someone else sits down and uses the computer with the previous user's passwords still in place.

You suspect there are other problems with the protection of passwords but you cannot provide it at this time.

What password management rules can you put in place to eliminate these problems? Include any other password problems that you suspect but cannot prove.

CASE 5-45

Electronic Health Record (EHR) Security Plan

You are the Data Security officer for Brownsville Town Hospital. The hospital is preparing to implement an EHR. You have been asked to determine the security measures that your facility will take to maintain confidentiality and prevent loss of data.

Write a security proposal to be presented to the CIO. Areas to be covered include, but are not limited to:

- Physical security of hardware
- Data security
- Confidentiality
- Access
- Disaster recovery
- Back-ups
- Business continuity planning
- Penalties for violating policies
- Other

This is not a paper, it is a proposal. Write a cover letter to the CIO to introduce the plan and begin the proposal with an executive summary.

Electronic Health Record (EHR) Training Plan

The EHR is being implemented in 6 months. Attention has turned to the training plan. Develop a training plan that will ensure that everyone who needs to be trained will be trained in a timely manner. Currently there are 500 employees, 350 of which are clinical staff. Sixty physicians will need to be trained. You currently have access to two training classrooms and can get access to one more room if needed. The vendor recommends 2 hours of training for nonclinical staff and 4–6 hours for clinical staff.

The plan should include:

- Content (What will the content of the training include?)
- Classes for employees (How will you break the students into different types of classes?)
- A schedule for training
- The skills that the trainers need
- Number of classes required
- Amount of time needed for course
- Number of trainers needed
- Format of class
- Resources needed
- When you should start training to be ready for a December 1 deadline (Assume today's date is July 10.)
- When the training will be completed

CASE 5-47

Strategic Planning

Bayside General Hospital, where you work, is in a community that is changing. It had been an industrial city, but many of the industries closed. The local college is growing and is now by far the number one employer; other major businesses include healthcare and a local amusement park. The population is changing also. There are a lot of young people because of the college and work available at the amusement park.

A new hospital is opening up in 1 year. It will be a high-tech facility. The only currently existing hospital competing against you is opening an OB service. This existing hospital also has the trauma center for the area. There is no children's hospital in the area. Both existing hospitals treat some pediatric patients; seriously ill pediatric patients, however, are sent to the closest children's hospital, which is 2 hours away. Bayside General Hospital has recently added physician offices, home health, and an occupational health center to their network. They have not networked and implemented existing systems to these organizations.

Administration developed the following business objectives:

- Improve quality of care provided to patients.
- Use hospital resources effectively and efficiently.
- Increase market share of healthcare services provided within Bayside.

Bayside General Hospital has the following information systems implemented:

- Lab information system was implemented 5 years ago.
- Radiology information system was implemented last year.
- Nursing information system was implemented 3 years ago.
- Hospital information system was implemented 10 years ago.
- Decision support system goes live in 6 months.
- Financial information system was implemented 2 years ago.

The hospital does not have the following systems:

- Knowledge-based system
- Order entry/results reporting
- Intensive care unit
- Data repository

Based on the information above:

1. How well are systems in place to meet the objectives?

2. Determine possible projects to ensure that the objectives are met.

3. How can you use technology to prepare for the changes in the community?

4. How will HIM be affected by your proposed projects?

CASE 5-48

Single Vendor or Best of Breed

You are the HIM Director of a 500-bed facility. Your HIM systems are sorely outdated, so you've decided that many of them need to be updated. You submitted a capital budget request and received approval to purchase the new systems that you need. These systems are transcription, encoder/grouper, chart locator, chart deficiency, and tumor registry. The only thing that you do not want to update is the digital dictation system that was installed 2 years ago. Before you can submit an RFP or even an RFI, you have a decision to make. You have to decide if you want to purchase systems from the same vendor or use the best of breed model. You know the up- and downsides to each. You do not have much time, since you want to have the RFP submitted to the vendors in 3 months and you cannot finish writing it until this decision is made.

1. Which would you choose, a single vendor or best of breed?

2. Why did you choose this model?

3. What are the downsides to the model that you selected?

4. What if you selected a single vendor and some have most but not all of the products you need? Will you send the vendor an RFP?

Functional Requirements of a Transcription System

As the transcription supervisor, you have been given the responsibility of developing the functional requirements for a new transcription system that you hope to purchase and install in the next year. You have met with your staff and done some brainstorming to come up with a comprehensive list of functions that you need and whether or not each of the functions is mandatory, desirable, or a luxury. The functional requirements must be comprehensive and include data entry, interfaces, data fields, reporting, and other functionality.

Develop the list of functional requirements in the format of Table 5-14.

Table 5-14 *Functional Requirements of a Transcription System*

Function	Mandatory	Desirable	Luxury

SECTION SIX

Management and Health Information Services

Developing an Organizational Chart for Health Information Management (HIM)

Before you can begin recruiting personnel, you will need to develop an organizational chart for the HIM Department.

Use the list of employees and the classifications in the department provided in Table 6-1 to develop your organizational chart.

Table 6-1 *Department Employees by Classification*

Classification	Number of Employees
Director	1
Coding Supervisor	1
Release of Information (ROI) Coordinator (contracted employee through ROI services)	1
Transcription Supervisor	1
Transcriptionists	4
Coders	3
Chart Completion Supervisor	1
HIM File Clerks	2
Secretary	1

CASE 6-2

Writing a Policy and Procedure

Write a policy and procedure for customer service for use by the receptionists at the front desk. Include procedures for dealing with voice-mail messages from overnight and telephone calls and for handling walk-in customers.

See Figure 6-1 for the formal format of the usual components found in a written policy and procedure. Include these elements in your final written policy and procedure. Remember, effective procedure writing requires great attention to detail.

You may use the format in Figure 6-1 for your policy and procedure.

PORT BISMARCK		
HOSPITAL		
Policy:		

Procedure:

Department Policy	**Title**	**Policy #**

Effective Date	**Revised Date**	**Department Effected**	**Approved By**

Figure 6-1 *Sample Policy and Procedure Format*

CASE 6-3

Work Measurement Study

Select a simple HIM-related task or task you perform at your current job to complete this exercise. You may need to get assistance in conducting the study to measure "how long" it takes to complete the task at least six different times.

Use Table 6-2 to record your work measurement study results. Then, use your data to calculate the average time to use in establishing a standard for a person performing the task. Remember to allow for external influences and fatigue when conducting the time study.

Design a productivity report on this task for a person to log and report weekly production to the supervisor.

Table 6-2 *Work Measurement Study Form*

WORK MEASUREMENT STUDY		Amount Completed
Times Task Was Studied		
Time 1	Start	
	Stop	
Time 2	Start	
	Stop	
Time 3	Start	
	Stop	
Time 4	Start	
	Stop	
Time 5	Start	
	Stop	
Time 6	Start	
	Stop	
Total Amount Completed		
Average Productivity		
Productivity Expected Per 8-Hour Day		
Comments/Calculations		

Evaluating Employees' Skills

You are the Assistant HIM Director of a regional medical center. The HIM Director has asked you to develop a general competency form that can be used when conducting HIM employees' performance appraisals. The competency form would be used to determine if the employees are meeting requirements necessary on an annual basis. The Director explains her goal is to maintain an Employee Competency and Staff Development Record that will provide evidence of the hours of continuing education and of staff training programs completed by employees. This form will be maintained throughout the year and reviewed with each employee at their annual evaluation period.

Which organizational agencies should be considered in determining what competency standards should be established?

Identify elements that should be met to remain competent.

CASE 6-5

Recruiting Resources

You have had trouble recruiting coders. You have advertised in the county *Herald Tribune* without success. The only applicants are people off the street without any coding background.

How should you proceed?

What are your options?

Which would you pick and why?

CASE 6-6

Recruitment Advertisement

You have been discussing the difficulty in recruiting coders with your director of Human Resources. She has agreed to place an advertisement in the local newspaper for you. After the ad was placed, you received many job applicants for the coding position. In reviewing the advertisement, you find that the ad misrepresented the job and the salary.

What should you do?

CASE 6-7

Interviewing Job Applicants

A variety of scenarios have been provided for interview simulations in Interview Situation 1 through Interview Situation 6. Select one of the interview situations and present it with a classmate, adding either appropriate or inappropriate questions according to compliance with employment laws.

Allow the class to analyze and critique the interaction by identifying the compliance or noncompliance with employment laws. In turn, you will critique each role-play portrayed by your classmates and identify compliance or noncompliance with employment laws.

Interview Situation 1   Vacant Position—Coder

The applicant has 2 years of experience in an acute care facility as a Tumor Registrar. She is a registered health information technician (RHIT) and now wants to get into coding. You have been unable to find an experienced coder, even though your salary is competitive. This person has noted on her application that she was terminated from her last position.

Interview Situation 2   Vacant Position—Health Information Management Director

The applicant has 10 years' experience managing HIM Departments but has spent the past 4 years as a consultant. The HIM Department is responsible for the traditional HIM functions, including Tumor Registry and birth certificates. The Department is preparing to implement an electronic health record (EHR) system and will be involved with implementation of a data warehouse.

Interview Situation 3   Vacant Position—Coder for Outpatient Records

(Emergency Room and Ambulatory Surgery)

The applicant has no work experience in an HIM Department and desires employment at this small acute care facility in her hometown. She is a recent graduate of a Health Information Technology (HIT) program and has registered to write her national RHIT exam in the upcoming fall. Her application reflects previous employment as a bank teller for 2 years following high school graduation. The application lists her supervisor from the bank as a work reference. The only other references are three personal references.

Interview Situation 4   Vacant Position—Evening Chart Analyst

The applicant has never worked in an HIM Department. However, she has experience in two healthcare settings, with the most recent in a nursing home as the Medical Records Coordinator. She maintained records at the Nursing Home for 6 years prior to leaving approximately 1 year ago. Her job prior to the Nursing Home was in a doctor's office as an Office Receptionist.

Interview Situation 5   Vacant Position—Transcription Supervisor

The applicant has many years' experience in an HIM Department. Her latest position was as a Transcriptionist at a large Medical Center in another state for the past 17 years. Prior to that, she had worked as an Assembler/Analyst for 10 years at the same facility. Her application reflects she graduated from high school in 1962 and that she obtained her Certified Medical Transcription (CMT) credentials in 1991.

Interview Situation 6   Vacant Position—File Clerk

The applicant has never worked in an HIM Department; however, she has worked in an insurance company for 6 months. She has held five jobs in the past 3 years. She performed filing in two of these positions. One position was working in a fast-food restaurant, another was at a day-care, and the fifth was in retail.

CASE 6-8

Job Applicant and the Americans with Disabilities Act (ADA)

An applicant has interviewed for the tumor registry position. He is in a wheelchair and has vision problems. He is an **RHIT** with tumor registry experience. You have several candidates with the same or fewer qualifications. No one has more qualifications than this applicant.

How should you proceed?

How would you determine who gets the position?

Developing a Training Plan

Most of your entry-level employees were hired with very little work experience. They are a good group in that they are hard working and want to learn. Unfortunately, they do not have all the skills needed to perform their jobs. This has resulted in breeches of privacy, subpoenas not arriving in court on time, wrong charts being pulled, misfiles, and deficiencies assigned to the wrong physician. Their frustration level is high, which sometimes manifests itself in rudeness to the customers. Develop a training plan for each of the following HIM functional areas.

- record analysis
- documentation improvement
- release of information
- reception and customer service
- maintaining the file area
- processing loose material

Include the specific topics to be covered, the amount of time that you plan to devote to training for each group, and how you will cover their responsibilities during the training.

How do you prioritize who gets trained first and what type of training is conducted first?

CASE 6-10

Department Coverage

You have problems with phone coverage when someone calls in sick or is on vacation. Administration and physicians have complained that there continue to be times when they have trouble reaching the department by telephone. The current policy is that whoever is available covers the phone.

What are your options?

What would you recommend and why?

Decision Making

The HIM Department is small and has very limited resources. Normally the director goes to the American Health Information Management Association (AHIMA) national meeting, but this year she will be unable to go because she will be on maternity leave. The director feels that the new employee, who is a registered health information administrator who will be covering while she is on maternity leave, should go. Another employee, who is also an RHIA and has been with the department longer, feels she should go.

How should the director choose which employee will go?

CASE 6-12

Progressive Disciplinary Approach

HIM managers may experience a variety of disciplinary situations.

How would you handle the following situations if you were an effective HIM Manager who practices progressive discipline measures?

Disciplinary Situation 1

Jean is 30 minutes to 1 hour late 2 to 3 days a week. You have talked to her about it repeatedly and even given her a written warning. It is now 2 weeks since the written warning and there has not been an improvement.

How would you discuss this with Jean? What would be your next step?

Disciplinary Situation 2

The quality of Carla's work has recently deteriorated. You have discussed this with her and have given her a verbal warning. There has not been any improvement.

How would you discuss this with Carla. What would be your next step?

Disciplinary Situation 3

You have been at a meeting and return to the department. As you walk in, you hear the ROI coordinator, Susan, talking on the phone to a requester. Susan becomes very upset with the person on the phone and tells him off. This is the first time that Susan has done this that you are aware of. Discuss this with Susan.

How would you handle the situation?

Disciplinary Situation 4

The HIM Department has a policy of no personal calls. You know employees make short calls to let family know they are working late and the like. Pam has begun to spend a lot of time on the telephone discussing personal business. You know she is going through a divorce, but employees are starting to talk.

How would you discuss the situation with Pam?

Disciplinary Situation 5

Cindy and Barbara work in the Analysis area. They got into an argument today that disrupted the workplace. They were both written up for fighting a month ago. You told them they would be suspended for 3 days if another incident happened. Discuss this with them.

What would you bring out in your meeting with them?

Disciplinary Situation 6

Kim is a new employee who is having problems with her performance. She is still in her probationary status.

How would you discuss the situation with Kim?

Disciplinary Situation 7

Kelly is your coding supervisor. She was berating one of her subordinate coders. She called the employee stupid and said that she was going to make the coder's life miserable. Your transcription supervisor overheard the conversation and reported it to you.

How would you discuss the situation with Kelly?

Falsification of Information on Employment Application

Jeremy is the director of the HIM Department. Laura, a transcriptionist, has been a wonderful employee. Through the grapevine, he heard that Laura had put on her employment application that she had an associate's degree but she did not have one. He called the college and found that she was two classes short of her degree. This was grounds for dismissal.

What should Jeremy do?

How should he handle the meeting with Laura?

CASE 6-14

Time Management

You are the HIM Director for a small 140-bed county-owned hospital in a rural area. The department has become backlogged in ROI since your Correspondence Coordinator's resignation was received 2 weeks ago.

The Correspondence Coordinator resigned following an extended leave due to injuries received from a car accident that occurred 3 months prior. She was out of work for major surgery and rehabilitation, with the intent to return when she was able. She worked for you for 3 years and was rarely out of work until the accident. In the interim, you had employees cross-trained to help cover the ROI work.

You approached Administration about hiring a temporary employee a month after your employee was out on leave, but Administration did not give approval. When the employee turned in her resignation, you submitted a request to replace her position and Administration has approved it. You are in the process of accepting applications and scheduling interviews.

The Business Office Claims Manager has been calling regarding "bills held" due to pending copies needed of medical records to support the claim. The Business Office Manager called just this morning, concerned that an increase in accounts receivable (AR) is due to the backlog in ROI.

Two days ago, the hospital Administrator requested that you submit a detailed report on the ROI status. It is due today. You are gathering the necessary data to compile the report for Administration when your inpatient Coder comes into your office and asks to meet with you. Your report is due in 2 hours and still needs a lot of work to be completed.

Might an alternative means be available that you could consider (other than hiring a replacement full-time employee [FTE]) in providing ROI service? If so, what?

How should you respond to the Business Office Manager?

What elements do you feel should be included in the report for Administration?

How should you respond to the Coder?

Interdepartmental Communications

Dr. Jenkins arrived in the Operating Room (OR) suite at 8:45 a.m. to perform surgery on a 9:15 a.m. scheduled elective surgery case. The OR supervisor requested to speak with the surgeon to explain that the case would have to be canceled, because a history and physical (H&P) report had not been completed for the patient's record.

Dr. Jenkins became obviously upset and began making accusations, saying that he dictated the H&P 3 days ago and that the HIM Department was at fault. The OR supervisor was already aware that her secretary had phoned Mr. Rheems, the HIM Director, the day prior to inquire on the H&P report. The dictation system transcription report reflected no dictation was available then. The OR supervisor informed Dr. Jenkins that as of yesterday afternoon there was no dictation found in the system but that she would inquire again with the HIM Department.

The transcription supervisor searched the dictation system again immediately upon receiving the call and noted the H&P report had been dictated 45 minutes earlier, at 8:15 a.m., by Dr. Jenkins, and informed the HIM Director it would be typed as soon as possible and delivered to the OR.

The transcription supervisor informed Mr. Rheems that Dr. Jenkins had done this on two other occasions over the past few months. Mr. Rheems knows the dictation system has tracking and audit capability for reports that reflects the date, time, and author of dictation, as well as identifies the date, time, and transcriber of each dictation.

How should Mr. Rheems respond to the OR regarding Dr. Jenkins' H&P report?

Should this individual incident be taken to administrative staff? If so, to whom?

Should this individual incident be taken to a medical staff committee? If so, to which committee?

If not, what actions should Mr. Rheems take to prevent recurrence of such activity against the HIM Department in the future?

Merit Raise

You graduated from a baccalaureate Health Information program 3 years ago. You obtained your RHIA credentials 6 months after graduation and have been coding at the county hospital since graduation. There are four inpatient coders, including you. The Coding supervisor has a long tenure with the hospital and has acquired her certified coding specialist (CCS) credentials, but she does not have a college degree to accompany it. Your short-term career goal is to advance in salary and obtain a managerial position. You suspect, and have heard, that your Coding supervisor is paid a salary much greater than yours.

How might you seek an increase in pay at your current employer that is a more comparable salary to the market scale for RHIA inpatient coders?

CASE 6-17

Incentive-Based Compensation Programs

There are several different payment scales for incentive-based transcription programs presented in Incentive-Based Compensations Programs 1 through 5. Review each program and complete the computation of incentive pay based upon the payment scale given for each program.

Incentive-Based Compensation Program 1

The incentive pay is $1.00 per dictated minute transcribed.

Calculate the incentive pay for each transcriptionist, using Table 6-3.

Table 6-3 *Transcriptionist Incentive-Based Pay: Program 1*

Transcriptionist Incentive-Based Pay: Program 1				
Transcriptionist	Number of Hours Worked	Number of Minutes Transcribed	Minimum Required Biweekly Production	Amount of Incentive Pay
Jeana	80	1,145	1,200	
Meagan	80	1,200	1,200	
Sandra	80	1,264	1,200	
Julia	80	1,320	1,200	
Tenille	80	1,410	1,200	

Incentive-Based Compensation Program 2

The incentive pay is $0.15 per line transcribed, based upon 65 characters per line.

Calculate the incentive pay for each transcriptionist, using Table 6-4.

Table 6-4 *Transcriptionist Incentive-Based Pay: Program 2*

		Transcriptionist Incentive-Based Pay: Program 2		
Transcriptionist	Number of Hours Worked	Number of Lines Transcribed	Minimum Required Biweekly Production	Amount of Incentive Pay
Jeana	80	7,400	8,200	
Meagan	80	8,010	8,200	
Sandra	80	8,215	8,200	
Julia	80	8,575	8,200	
Tenille	80	8,885	8,200	

Incentive-Based Compensation Program 3

The incentive pay per dictated minute is $1.00. You are given the daily production in Table 6-5.

Calculate the weekly incentive pay for each transcriptionist using Table 6-6.

Table 6-5 *Weekly Transcription Totals for Incentive-Based Pay: Program 3*

	Weekly Transcription Totals for Incentive-Based Pay: Program 3					
Transcriptionist	Monday Minutes	Tuesday Minutes	Wednesday Minutes	Thursday Minutes	Friday Minutes	Total Minutes
Jeana	90	90	90	90	90	450
Meagan	90	90	89	95	122	486
Sandra	112	110	124	98	106	550
Julia	105	123	145	107	131	611
Tenille	157	132	137	123	116	665

Table 6-6 *Transcriptionist Incentive-Based Pay: Program 3*

		Transcriptionist Incentive-Based Pay: Program 3		
Transcriptionist	Total Hours Worked	Total Completed Dictated Minutes	Minimum Required Minutes per Week	Total Amount of Incentive Pay
Jeana	40	450	600	
Meagan	40	486	600	
Sandra	40	550	600	
Julia	40	611	600	
Tenille	40	665	600	

Incentive-Based Compensation Program 4

The incentive pay per line, above required production, is $0.15. You are given the daily production in Table 6-7. Calculate the weekly incentive pay for each transcriptionist using Table 6-8.

Analyze the production of each transcriber and determine if minimum lines of transcription is met for incentive pay.

Table 6-7 *Program 4 Weekly Transcription Totals*

Weekly Transcription Line Totals: Incentive-Based Compensation Program 4						
Transcriptionist	Monday	Tuesday	Wednesday	Thursday	Friday	Total
Jeana	1,070	1,250	1,135	1,030	1,290	5,775
Meagan	1,260	1,395	1,315	1,205	1,300	6,475
Sandra	1,325	1,415	1,300	1,205	1,395	6,640
Julia	1,140	1,255	1,230	1,335	1,230	6,190
Tenille	1,175	1,265	1,380	1,290	1,185	6,295

Table 6-8 *Transcriptionist Incentive-Based Pay: Program 4*

Transcriptionist Incentive-Based Pay: Program 4					
Transcriptionist	Total Hours Worked	Total Completed Dictated Minutes	Minimum Required Lines per Week	Incentive Pay above Base	Weekly Incentive Production Met? Y/N
Jeana	40	5,775	6,000		
Meagan	40	6,475	6,000		
Sandra	40	6,640	6,000		
Julia	40	6,190	6,000		
Tenille	40	6,295	6,000		

Incentive-Based Compensation Program 5

The daily incentive pay per line is $0.13 from 800 to 1,099 lines, $0.15 for 1,100 to 1,399 lines, and $0.20 for 1,400 and more. Use the information in Table 6-9 to calculate the daily incentive pay for each transcriptionist. Enter the daily incentive pay for each transcriptionist in Table 6-10.

Table 6-9 *Program 5 Daily Transcription Totals*

	Daily Lines of Transcription: Incentive-Based Compensation Program 5				
Transcriptionist	Monday	Tuesday	Wednesday	Thursday	Friday
Jeana	990	990	990	990	990
Meagan	990	990	989	995	1,122
Sandra	1,112	1,110	1,124	998	1,106
Julia	1,105	1,123	1,145	1,107	1,131
Tenille	1,157	1,132	1,137	1,123	1,116

Table 6-10 *Program 5 Daily Incentive Pay*

	Daily Incentive Pay Earned: Program 5				
Transcriptionist	Monday	Tuesday	Wednesday	Thursday	Friday
Jeana					
Meagan					
Sandra					
Julia					
Tenille					

CASE 6-18

Payroll Budget Decisions

The HIM Directors in the following situations have been approached by Administration with personnel budget concerns and given constraints to apply. Review the four budgeting issues presented and make calculations as appropriate.

Budget Decision 1

The HIM Director, Linda, has been given $1,500.00 for the overtime needed to catch up on the loose filing.

If the average salary of the HIM clerical staff is $6.65, how many hours of overtime can be worked?

Budget Decision 2

The HIM Director, Carlotta, has been given $2,350.00 to hire temporary employees.

If the temporary agency is charging $15.00 per hour, how many hours of temporary help will be available to Carlotta's department?

Budget Decision 3

The HIM Director, Jose, has been given instructions that he cannot go over $2,100.00 in salary (overtime) for the week of June 2–8. Based on the information provided in Table 6-11, how close is he to using the allotted overtime budget for loose filing?

Table 6-11 *Salary Expense Calculation*

Salary Expense for June 2–8			
Employee	Number of Hours Worked	Salary/Hour	Total Earnings
Michaela	40	$5.35	
Glenn	40	$12.46	
Jerome	22	$8.78	
Natasha	32	$6.88	
Sarah	40	$14.66	

Budget Decision 4

As the HIM Imaging Coordinator, you are in charge of reporting your staff payroll. Overtime is based on 80 hours per 2 weeks. The weekly hours for the past 2 weeks are shown in Table 6-12 and Table 6-13. Your HIM Director has asked you if you have had any overtime for this payroll. If so, who worked overtime and how many overtime hours did they work?

Table 6-12 *Hours for Week 1*

Hours Worked Per Employee in Week 1						
Employee	Monday	Tuesday	Wednesday	Thursday	Friday	Total
Michaela	8.0	7.5	8.5	6.25	8.0	
Glenn	8.0	8.5	9.0	10.5	8.0	
Jerome	8.0	7.5	3.0	10.0	8.0	
Natasha	9.0	8.0	9.0	8.0	7.5	
Sarah	8.0	9.0	8.0	8.0	7.5	

Table 6-13 *Hours for Week 2*

Hours Worked Per Employee in Week 2						
Employee	Monday	Tuesday	Wednesday	Thursday	Friday	Total
Michaela	8.0	8.0	8.0	8.0	7.75	
Glenn	10.5	8.0	8.0	8.0	8.25	
Jerome	9.0	8.0	8.0	8.0	8.5	
Natasha	8.0	8.0	8.0	8.0	9.0	
Sarah	7.75	8.0	8.0	8.0	7.75	

CASE 6-19

Budgeting for Reducing Payroll

Two of the facilities in the healthcare corporation you work for are going through a transitional period. As the divisional HIM Director, you have been given the assignment to help with corporate finances by reducing payroll in the HIM Department in each of these facilities.

Follow the instructions and complete the calculations, so that you can report the results for each of the HIM Departments undergoing reductions.

Facility 1

You have been given the difficult assignment of reducing your payroll by 4% per week.

If the payroll is $8,348.45 for the week, how much will have to be eliminated?

What will be the new weekly payroll?

Facility 2

All of the departments have been given instructions to reduce payroll costs.

The HIM Department is instructed to reduce payroll by 6% per week.

If your payroll is $9,149.99 for the week, how much should the new reduced payroll be?

CASE 6-20

Calculating Salary Increases

The five HIM Departments that you manage have just completed the annual evaluations for your staff. Now you need to calculate the increase in payroll for each one.

Facility 1

The hospital just announced a 3.5% raise across the board. What would be the new salaries after the 3.5% increase? Use the information in Table 6-14 to calculate the new salaries (round to the nearest cent).

Table 6-14 *Facility 1 Salary Increase Calculation Form*

Salary Increase Calculation Form: Facility 1			
Employee	Current Salary	Amount of Raise	New Salary
Michaela	$5.35		
Glenn	$12.46		
Jerome	$8.78		
Natasha	$6.88		
Sarah	$14.66		

Facility 2

The hospital just announced a 5% raise across the board. Use the information in Table 6-15 to calculate the new salaries (round to the nearest cent).

Table 6-15 *Facility 2 Salary Increase Calculation Form*

Salary Increase Calculation Form: Facility 2			
Employee	Current Salary	Amount of Raise	New Salary
Nicole	$25.54		
Brad	$18.53		
Jared	$12.22		
Sophie	$14.22		
Elizabeth	$9.66		

Facility 3

The hospital just announced raises. The amount of the raise is based on the employee's performance evaluation. Based on the employee information in Table 6-16, calculate the new hourly salary for each employee (round to the nearest cent) and enter the information in Table 6-17.

Table 6-16 *Facility 3 Evaluation Score and Amount of Raise*

Evaluation Score and Corresponding Amount of Raise	
Evaluation Score	Amount of Raise
5	5.0%
4	4.0%
3	2.5%
2	1.0%
1	0.0%

Table 6-17 *Facility 3 Calculation Form for Increase in Salary*

Calculations for Increase in Hourly Salary: Facility 3				
Employee	Current Hourly Salary	Evaluation Score	Amount of Raise	New Hourly Salary
Toni	$15.23	5		
LaSha	$13.54	3		
Lori	$7.75	1		
Gloria	$9.22	5		
Thaddeus	$5.85	3		
Gregg	$6.22	3		

Facility 4

The hospital just announced raises. The amount of the raise is based on the employee's performance evaluation. The evaluation score and corresponding raise amount is shown in Table 6-18. Using the information in Table 6-18, calculate the new hourly salary for each employee and enter the information in Table 6-19.

Table 6-18 *Facility 4 Evaluation Score and Corresponding Amount of Raise*

Evaluation Score and Corresponding Amount of Raise	
Evaluation Score	Amount of Raise
5	6.0%
4	5.0%
3	3.0%
2	1.0%
1	0.0%

Table 6-19 *Facility 4 Calculation Form for Salary Increase*

Calculation Form for Salary Increase				
Employee	Current Hourly Salary	Evaluation Score	Amount of Raise	New Hourly Salary
Jennifer	$15.55	5		
Grant	$9.65	1		
Flora	$6.61	2		
Louise	$8.55	5		
Laura	$7.69	5		
Mark	$12.93	4		
Abigail	$14.22	3		

Facility 5

The hospital just announced raises. The amount of the raise is based on the employee's performance evaluation as shown in Table 6-20.

Table 6-20 *Facility 5 Evaluation Score and Corresponding Amount of Raise*

Evaluation Score and Corresponding Amount of Raise: Facility 5	
Evaluation Score	Amount of Raise
5	5.0%
4	4.0%
3	2.5%
2	1.0%
1	0.0%

Based on the employee information in Table 6-21, calculate the new annual salary for each employee and the total salary budget (round to the nearest cent).

Table 6-21 *Facility 5 Calculation Form for Salary Increase*

Calculation Form for Salary Increase: Facility 5				
Employee	Current Annual Salary	Evaluation Score	Amount of Increase	New Annual Salary
Toni	$35,248.77	5		
LaSha	$28,599.47	3		
Lori	$15,657.44	1		
Gloria	$16,555.95	5		
Thaddeus	$22,578.33	3		
Gregg	$19,558.04	3		
Total Salary Budget				

The salary budget is based on the fiscal year (FY), which begins June 1. Salary increases will not take effect until October 1. Based on the employee information that you have calculated in Table 6-21, determine your payroll budget for the year (beginning in June and ending in May). Then enter the information by month in Table 6-22.

Table 6-22 *Payroll Budget for Year Beginning June 1*

Name	Jun	Jul	Aug	Sep	Oct	Nov	Dec	Jan	Feb	Mar	Apr	May	Total
Toni													
LaSha													
Lori													
Gloria													
Thaddeus													
Gregg													
Totals													

CASE 6-21

Planning for Paper-Based Record Retention

You have been given the task of planning for paper-based record retention needs for each of the departments given below. Calculate the information needed to generate your report to administration.

Department 1

Use the information in Table 6-23 to calculate the average chart thickness (round to 1 decimal place).

Table 6-23 *Samples Taken to Determine Average Size of Chart Thickness*

Department 1	Sample Inch Measurements to Determine the Average Chart Thickness				
0.2	4.0	0.5	3.5	0.5	0.25
0.5	0.4	0.25	2.75	0.5	0.75
0.75	0.75	0.75	4.0	0.5	0.75
1.25	1.25	1.25	1.5	1.75	1.0
3.25	1.5	1.75	3.75	0.25	0.75

Department 2

Calculate the linear filing inches required for 175,000 charts with an average size of 0.5 inch each.

Department 3

Calculate the linear filing inches required for 576,000 charts with an average size of 0.75 inch each.

Department 4

Calculate the linear filing inches required for 326,000 charts with an average size of 0.2 inch each.

Department 5

Calculate the linear filing inches required for 175,000 charts with an average size of chart 0.5 inch and a 25% allowance for future growth.

Department 6

Calculate the linear filing inches required for 576,000 charts with an average size of 0.75 inch and a 20% allowance for future growth.

Department 7

Calculate the linear filing inches required for 326,000 charts with an average size of 0.2 inch each and include a 35% allowance for future growth.

Department 8

Use the information in Table 6-24 to calculate the average chart thickness. Then calculate the linear filing inches required for 217,000 charts, including a 25% allowance for growth.

Table 6-24 *Samples Taken to Determine Average Size of Chart Thickness*

Department 8	Sample Measurements (in Inches) to Determine the Average Chart Thickness				
0.75	3.0	0.75	2.25	4.0	1.5
0.25	0.5	0.25	2.50	4.0	1.75
0.10	1.75	0.75	3.0	4.0	0.75

Department 9

Use the information in Table 6-25 to calculate the average chart thickness (round to 2 decimal places). Then calculate the linear filing inches required for 452,000 charts, including a 25% allowance for growth.

Table 6-25 *Samples Taken to Determine Average Size of Chart Thickness*

Department 9	Sample Measurements (in Inches) to Determine the Average Chart Thickness				
1.0	2.25	0.25	1.75	3.75	2.50
3.0	2.5	0.75	2.75	2.25	0.50

Department 10

Macon General Hospital has 248,000 medical records with an average size of 0.75 inch per chart.

How many shelving units are required if the shelves are 36 inches wide and there are 7 shelves in each unit?

Department 11

Atlanta General Hospital has 758,200 medical records with an average size of 1.0 inch per chart.

How many shelving units are required if the shelves are 36 inches wide and there are 6 shelves in each unit?

Department 12

Perry Medical Center has 150,000 medical records with an average size of 0.5 inch.

How many shelving units are required if the shelves are 33 inches wide, there are 8 shelves in each unit, and a growth rate of 25% is desired?

Department 13

Birmingham Pediatrics currently has 467,000 linear filing inches. The current shelves are nearing capacity. They want to increase filing capacity by 40%. They want to continue utilizing shelving units that are 33 inches wide and 7 shelves tall.

How many new shelving units will be required?

Planning for Electronic Record Retention

You have been given the task of planning for electronic record retention needs for each of the departments given in the following sections. Perform the calculations necessary to report to administration.

Department 1

You must decide how many CDs you will need to store the scanned images of the existing medical records. Each CD stores 12,000 images. It is estimated that there are 750,852,214 images to store on the CDs.

How many CDs would you need?

Department 2

You must decide how many CDs you will need to store the scanned images of the existing medical records. Each CD stores 12,000 images. It is estimated that there are 1,538,535,515 images to store on the CDs.

How many CDs would you need?

Department 3

The 12-inch platters that have been selected for the new imaging system will each store 1,400,000 images via computer output laser disk (COLD). It was calculated that over the next 5 years there would be 129,956,493,345 images via COLD.

How many of these platters should be purchased for the department?

Department 4

The platters that have been selected for the new imaging system will store 14 gigabytes. There are 2,000,000 images and a scanned image averages 199 kb.

How many platters will be needed?

Calculating Department Operations Budget

As HIM Divisional Manager over four facilities, you are responsible for submitting the operations budgets for the HIM Departments. Use the information that is provided for each of the HIM Departments to calculate the budgets for reporting to administration.

Facility 1 Operations Budget

You have been asked to calculate the operations budget for the HIM Department for the new FY. The hospital has announced that there will be a 2% increase in the operations budget across the board. Based on the current line items and FY budget shown in Table 6-26, calculate the new budget.

Table 6-26   *Line Items—Facility 1 Operations Budget*

Line Items for Operations Budget		
Line Item	Current Budget	New Budget
Supplies	$7,500.00	
Maintenance	$2,000.00	
Equipment	$12,000.00	
Software Licensing	$1,000.00	
Copy Machines	$5,000.00	
Folders	$15,000.00	

Facility 2 Operations Budget

You have been asked to calculate the operations budget for the HIM Department for the new FY. The hospital has announced that there will be a 2% increase in the operations budget across the board. In addition, there will be a 5% increase in the maintenance costs and your software. Based on the current FY budget shown in Table 6-27, calculate the new budget.

Table 6-27 *Line Items—Facility 2 Operations Budget*

Line Items for Operations Budget		
Line Item	Current Budget	New Budget
Supplies	$5,500.00	
Maintenance	$2,000.00	
Equipment	$15,000.00	
Software Licensing	$1,500.00	
Copy Machines	$3,000.00	
Folders	$8,000.00	

Facility 3 Operations Budget

You have been asked to calculate the operations budget for the HIM Department for the new FY. The hospital has announced that there will be a 6% decrease in the operation budget across the board. Based on the current FY budget shown in Table 6-28, calculate the new budget.

Table 6-28 *Line Items—Facility 3 Operations Budget*

Line Items for Operations Budget		
Line Item	Current Budget	New Budget
Supplies	$6,000.00	
Maintenance	$3,000.00	
Equipment	$20,000.00	
Software Licensing	$1,500.00	
Copy Machine	$2,500.00	
Folders	$5,500.00	

Facility 4 Operations Budget

You have been asked to calculate the operations budget for the HIM Department for the new FY. The hospital has announced that there will be a 5% decrease in the operation budget across the board. The budget must be cut even though maintenance and software licensing is being increased by 2%. Based on the current FY budget shown in Table 6-29, calculate the new budget.

Table 6-29   *Line Items—Facility 4 Operations Budget*

Line Items for Operations Budget		
Line Item	Current Budget	New Budget
Supplies	$4,500.00	
Maintenance	$3,000.00	
Equipment	$4,500.00	
Software Licensing	$750.00	
Copy Machine	$800.00	

CASE 6-24

Net Present Value (NPV) Method of Evaluating a Capital Expense

You are requesting approval of a capital expenditure for a new dictation system. The cost of the system is $65,000.00. You expect that the system will save the HIM Department $20,000.00 per year by eliminating the cost of outside contract transcription. You anticipate the system life will be 5 years. Your facility uses straight line depreciation for the life of any capital expenditure. Assume that Management requires the use of a net present value (NPV) of capital at 10%. Use the net present value shown in Table 6-30.

Calculate the net cash flow.

Would the dictation system meet the criteria to have a 10% return and exceed the initial capital outlay?

Table 6-30 *Net Present Value at 10.0%*

	Net Present Value at 10%		
Years	Net Cash Flow	Factor for NPV at 10.0%	Present Value of Cash Flow
1		$0.909091	
2		$0.826446	
3		$0.751315	
4		$0.683013	
5		$0.620921	

CASE 6-25

Accounting Rate of Return Method of Evaluating a Capital Expense

You want to get approval for a capital expense to bring the copy service back in-house. You estimate that it will bring in a net cash flow of $40,000.00 over the next 5 years. An initial outlay of $24,000.00 cash will be needed for two networked, dedicated computers and a new copy machine to support the ROI staff you already have.

Use straight-line deprecation in calculating the average net income and enter the information in Table 6-31. The accounting rate of return needs to be at least 10% for the project to be accepted.

Will the accounting rate of return for the capital expense be acceptable?

Table 6-31 *Accounting Rate of Return*

Accounting Rate of Return		
Net cash flow per year	Cash flow/number of years	40,000/5 = 8,000
Depreciation	Cost/number of years	
Average net income	Net cash flow per year less depreciation	
Investment	Cost of project	
Accounting rate of return for project	Average net income/investment	

CASE 6-26

Payback Method of Evaluating a Capital Expense

You want to get approval for a capital expense to bring the copy service back in-house. An investment of $24,000.00 for a dedicated computer and a new copy machine will support the ROI staff you already have. You estimate that it will bring in a cash income of $40,000.00 over the next 5 years. Your facility uses straight-line depreciation to calculate the average net income.

Use Table 6-32 to figure the rate of return on the net present value and Table 6-33 to determine the number of years it will take for the payback. Then, use the formula in Figure 6-2 to calculate the payback period.

How many years will it take to pay back the investment?

Table 6-32   *Net Present Value at 10.0%*

Net Present Value at 10.0%			
Years	Net Cash Flow	Factor for NPV at 10.0%	Present Value of Cash Flow
1	$2,000	$0.909091	
2	$5,000	$0.826446	
3	$9,000	$0.751315	
4	$11,000	$0.683013	
5	$13,000	$0.620921	

Table 6-33 *Payback Method of Evaluating the Capital Expense for the In-House Copy Service*

Payback Method of Evaluating the Capital Expense for the In-house Copy Service			
Year	Average Net Income	Initial Investment	Remaining
0		$24,000	
1			
2			
3			
4			
5			
6			
Total			

$$\frac{\text{Initial Outlay (Investment)}}{\text{Average Net Income}} = \text{Payback Period}$$

Figure 6-2 *Formula for the Payback Method*

CASE 6-27

Developing the HIM Operations Budget

Develop the HIM Department operations budget on a spreadsheet for the next FY. Allocate the funding throughout the FY on a monthly basis. The FY at General Hospital begins July 1.

Personnel Salaries and Wages

Calculate amounts for salaries with fringe benefits, allowed overtime, and total personnel budget.

Salaries With Fringe Benefits

Allowed Overtime

Use the information in Table 6-34 to calculate the payroll costs for the new FY. New salaries include:

- A new approved Analyst/Coder/Abstractor position that will go into effect at the beginning of the new fiscal year with the salary of $22,500.00.
- Fringe benefits of 30% of monthly salaries.
- A merit raise of 5% that will go into effect in December.
- Overtime limits not to exceed $4,000.00 for the year.

Table 6-34 *Personnel Salary Information*

Personnel Salary Information			
Classification	Number of Employees	Current Salaries	Salaries for New FY
Director	1	$50,000.00	
Assistant Director	1	$36,000.00	
Coding Supervisor	1	$28,000.00	
Receptionist/Clerk	1	$18,000.00	
Transcription Supervisor	1	$28,000.00	
Transcriptionists	4	$26,000.00	
Coders	3	$24,500.00	
Chart Completion Supervisor	1	$25,000.00	
HIM File Clerks	2	$17,500.00	
Secretary	1	$20,000.00	

Operations expenses are shown in Table 6-35 and should be allocated throughout the FY.

Table 6-35 *Operations Expenses for New FY*

Operations Expenses for New FY	
Expense	Budget
Telephone	$1,000.00
Supplies	$7,500.00
Folders	$15,000.00
Equipment	$12,000.00
Copy Machine	$5,000.00
Education	$1,500.00

CASE 6-28

Developing the HIM Department Budget

Develop a budget for the HIM Department for the next FY at Sea Crest Healthcare Center. The FY begins July 1. Utilize spreadsheet software to develop the budget parts and then develop the department budget for the next fiscal year.

There are three parts to the budget:

- Personnel (see Figure 6-3)
- Operational (see Figure 6-4)
- Capital Equipment (see Figures 6-5, 6-6, and 6-7)

Calculate the budget for each month and a total for the year. Line items to be included are identified in each of the three parts of the budget. Any limitations/instructions from administration are also provided.

Use the Capital Expenditure Approval Form (Figure 6-7) in completing and submitting a capital expenditure request for a new dictation system.

Personnel Budget

Position	Current Salary	20xx–20xx Salary
Director	$45,000.00	
Assistant Director	$36,000.00	
Receptionist/Clerk	$18,000.00	
Analysts/Coder/Abstractor	$25,000.00	
Analysts/Coder/Abstractor	$22,500.00	
Assembly Clerk	$19,000.00	
Transcriptionist	$25,000.00	
Transcriptionist	$27,000.00	
Part-Time File Clerk	$6,500.00	

Line Items   Salaries
                  Fringe Benefits
                  Overtime

Instructions: Calculate fringe benefits as 25% of monthly salary. A 5% raise will go into effect in October.

Limitations   Overtime cannot exceed $4,000.00 for the year. No new employees.

* Student should use a spreadsheet to calculate and reflect the monthly personnel budget.

Operational Budget

Operation	Fiscal Year 20xx–20xx
Telephone	$2,000.00
Supplies	$7,500.00
Folders	$15,000.00
Equipment	$12,000.00
Copy Machine	$5,000.00
Education	$1,000.00

Justification for New Transcription System

The current dictation system is fifteen years old. It requires service a couple of times per month. The downtime of the system averages fifty minutes each time the serviceman comes out to service it.

The medical staff has complained of not being able to access the system due to getting busy signals. Dr. Delinco complains that his Operative Reports are taking 1½ weeks to be typed. Dr. Smith has complained that the current system doesn't allow him to call in and listen to his dictations as an alternative when the report is not available on the patient chart.

Also, prioritizing reports among the transcriptionists is not as automated as newer systems allow, therefore consuming transcribers' time and impacting production.

Figure 6-5 *Justification for New Transcription System*

Capital Equipment

Item: New Dictation System

Cost for System: $65,000.00
Annual Income Produced: $20,000.00
Depreciation over 5 Years:

Instructions: Complete the HIM Department's Capital Equipment Budget for fiscal year 20xx-20xx. Note: the only major equipment request is to replace your current dictation system.

Administration has distributed budget requests to each department at General Hospital with a memo indicating a due date of 1 month.

Instructions state that the capital budget is "zero-based," requiring justification of any proposed capital expenditures. You have listed some justifications for a new digital dictation system for the upcoming year in Figure 6-5. You need to complete the Capital Expenditure Approval Form shown in Figure 6-7 and return it to administration with your budget.

As the HIM Director, you know that after Administration's review of submitted department budgets, only those foreseen as most important will be approved and funded. For this exercise, include the dictation system in your capital budget as if it were approved.

Figure 6-6 *Information for Capital Equipment Budget*

Capital Expenditure Approval Form	
Description_____	
Budget Year_____	Budget Cost $_____
Type of Expenditure:	Replacement:____ New:____

Briefly define function of capital expenditure:_____

_____

Briefly describe why item is needed :

Justification for New Transcription System is attached (see Figure 6-5)_____

Financial Analysis	Annual
A) Gross Revenue	$_____
B) Less Depreciation	(_____)
C) Gross Profit	_____
D) Asset Cost	$_____
E) Return on Asset	_____ %
F) Payback- years	_____

Requested by:_____ (Department Manager)

Approved by:

_____ (Operations Manager)   Date_____

_____ (Finance Manager)   Date_____

_____ (Administrator)   Date_____

Figure 6-7   *Capital Expenditure Approval Form*

CASE 6-29

Filing System Conversions

As an HIM Assistant Director, you have been asked by administration to help with the filing system conversions at two of the outpatient service facilities of your healthcare system. They have asked you to help them in calculating the number of employees needed to complete their projects.

Project 1

Orthopedics of Central Omaha is converting the filing system from alphabetic to terminal digit. The front office staff consists of 8 FTEs. The Practice Manager has given instructions that the work can begin on Friday afternoon as soon as the last patient leaves, which is typically 5:00 p.m. The project must be completed by 8:00 a.m. Monday morning.

The HIM Coordinator has been collecting information for you to use in the planning process. There are 8,950 medical records. It takes 2 minutes per chart to convert from alphabetic to terminal digit.

Determine the number of hours that you expect it to take.

Can everything be done by working the day shift, or will you need an evening and/or night shift to get the job completed on time?

How many people will be needed to complete the project in the time frame given?

Project 2

Eastern Omaha Neurology Center is converting the filing system from alphabetic to terminal digit. There are 15 office staff members. The Practice Manager has given instructions that the work can begin on Friday afternoon as soon as the last patient leaves, which is typically 2:00 p.m. The project must be completed by 8:00 p.m. Sunday night.

The HIM Coordinator has been collecting information for you to use in the planning process. There are 54,760 medical records. It will take 3½ minutes per chart to convert from alphabetic to terminal digit filing.

How many hours do you expect it to take?

How long will a shift be?

How many people will be needed to complete the project in the time frame given?

Can everything be done by working the day shift, or will you need an evening and/or night shift?

SECTION SEVEN

Project and Operations Management

Organizational Chart

The current organizational chart for the HIM Department is shown in Figure 7-1.

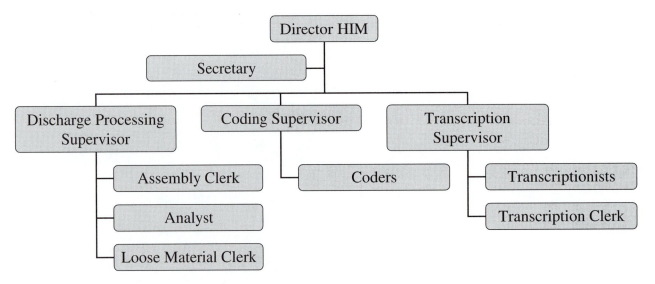

Figure 7-1 *HIM Department Organizational Chart*

The hospital has just undergone a massive reconstruction in which the HIM Department has added three new functions: quality improvement, birth certificates, and research/institutional reporting. With the functions, the positions being moved to the HIM Department include Quality Improvement Coordinator, Physician Advisor, Quality Improvement Clerk, Research Coordinator, Report Writer, and Birth Certificate Coordinator. You have also received approval to hire two assistant directors. You plan to have two supervisors moving with the new staff to the HIM Department.

Update the organizational chart to indicate the changes.

CASE 7-2

Job Description Analysis

You are the coding supervisor at a hospital that just increased its bed size from 75 beds to 150 beds. The facility offers inpatient services, outpatient surgery, ancillary services, and emergency room services. As the volume increases with the increased bed capacity, you will have to increase the number of coders who are in your department. Currently there is only one coding job classification—HIM Coder. This position is responsible for coding all services. You are evaluating this practice to determine if you want to continue with the one job classification.

What would you recommend?

If you recommend more than one job classification, what would they be?

How would you divide the work load?

CASE 7-3

Productivity Study

Your inpatient coders are always behind. The supervisor has asked for more staff and the HIM Director agrees with the request. When the Director submitted her request to administration, the Vice President asked her to conduct a productivity study of the local hospitals. She called four hospitals, and her findings are shown in Table 7-1. The Director knows that if she shows this to the Vice President, not only will she not get the positions, but she will be asked to increase her productivity. She can see that she needs to do some more research. You know that the coders at your facility code the charts and also abstract quality indicators. Your research shows that at the other hospitals, the quality indicators are abstracted by staff in the quality management department.

Table 7-1   *Productivity Study of Local Hospitals*

Productivity Study of Local Hospitals					
	Our Hospital	Hospital A	Hospital B	Hospital C	Hospital D
Inpatient charts coded per day	15	20	22	23	21

Do you need any additional information?

If so, where would you go get the information?

What arguments can you use to support your need for the additional staff?

CASE 7-4

Performance and Quality Improvement in a Coding Department

Molly, the coding supervisor of Homer General Hospital, has a problem. Her Discharged Not Final Billed (DNFB) report is staying significantly over the limit that administration desires. She is also behind in some of the compliance monitoring that needs to be completed. Molly has been given the mandate to determine what needs to be done to bring the DNFB down and still maintain quality, as well as keep current in the compliance monitoring. She pulls together the information shown in Table 7-2. Analyze this situation from every aspect, including but not limited to quality, legal, and management, and answer the following questions:

1. What additional information should Molly gather?

2. What are Molly's options?

3. How can you ensure quality of coding while at the same time emphasizing volume?

4. What would you recommend to solve Molly's problems?

Table 7-2 *Analysis for Discharged Not Final Billed (DNFB)*

Number of current employees	Coding supervisor	1
	Coders (all types of charts)	3
Number of vacant positions	Coders	1
Volume (average per day)	Inpatient	70
	Outpatient	177
	Emergency Room	122
	Outpatient Surgery	90
Productivity Standards	Inpatient	25–28
(per 8-hour day)	Outpatient	170–185
	ER	120–125
	Outpatient Surgery	85–100
Amount of time currently spent on compliance issues	Hours per week	10
Amount of time that Molly feels should be dedicated to compliance to do it right	Hours per week	32
Current DNFB	$1.2 million	
Desired DNFB level	$600,000	
Aging	Current charts (3-day bill hold)	35%
	4–10 days old	20%
	11–21 days old	15%
	22–30 days old	15%
	more than 30 days old	10%

Performance Improvement for a File Area

You are the new archives (file area) supervisor. The previous supervisor was terminated for incompetence, and the position remained vacant for 6 months before you were hired. There are major problems with the quality of the work provided by your staff, resulting in a lot of time spent searching for misfiled charts. Many of the misfiled charts are not just transposed numbers or 1–2 charts off, but are grossly misfiled. The loose material on the chart has been found filed in the wrong order and, in addition, frequently in the wrong chart.

The customers have several complaints:

- They are not getting the charts as requested.
- The records that they do receive are in shambles.
- Sometimes the charts are never provided.
- Sometimes they get the wrong patient record.
- At times, the requested visit is not in the volume that they received.

Your staffing is currently structured as follows:

- Six full-time employees (FTEs) on the day staff. The day staff retrieves charts for the ER, finishes up anything not completed by the night shift, and files loose material.
- Two FTE evening staff. The evening shift files back all of the charts returned throughout the day and pulls for the ER.
- Two FTE night staff. The night shift pulls for the clinic, for scheduled admissions, for the ER, and for administrative purposes.

The daily work assignment can be described as follows:

- Staff members grab the first stack(s) of charts that they get to, sort them into terminal digit order, and then file them.
- Staff members grab the first stack(s) of loose material that they get to, sort the sheets into terminal digit order, and then file them.
- There is no control over the number of charts picked up by the employee or the area in which the charts are filed.

The first thing that you evaluated is the work volume and found that the number of staff is appropriate. You also looked at the overall flow of the process and found that to be appropriate. However, as an experienced supervisor, you realize that there is no accountability for quality in this method of work distribution. By the end of the first week, you need to give a proposal to the HIM Director regarding your plan to solve the quality problems in the department.

What changes would you recommend?

How would you implement your plan, if it is approved by the director?

Instituting Productivity and Quality Standards for Imaging or Scanning Records

You are the new imaging supervisor. The previous supervisor recently retired after 35 years of service to the hospital. The facility has had the imaging system for only the past 6 months.

The scanners are responsible for prepping the medical record as well as the actual scanning. They do not index, nor do they conduct quality checks. If the quality control clerks find more than 1–2 pages in a chart that need to be rescanned, the chart is returned to the scanners for rework.

The first thing that you noticed is the significant backlog of charts to be scanned. You learn that the previous supervisor did not want to create productivity standards until the system had been used for at least a year. The scanners do not even turn in a report of their work each day. It is going to take some time to develop the appropriate productivity standards. In the meantime, you plan to have the scanners report their productivity each day.

Use forms design principles to develop the productivity report required.

What would you recommend to get them caught up?

How will you establish productivity standards?

Evaluation of Transcription Department

Because you have been having difficulty recruiting transcriptionists, you are considering outsourcing the transcription services. You have the responsibility of making the decision.

Based on the information that has been collected, you have to decide which is more cost-effective. Table 7-3 shows the current in-house transcription services with the transcriptionist positions and salaries. The following list includes additional information regarding in-house transcription:

- Expenses caused by overhead are $3,500.00 per year
- 500 square feet of space have been allocated
- Number of lines transcribed a month: 225,000
- Benefits are 24% of salaries
- If you retain transcription in-house:
  - You will have to increase salaries by 20% to be competitive. (This figure is based on salary surveys of local hospitals and major transcription services.)
  - You will need an additional 50 square feet to accommodate two more transcriptionists.

Table 7-3 *In-house Transcription Positions and Salaries*

Transcriptionist Positions and Salaries	
Position	Current Salary
Transcriptionist 1	$14.76
Transcriptionist 2	$12.23
Transcriptionist 3	$15.47
Transcriptionist 4	$18.72
Transcriptionist 5	$16.06
Transcriptionist 6	$15.76
Transcriptionist 7	$16.84
Transcriptionist 8	$17.37
Transcriptionist 9	$15.27
Transcriptionist 10	$16.84
Transcriptionist 11	Vacant position
Transcriptionist 12	Vacant position
Supervisor	$22.02
Transcription Clerk	$6.75

An RFP was utilized to gather information on several transcription companies. You have decided which company you will go with if the decision is made to outsource.

Key information regarding outsourcing transcription and your projected volume is shown in Figure 7-2.

Information Needed for Outsourcing Transcription

- A transcription coordinator will be needed to handle problems, monitor quality, and be the contact for the transcription company.
- The salary range for the transcription coordinator is $15.27–$25.32.
- The current Transcription Supervisor would probably be placed in the transcription coordinator role.
- The transcription company will charge 17¢ per line.
- A 12% increase in the work load over the next year is expected.
- Fifty square feet of space will be needed to support the transcription functions (not including the servers in the computer room).

Figure 7-2 *Outsourcing Transcription*

Which method would you recommend from strictly a financial aspect?

What other aspects should be reviewed before making this decision?

What additional information do you need to make a decision?

Performance and Quality Evaluation and Improvement of the Health Information Management (HIM) Department

You have just been hired as the HIM Quality Coordinator. This is a new position in the HIM Department. Your job tasks read as follows:

- Develop and implement the HIM Department Quality Plan.
- Develop data collection, data analysis, and data presentation tools for use in the quality plan.
- Report findings to the HIM Director, Administration, Medical Staff Director, and Medical Staff Committees as appropriate.
- Other duties are as assigned.

The facility is a 338-bed hospital with active ER and outpatient services. There are 45 employees in the HIM Department. About 75% of the medical record is electronic. Those documents are not printed out. The remaining 25% of the record is paper and is scanned into the system by the HIM Department. These documents are scheduled for destruction in 60 days from scanning.

The former Director of HIM was successful in working with administration to get the EHR and imaging in place and to get approval to destroy the paper records. She failed at managing the day-to-day operations of the department. Now, the department has quality issues in the HIM functions. The former director also did a great job preparing the medical staff for the EHR, and the transition went smoothly; however, many physicians and other users are frustrated by the quality issues. Administration is also becoming concerned with the high billing hold report. The director's position was vacant for 5 months before the new director started work. She has only been here a month.

Today is your first day. The HIM Director has her instructions from administration and the medical staff. She has passed these instructions on to you. Your instructions boil down to two words—FIX IT. While the director will be actively involved in this clean-up, she cannot do it by herself with the other demands on her time. This is why she requested your position. It is almost unheard of for a new position to be approved in the middle of the fiscal year. Adding the extra position shows how serious administration is about getting the problems solved. The problems are as follows:

- Scanning:
  - There is a 2-month backlog in scanning the paper records.
  - The quality of the scanning has problems.
    1. Sometimes pages are fed two at a time, and the backs of pages are not always scanned.
    2. This requires 100% audit, which is 3 months behind.
    3. The staff members conducting the quality audits do not catch all of the errors.

- Billing:
  - The billing hold report is over $2,000,000.00.
  - Administration wants the billing hold report held at $500,000.00.
- Coding:
  - Coding is 2 weeks behind.
  - There are three vacancies in the coding area.
  - One of your coders is a new graduate of the local HIT program and is slower than the experienced coders.
  - The last coding audit conducted by corporate showed an 80% coding accuracy report.
- Release of Information:
  - The release of information area is 2 days behind.
  - The release of information area has received repeated complaints that the wrong information is being sent. The errors include:
    1. Not everything requested was released.
    2. Wrong admissions are being released.
    3. Information on wrong patients are being released.
    4. Wrong documents are being released.
- Transcription:
  - An outsourcing company is used, since the hospital had trouble recruiting and retaining qualified transcriptionists.
  - Although the transcription is current, the quality of the work is inconsistent. Most of the reports are perfect, but a significant number of reports are totally inaccurate because of:
    1. multiple typos
    2. abbreviations that are not spelled out
    3. poor grammar
    4. in some cases, wrong medications with names similar to the right medications

Your assignment for this project is to develop a plan to solve the problems identified above and to prevent them and other problems from occurring in the future. Your plan should include AT LEAST:

- Who should be involved
- What reporting mechanism you should have
- Who you should report to
- What accuracy rates you expect
- What you will do to solve problems (training, outsourcing, new policies, etc.)
- What will be monitored
- Frequency of monitoring
- Frequency of reporting
- What investigations you will do
- How you will build quality into your process
- How you prioritize problems to be addressed
- Forms
- Graphs

Be creative, but use sound HIM principles as the foundation for your project. If you make assumptions, identify the assumptions in your narrative. Please take into consideration all aspects of the issues, including but not limited to legal, data quality, compliance, and quality improvement.

Creating a Workflow Diagram for Discharge Processing

You have been asked to draw a workflow diagram to illustrate the discharge processing workflow in your HIM Department. Show key steps in the process, not every step.

The process is:

- The charts are picked up at midnight on the day of discharge.
- The charts are brought to the HIM Department via a buggy.
- The charts are checked off the discharge list.
- The charts are sorted based on the primary terminal digits into the following stacks: 00–24, 25–49, 50–74, 75–99.
- The charts are placed on the appropriate assembly clerk's desk.
- Each chart is assembled into proper chart order.
- The person assembling the chart writes his or her initials on the facesheet.
- The chart is placed on the analyst's desk.
- The analyst reviews the medical record for deficiencies.
- Colored tags are placed on the page where signatures are required.
- The deficiencies are entered in the chart deficiency system.
- The deficiency sheet is placed on the chart.
- The person analyzing the chart writes his or her initials on the facesheet.
- The charts are placed on the shelf in coding (terminal digit filing) by discharge date.
- Each chart is pulled from the shelf for coding.
- Each chart is reviewed.
- Codes are assigned.
- Discharge disposition abstracted, service, and attending physician are confirmed.
- Code summary is printed out.
- Information is filled in chart folder.
- If complete, chart is sent to permanent files.
- If incomplete, chart is sent to incomplete chart room.
- Chart is filed in terminal digit order on wall.
- Incomplete charts are pulled for physician.
- Deficiency sheet and system are updated.
- If complete, chart is sent to permanent files.
- If incomplete, chart is returned to incomplete files.
- Process is repeated until chart is complete.
- Chart is filed.

CASE 7-10

Improving Workflow Process for Performance Improvement for Discharge Processing

The current workflow process has worked well for the past 10 years. The new CFO wants the DNFB to drop from $2.4 million to $750,000.00. Coding is the only thing preventing the bill from being dropped within 3 days. In addition, there are complaints from some of the new physicians on staff that they have to wait too long to get charts to dictate. They want to be able to dictate the discharge summary within a day or two after patient discharge. To satisfy the CFO and the physicians, you will need to make changes. You need to speed up the process to get the codes entered into the system faster, as well as to get charts to the incomplete chart room quickly. To accomplish this, you need to reengineer the current workflow. The current process is:

- The charts are picked up from the unit at midnight of the day of discharge.
- The charts are checked off the discharge list.
- The charts are placed on the "wall" to await loose material that is needed for analysis, coding, and quality indicator monitoring.
- Loose material is filed in the charts for three days.
- On the fourth day, each chart is coded.
- On the fifth day, each chart is assembled.
- On the sixth day, each chart is analyzed.
- On the seventh day, the quality indicator abstracting is conducted and the charts are sent to the incomplete chart room or the permanent file.

What changes can you recommend to accomplish your goals?

What impact (positive and negative) do you expect?

What could you do to diminish the impact of the negative outcomes?

Physical Layout Design for the Health Information Management (HIM) Department

Design the physical layout for the HIM Department for a 250-bed acute care hospital. When designing the department, consider the equipment needs, the workflow, and the tasks involved. The department has implemented an imaging system for scanning records upon discharge; however, it still retains 2 years of old records on the completed shelf. Records older than 2 years are stored on microfilm for access. The department houses two main areas: the Physician's Incomplete/Research Room and the HIM Room. The Physician Room serves as an area for digital completion of patient records and dictating per telephone, as well as access to the Internet for research purposes to knowledge-based healthcare information. The specifications for both areas of the HIM Department are shown in Figure 7-3.

Data for HIM Department Layout Design

I. HIM Department
Size: 65 feet by 45 feet
Staff: 1 Director
1 Imaging Coordinator
1 Receptionist/Secretary
2 Analysts
2 Coder/Abstractors
1 ROI Coordinator
1 Assembly Clerk
2 Transcriptionists
4 File Clerks

II. Physician Incomplete/Research Room
Size: 10 feet by 20 feet

III. Guidelines
Equipment needed for each HIM employee includes, but not limited to:

1. desk with overhead file shelf
2. chair
3. computer
4. telephone

IV. Equipment needed elsewhere in department includes, but not limited to:

- open file shelving units (stationary or mobile units)
- 1 Imaging System
- 1 Microfilm/Reader Printer
- 1 Copy Machine
- 2 chairs for visitors near correspondence desk
- 1 Network printer in transcription
- 2 Network printers in main area
- 1 printer for director
- 1 printer for secretary
- 4 computer workstations for Physician's Incomplete Room/Research Room

V. Other Pertinent Information

- Labeling: Identify each piece of equipment (legend or text labeling).
- Title of Project: The floor plan should include facility and department name.
- Offices: Include Private Office Areas for Director and Transcriptionist.
- Scale: 1/4 inch per 1 foot
- Complete Shelf: Design area for 30 open shelf filing units. Units are 36 inches wide, 8 shelves high and 12 inches deep.
- Aisle space: 36 inches

Figure 7-3 *Data for HIM Department Layout Design*

Revision of the Information Management Plan

As the HIM Director, you have been assigned the responsibility of revising the outdated information management plan. Although the Joint Commission conducts unannounced surveys, you know that you can expect a visit in about a year. The information management plan has to be revised and in place before the surveyors arrive. You only have 6 months in which to have the new plan developed, approved, and implemented. Obviously you cannot do this alone. You do not know how Physical Therapy (PT) and other departments use information. After reflection, you decide to make each department head responsible for developing the portion of the information management plan applicable to them. You will write the overall information management portion of the plan as well as the HIM Department's portion. You decide to have a training session for all of the department heads who will be involved. There are 30 people to be trained on what needs to be included, the time table, and the format.

Develop a project plan for the revision of the information management plan.

What steps need to be done?

Who is responsible for each?

How long will you allocate to each step?

Develop a Program Evaluation Review Technique (PERT) chart of the project.

CASE 7-13

Defining a Project

One of your employees is confused about what is a project and what is a new process/procedure. She has given you a list of changes going on at your facility and asked you to help her understand. Review the situations described in Table 7-4. Indicate whether each situation meets the definition of a project or not. Explain to her why it is or is not a project.

Table 7-4 *Which Scenarios Are a Project*

Scenario	Project	
	Yes	No
The Assistant Director is ordering the annual supply of medical record folders. He is taking bids from vendors to get the best price.		
You are developing a new PI program. Data will be abstracted into an information system with reports being generated monthly.		
You are converting your filing system from alphabetic to terminal digit.		
You are installing new cubicles in the HIM Department.		
The state is updating its electronic birth certification software. It will be rolling out to all of the hospitals over the next 6 months.		
The Information Management plan is being revised. The HIM Special Projects Coordinator has been given sole responsibility of the revision.		
You are developing new productivity standards for your HIM functions.		
Your Joint Commission survey is scheduled sometime around the end of the year. You have a lot of work to ensure that everything is in place.		
The annual coding update has been sent to you for installation.		
The monthly employee newsletter is being written for release next week.		

CASE 7-14

Job Description for Project Manager

It is time to review all of the job descriptions in the organization to determine if they are still valid. The next one in your stack to review is for Project Manager.

What problems do you see with the Project Manager Job Description in Figure 7-4?

Taos General Hospital

Job Description

Department: HIM
Title: Project Manager
Classification: Level 36
Education: Master's Degree preferred, BS, HIM required.
                      RHIA certification required
Experience: 1 year of management experience.
Skills: leadership and computer skills.
Job Responsibilities:

                      Manage assigned projects efficiently and effectively.
                      Develop project plans.
                      Manage large budgets.
                      Supervise large numbers of people on project team.
                      Ensure the quality of the projects assigned.

Revised: 4/5/XX

Figure 7-4 *Project Manager Job Description*

Forming Committees

You are the chairperson of a large IS Committee in charge of implementing a new EHR. The committee is so large that you are not getting anything done. For example, you met for 4 hours yesterday and only got through 3 of the 15 items on the agenda, because everyone wants to have his or her say in each issue. The committee make-up is as follows:

- Project leader
- HIM Director
- Vice President, Finance
- Vice President, Clinical Services
- Chief Information Officer
- Director, Lab
- Director, Radiology
- 4 computer programmers
- Vice President, Nursing
- 2 vendor representatives
- Director, Cardiopulmonary Services
- Director, Materials Management
- Director, Research
- 3 systems analysts
- 2 database administrators
- Director, Training

The decision has been made to create subcommittees. The subcommittees will be:

- Training
- Data Management (data quality, data collection, and data retrieval)
- Development (programming, customization)
- Conversion
- Interfaces

All representatives should be on at least one subcommittee.

Who would you place on each subcommittee?

Why did you choose them?

What charge would you give to each subcommittee?

Committee to Perform System Benefits Analysis

As the HIM Director of a large medical center, you employ 88 FTEs in your department. Your hospital still maintains a paper medical record, although it has several systems throughout the hospital that could directly feed into an EHR. You are certain that the efficiency of your department and the hospital can be achieved with the implementation of an EHR. The efficiencies that can be achieved in the HIM Department alone are abundant if the EHR can interface directly to the dictation and transcription system, coding, release of information, and chart completion systems.

You chair the intradepartmental Clinical Information System Committee for the hospital, which is represented by every clinical department, administration, and Information Services staff. In developing the criteria for sending an RFP out to various vendors, it is important to identify benefits and efficiencies the hospital expects to achieve from an EHR. The task assigned was to have the committee identify benefits to be achieved in justifying the EHR for the hospital.

What benefits can be achieved with the implementation of an EHR for the HIM Department?

What benefits might impact the delivery of patient care?

CASE 7-17

Project Management and Program Evaluation Review Technique (PERT) Chart

You have been given the responsibility of conducting a purge of your files. You have just developed a first draft of the PERT chart for the project.

Review the PERT chart shown in Figure 7-5.

What is the critical path?

What problems can you identify?

How can you improve on this plan?

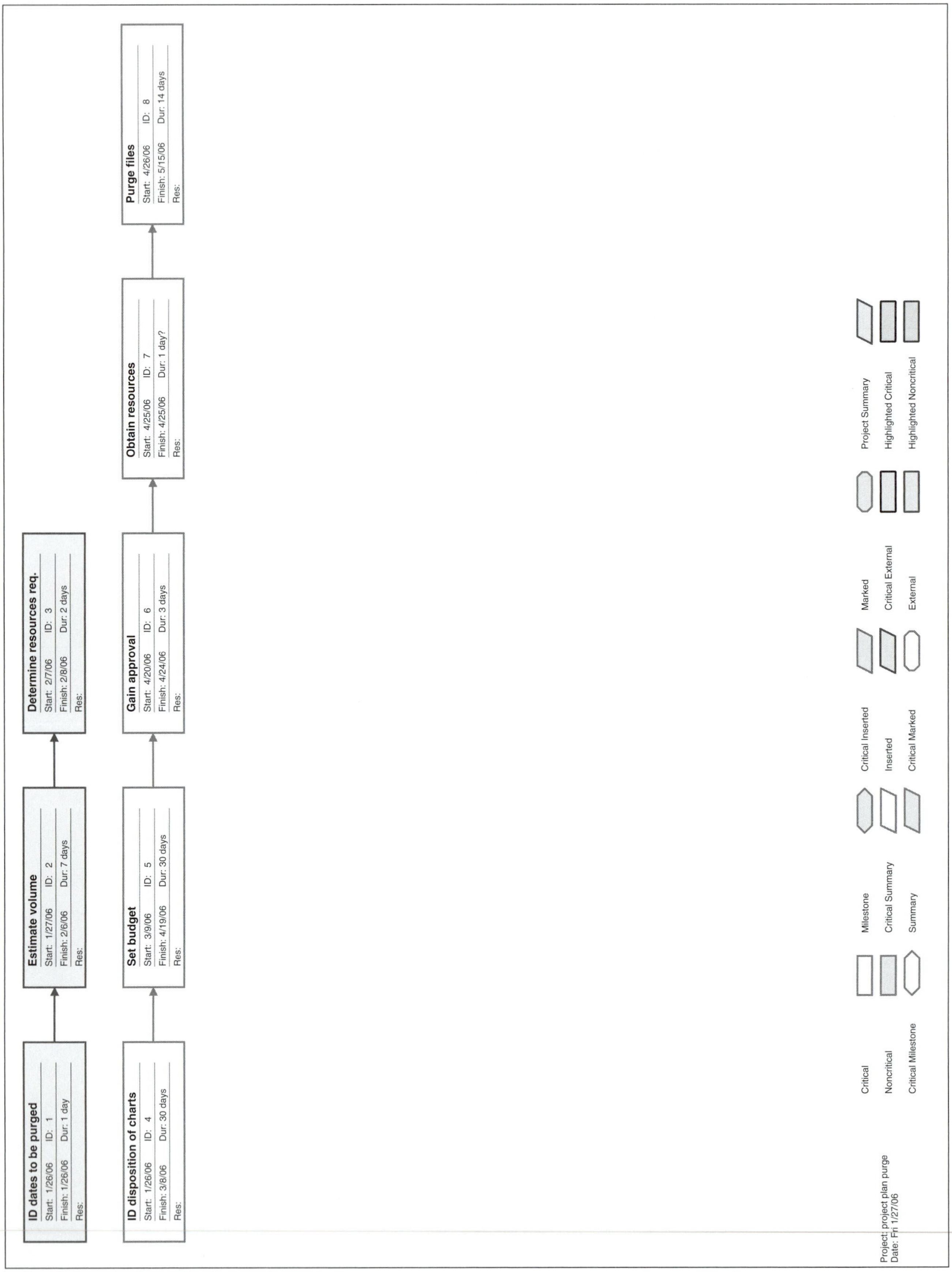

ID dates to be purged		
Start: 1/26/06	ID: 1	Dur: 1 day
Finish: 1/26/06		
Res:		

Estimate volume		
Start: 1/27/06	ID: 2	Dur: 7 days
Finish: 2/6/06		
Res:		

Determine resources req.		
Start: 2/7/06	ID: 3	Dur: 2 days
Finish: 2/8/06		
Res:		

ID disposition of charts		
Start: 1/26/06	ID: 4	Dur: 30 days
Finish: 3/8/06		
Res:		

Set budget		
Start: 3/9/06	ID: 5	Dur: 30 days
Finish: 4/19/06		
Res:		

Gain approval		
Start: 4/20/06	ID: 6	Dur: 3 days
Finish: 4/24/06		
Res:		

Obtain resources		
Start: 4/25/06	ID: 7	Dur: 1 day?
Finish: 4/25/06		
Res:		

Purge files		
Start: 4/26/06	ID: 8	Dur: 14 days
Finish: 5/15/06		
Res:		

Project: project plan purge
Date: Fri 1/27/06

Critical
Noncritical
Critical Milestone

Milestone
Critical Summary
Summary

Critical Inserted
Inserted
Critical Marked

Marked
Critical External
External

Project Summary
Highlighted Critical
Highlighted Noncritical

Figure 7-5 *PERT Chart for File Purge*

CASE 7-18

Project Management and Analysis of a Gantt Chart

Review the Gantt chart in Figure 7-6 and identify any problems with the project plan.

How can the Gantt chart be improved?

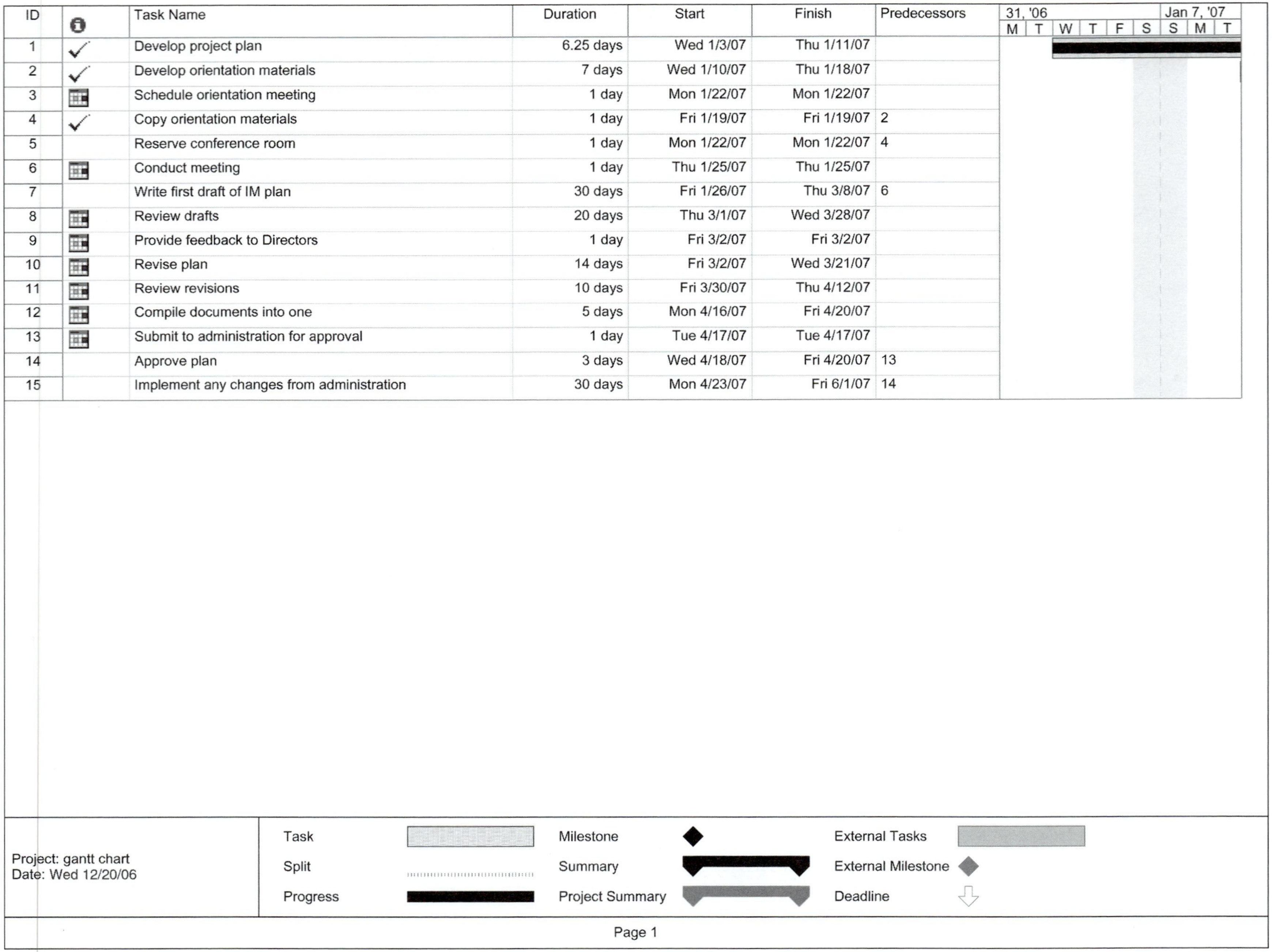

ID		Task Name	Duration	Start	Finish	Predecessors
1		Develop project plan	6.25 days	Wed 1/3/07	Thu 1/11/07	
2		Develop orientation materials	7 days	Wed 1/10/07	Thu 1/18/07	
3		Schedule orientation meeting	1 day	Mon 1/22/07	Mon 1/22/07	
4		Copy orientation materials	1 day	Fri 1/19/07	Fri 1/19/07	2
5		Reserve conference room	1 day	Mon 1/22/07	Mon 1/22/07	4
6		Conduct meeting	1 day	Thu 1/25/07	Thu 1/25/07	
7		Write first draft of IM plan	30 days	Fri 1/26/07	Thu 3/8/07	6
8		Review drafts	20 days	Thu 3/1/07	Wed 3/28/07	
9		Provide feedback to Directors	1 day	Fri 3/2/07	Fri 3/2/07	
10		Revise plan	14 days	Fri 3/2/07	Wed 3/21/07	
11		Review revisions	10 days	Fri 3/30/07	Thu 4/12/07	
12		Compile documents into one	5 days	Mon 4/16/07	Fri 4/20/07	
13		Submit to administration for approval	1 day	Tue 4/17/07	Tue 4/17/07	
14		Approve plan	3 days	Wed 4/18/07	Fri 4/20/07	13
15		Implement any changes from administration	30 days	Mon 4/23/07	Fri 6/1/07	14

Project: gantt chart
Date: Wed 12/20/06

Task		Milestone		External Tasks
Split		Summary		External Milestone
Progress		Project Summary		Deadline

Page 1

Figure 7-6 *Gantt chart*

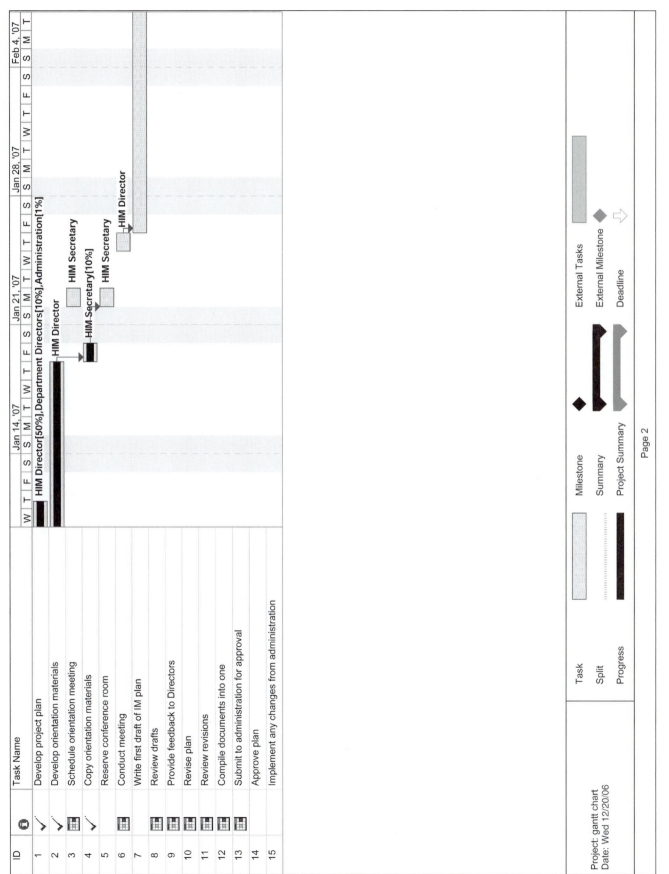

Figure 7-6 *Gantt chart (continued)*

ID		Task Name
1		Develop project plan
2		Develop orientation materials
3		Schedule orientation meeting
4		Copy orientation materials
5		Reserve conference room
6		Conduct meeting
7		Write first draft of IM plan
8		Review drafts
9		Provide feedback to Directors
10		Revise plan
11		Review revisions
12		Compile documents into one
13		Submit to administration for approval
14		Approve plan
15		Implement any changes from administration

HIM Secretary

Project: gantt chart
Date: Wed 12/20/06

Task		Milestone	◆	External Tasks	
Split	....	Summary		External Milestone	◆
Progress	▬▬	Project Summary		Deadline	⇨

Page 3

Figure 7-6 *Gantt chart (continued)*

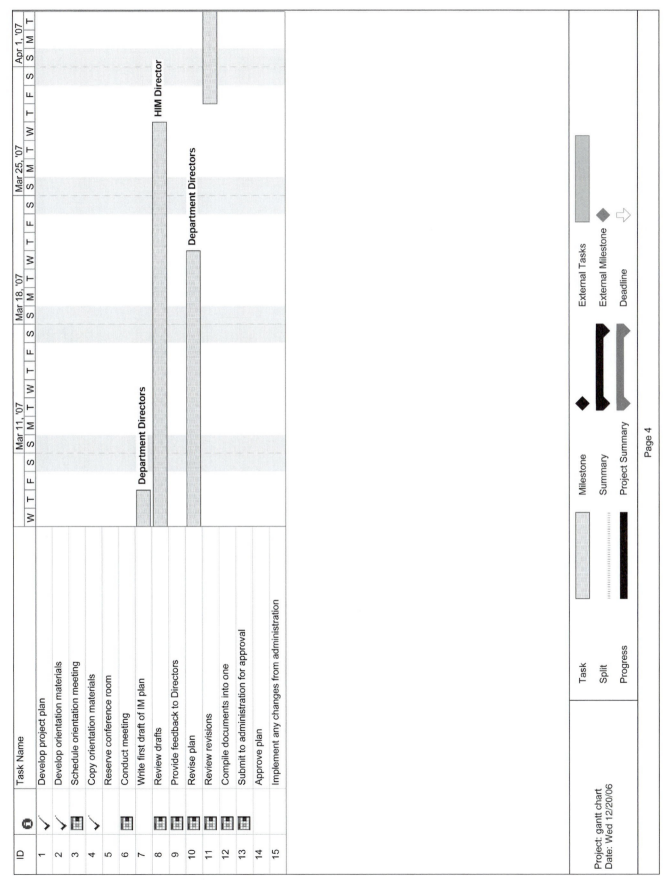

Figure 7-6 *Gantt chart (continued)*

ID		Task Name
1		Develop project plan
2		Develop orientation materials
3		Schedule orientation meeting
4		Copy orientation materials
5		Reserve conference room
6		Conduct meeting
7		Write first draft of IM plan
8		Review drafts
9		Provide feedback to Directors
10		Revise plan
11		Review revisions
12		Compile documents into one
13		Submit to administration for approval
14		Approve plan
15		Implement any changes from administration

Timeline headers: Apr 8, '07 — Apr 15, '07 — Apr 22, '07 — Apr 29, '07

Bar labels: HIM Director, HIM Director, HIM Secretary, HIM Director, Administration

Project: gantt chart
Date: Wed 12/20/06

Legend:
- Task
- Split
- Progress
- Milestone
- Summary
- Project Summary
- External Tasks
- External Milestone
- Deadline

Page 5

Figure 7-6   *Gantt chart (continued)*

ID	◎	Task Name
1	➘	Develop project plan
2	➘	Develop orientation materials
3	▦	Schedule orientation meeting
4	➘	Copy orientation materials
5		Reserve conference room
6	▦	Conduct meeting
7		Write first draft of IM plan
8	▦	Review drafts
9	▦	Provide feedback to Directors
10	▦	Revise plan
11	▦	Review revisions
12	▦	Compile documents into one
13	▦	Submit to administration for approval
14		Approve plan
15		Implement any changes from administration

Project: gantt chart
Date: Wed 12/20/06

Task		Milestone ◆		External Tasks
Split		Summary		External Milestone ◆
Progress		Project Summary		Deadline ⇨

Page 6

Figure 7-6 *Gantt chart (continued)*

Figure 7-6 *Gantt chart (continued)*

ID	Task Name
1	Develop project plan
2	Develop orientation materials
3	Schedule orientation meeting
4	Copy orientation materials
5	Reserve conference room
6	Conduct meeting
7	Write first draft of IM plan
8	Review drafts
9	Provide feedback to Directors
10	Revise plan
11	Review revisions
12	Compile documents into one
13	Submit to administration for approval
14	Approve plan
15	Implement any changes from administration

Project: gantt chart
Date: Wed 12/20/06

Page 7

CASE 7-19

Creating a Gantt Chart

You are in charge of the implementation of the new ADT/MPI installation. Your go-live date is December 1. Today's date is March 3. The contract has been agreed to but not officially signed. Assume that the contract will be signed within the week. You have been asked to create a first draft of a Gantt chart for the implementation process.

Use Microsoft Project to develop a Gantt chart that will include at a minimum:

- A list of tasks that must be completed
- The date each task must be started
- The date to be completed, with estimated number of days to completion
- Who will be responsible for each task (can include more than just the employees listed below)
- Enter any predecessors (what has to be done before the step can be done; for example, you cannot start implementing the computer system until a contract is signed and hardware has been installed)

Use the information listed below when developing the Gantt chart.

- The committee is made up of:
  - HIM Director
  - Admissions
  - Business Office Director
  - Project Manager
  - Network Administrator
  - Chief Information Officer
  - Vendor representative
  - Programmer

Evaluation of Project Management Budget Variance

Your hospital has a major problem with duplicate medical record numbers. You are implementing a new EHR and need to get this problem solved before implementation. You decide to hire a consultant to act as the project manager and to use temporary staff to do the actual work. The use of temporary staff is at the suggestion of the consultant. You have to train the registration staff on ways to avoid creating duplicate medical record numbers. Some of the temporary staff members have to be trained to pull and file charts. Other temporary staff members are trained to review the charts and determine if there is a duplicate and combine the physical chart where appropriate. A temporary RHIA is responsible for conducting data quality checks. You have a significant amount of temporary staff turnover, resulting in constant training and fluctuation of productivity on a daily basis. This results in the RHIA having to do a 100% audit for the entire project, instead of just at the beginning as planned. You really have had to speed up the process the last 2 months to complete the project on time. The project is completed 2 days ahead of time; the quality of the work is great. Now you need to review the final budget for the MPI clean-up.

Based on the project description and the budget shown in Table 7-5, what problems do you see?

From a project management standpoint, what could have been done to make this project work better?

To what do you contribute the budget variance?

Does the budget reflect the description of the project?

If you had to do this again, what would you do differently?

Table 7-5 *Master Patient Index (MPI) Clean-Up Budget*

MPI Clean-Up Budget							
Actual Monthly Expenses							
Line Item	April	May	June	July	Budgeted	Actual	Variance
Temp Staff	12,345.44	13,764.45	21,546.63	24,454.44	60,000.00	72,110.96	(12,110.96)
Equipment	602.67	0	0	0	1,000.00	602.67	397.33
Project Manager	5,000.00	5,000.00	5,000.00	5,000.00	20,000.00	20,000.0	0
Training	2,000.00	1,200.00	300.00	300.00	8,000.00	3,800.00	4,200.00
Total	19,948.11	19,964.45	26,846.63	29,754.44	89,000.00	96,513.63	(7,513.63)

CASE 7-21

Developing a Filing System and Evaluating Equipment Needs

South Utah Community Hospital is a new hospital that is opening January 2. The facility will have an active clinic and Emergency Room in addition to inpatient services. Unfortunately, it will not have an EHR when it opens because of budget constraints. You have been hired as the HIM Director. You are developing a filing system and determining the number of shelves and the like that you will need. The hospital has asked you to keep hard copy records for 4 years. To simplify the project, the number of discharges includes inpatient, outpatient, and ER.

- Expected number of discharges year 1:   25,000
- Expected number of discharges year 2:   28,000
- Expected number of discharges year 3:   32,000
- Expected number of discharges year 4:   40,000
- Average expected size of chart   3/4 inch

Determine the following:

- Amount of filing space required
- Type of shelving desired
- Number of shelves per unit
- Number of shelving units required
- Number of guides required
- Type of filing system to be used (centralized, decentralized, terminal digit, alphabetic, etc.)
- Method used to get information from HIM Department to the requestor
- Type of equipment needed to file and retrieve records
- Method of chart location system
- If outguides will be used
- Security measures to be taken
- Design of medical record folder

Justify your decisions. Include the advantages and disadvantages of the system that you select, where appropriate.

Identify how you will work around the disadvantages of the system, where appropriate.

CASE **7-22**

Project Planning for Conversion from Alphabetic to Terminal Digit Filing

You work in a physician office as the office manager. Several new physicians have been added to the practice over the past year. There are approximately 32,000 records. Based on time and motion studies, one employee can convert 50 records from alphabetical to terminal digit filing in an hour. The alphabetic filing system is no longer working for your office. Your job is to plan the conversion from alphabetic to terminal digit filing.

Create a plan for this conversion that includes:

- Number of staff
- Space
- Supplies required
- Staff training required
- Time schedule
- The process that will be followed

CASE 7-23

Planning the Health Information Management (HIM) Department for a New Facility

You have been hired by West Texas Hospital as their HIM Department Director. West Texas Hospital is a new 200-bed hospital that will open on January 1. The HIM Department will contain the following functions: assembly, analysis, coding, tumor registry, filing charts, chart completion, filing loose material, transcription, and birth certificates.

Use data in Table 7-6 to determine number of employees needed, their job title, and their job description.

Table 7-6 *Data for Health Information Management (HIM) Functions*

Description	Expected Amount for 2007
Discharges	25,000
Admissions	24,750
Outpatient admissions	57,000
ER	36,000
Number of pages per discharge	125
Number of pages per ER visit	10
Number of pages per outpatient visit	7
Number of different patients	62,000
Number of births	700
Number of new cancer cases	145
Amount of loose reports	250,000
Expected records to file/pull	300,000
Number of requests for information expected	3,000
Transcription lines expected	7,000,000
Time assemble charts—inpatient per chart	10 minutes
Time assemble charts—outpatient per chart	2 minutes
Time assemble charts—ER per chart	2 minutes
Time analysis—inpatient per chart	15 minutes
Time analysis—outpatient per chart	2 minutes
Time analysis—ER per chart	2 minutes
Transcription lines per hour per transcriptionist	300
Time—release of information	20 minutes
Time—tumor registry abstract records	1 hour
Loose material per day	800 reports per day
Time—birth certificates	45 minutes
Time—pull/file chart	2 minutes

Designing the Health Information Management (HIM) Department Functions for a New Facility

You have been hired as the Director of HIM for Lower Boston General Hospital, which is a new 100-bed hospital that opens on June 1. You are responsible for designing the HIM functions from the ground up. Write a detailed proposal to the hospital administrator outlining what functions must be performed, why they must be included, and what needs to be done to prepare for the implementation of the department. Include HIM-related tasks that impact the entire enterprise that you recommend the Director of HIM coordinate. Tasks should include, but not be limited to, budget, department design, writing policies, determining salary ranges, developing productivity standards, Medicare compliance, form design, quality, statistics, and hiring staff.

Your report should begin with an executive summary and then go into the detailed report by function. This is a comprehensive project that includes all HIM functions.

This assignment is about planning the department. You do not actually have to write policies and procedures, develop the budget, and so on.